WWII FRANCE

A Writer's Guide

Geneviève Montcombroux

ISBN 978-1-987946-24-6

1. Writing WWII guide for authors
2. France in WWII
3. Language for writers of WWII novels
4. French culture and customs in WWII
5. History of the Occupation of France

Cover by mmontcombroux

Solitude Publishing
solitudepublishing@gmail.com

TABLE OF CONTENT

Introduction

The idea for this work was born of my extensive study of the history of WWII, particularly how the war affected France, coupled with the desire to help authors avoid historical and cultural inaccuracies about French life during this era. This may involve relatively small things, like food and customs, or outright historical errors concerning times, dates, places and actual people or political figures. I hope that my bringing together in one handy volume details of life in France during WWII, you, as an author, will have an authoritative reference to help in your research. There is a bewildering array of information available on the internet but not all of it can be trusted.

This work is confined to France, because it is the country I know well, having been born and raised in Paris. I have done meticulous research in the Bibliothèque Nationale, National Archives, local archives, museums, consulted books by reputed historians, as well as diaries, maps of the era and memoirs particularly those written prior to 1950 whenever possible.

If there appear to be many more details about Paris it is simply because the capital city influenced what happened elsewhere in the country. It is also because there was a much larger German presence in Paris than anywhere else. What happened in Paris resonated throughout the rest of France, including the free zone. Paris *was* France. This de Gaulle understood perfectly but the Americans did not. Fortunately, de Gaulle prevailed and Paris was liberated early, thus giving a final boost of energy to the résistance in the rest of the country.

The mountain ranges have not moved and the rivers still flow the same as they have always done, but do remember that in the mid-twentieth century, glaciers were larger than today, snow more abundant, especially in the mountains, where roads could be blocked for weeks, affecting movement. In contrast, today's transportation routes, urban development, reconfiguration of departments and provinces for administrative purposes have all undergone significant change.

If one looks at today's Google maps of France, one sees a land crisscrossed with roads and multi-lane *autoroutes* (freeways). High-speed TGV railroads and regular rail lines are everywhere. The maps will also show a vast network of hiking trails through forested and mountainous regions,large areas of which have been made into nature parks. What trails existed before and during the war were unmarked and appeared only on unofficial maps (that is a hand-drawn map in the municipal office), if at all. Many of the mountain passes were known only to the local inhabitants. This is why the resistants, the *maquisards*, were able to operate so effectively without detection, until they engaged enemy troops or were betrayed.

Unfortunately, these modern maps and photographs do not reflect the France you are striving to depict in your WWII novel. Train service did not extend to every remote corner of the country. The road system was much the same as when laid out by Napoleon III in the mid-nineteenth century. It consisted of a few major highways, *routes nationales*, which were still only two-lane roads, with shoulders in some places but not everywhere. On the level plains, these routes were lined by regularly spaced tall poplars. Secondary roads, or *routes départementales,* were narrow and bordered by local trees. Local roads, or *routes municipales* were even narrower and also bordered by trees or hedges. In most villages, houses lined the roads and opened directly onto usually narrow streets.

Everything was simpler and less developed than today. People did not jump into cars and buses. They tended to walk or bicycle. France was still very much an agrarian country in 1939. The landscape would have consisted of scattered farms, not all of them with electricity. Villages were compact, usually clustered around the church and the village square, and largely self-sufficient. Nowadays, there are fewer but larger farms and many new houses or tastefully remodeled vacation homes belonging to urbanites.

Wartime bombing by the Allies, along with sabotage by the résistance, destroyed ninety percent of the rail network and its rolling stock. After the war the system was rebuilt and expanded, as was the road network. The Métro underground, not only in Paris but also in other cities, was expanded or rebuilt. Therefore, do not use modern maps. Many road numbers as well as the roads themselves have changed since the 1930s and 1940s.

In every city, town and village, streets and other local landmarks have been renamed, often after heroes of WWII. This goes for Parisian Métro stations. When your fictional characters need to rendez-vous in a street, a station or some identified place in your novel, keep to the names of prewar literary or military figures, famous battles or well-known music composers. Streets and squares named after Victor-Hugo, Foch, Lamartine, Verdun, Voltaire, Hector-Berlioz, Jules-Ferry, Solférino,etc. were to be found in even the smallest village.

During the war, few towns escaped some degree of destruction, first during the German invasion and secondly during the Occupation when Germans retaliated against the resistance groups and maquis camps and the Allies bombed military and industrial installations. A third wave of destruction occurred after the Allied landings and the liberating forces bombed and shelled their way across the country on their way to Germany. Some areas of Paris suburbs have been completely rebuilt as a consequence of the bombing, as was a swatch of Paris when the Luftwaffe bombed Paris the night of her liberation.

When trying to recreate the wartime era, one has to take into account the natural march of modernization, where the normal attrition of buildings no longer deemed suitable have been replaced. At the time of the Occupation, stone buildings in Paris and towns were smoke-blackened from the universal use of coal for heating and cooking. Today, these same buildings have been cleaned and appear creamy and honey-colored.

Before the war, and for several decades after it, the geographical departments were still grouped into provinces. In the 1970s and 1980s, provinces were regrouped into larger regions for administrative purposes. The resulting eighteen regions must not be mistaken for the former historical provinces in use during WWII and used for several decades afterward (see under Administration of France).

In addition, natural parks or natural areas (nature reserves) were created within the regions and also got a separate designation, for example, the region of Grand-Est is the administrative region of the old provinces of Champagne, Ardennes, Alsace and Lorraine, which included the departments of Ardennes, Aube, Marne, Haute-Marne, Meurthe-et-Moselle, Moselle, Bas-Rhin and Haut-Rhin. It includes six regional natural parks: Ardennes, Montagne de Reims, Forêt d'Orient, Ballon-des-Vosges, Lorraine and Vosges-du-Nord. To confuse you even more, the old departments still exist but are referred to by a number: Ain is No 1. Aisne is No. 2. Allier is No.3, Seine is No. 75.

Quite a complication, I am sure you will agree. Because of this, unless it is absolutely vital for your novel, avoid naming the departments or provinces unless you have access to prewar maps.

In more recent times, the French way of life and customs have also been affected by entry into the European Union and the Schengen Agreement, signed in June 1984. The French school system (which had already undergone reforms from 1968 to 1970) also changed to reflect France's membership in the EU. To conform with EU regulations, schools became co-educational. The EU school calendar was adapted (a September start instead of October, etc.). Hence, do not rely on references post-1960.

In their appropriate sections, you will find a few names of well-known artists, performers, writers, songs, plays, operas, politicians, résistants and newspapers of that era. Careful attention to these relatively minor elements of French life will mean that a reader will not be confronted by a character sitting in a café in 1940 reading the news in *Le Monde* newspaper, which was founded in August 1944.

This work is presented in alphabetical order under main category headings and their sub-categories to make it easier to check references. Some of the sections are repeated when that section applies to other categories. This is to reduce the need for page flipping. Where applicable, sub-categories are further divided by years as the situation on the ground evolved. The timeline at the front of the book is to help anchor the turning points in the war concerning the Occupation of France, in particular the announcements of the Allied landings June 1 and June 5, 1944, which are frequently confused in novels. A brief (too many documents to be listed) bibliography is included at the end.

A note of caution about relying on internet AI-software translation when a text is only available in French. There are terms in French that have no equivalent in English. AI will give idiotic results. French and English words that look like cognates can lead to confusion. For example, the word *librairies* means bookstores. The French for libraries is *bibliothèques*.

The section on Weather gives a month by month general view of the prevailing weather in France during the five years of war. This should help you avoid describing an event such as a parachute drop occurring in an area during gale force winds or have a character fly fishing when it was actually flooding.

Annex I is a short list of common male and female first names that were popular prior to 1940. Nothing is more jarring for a reader of a WWII novel than to be presented with characters called Zoé, Romy or Taylor, and males called Maël, Sacha or Liam, and other first names that were not in use at that time.

I sincerely hope that my efforts in putting together this compendium of wartime information will help you write the best novel ever.

Main abbreviations used in this book

BBC – British Broadcasting Corporation, based in London, England

BCRA – Bureau Central de Renseignements et d'Actions, based in London under de Gaulle – Central Office for Intelligence and Action

CFLN – Comité Français de Libération National – French National Committee for the Liberation of France

CMP – Compagnie du Chemin de fer Métropolitain – Métro for short

ERR – Rosenberg Institute for Occupied Territories

FFI – Forces Françaises de l'Intérieur – French Forces of the Interior, the military setup of the Résistance

FFL – Forces Françaises Libres – Free French Forces, the army under General de Gaulle in London

Gestapo – the shorthand title of the Geheime Staatpolizei or German secret police

GMT – UTC – Greenwich Mean Time, now UTC, Coordinated Universal Time

GPRF – Gouvernement Provisoire de la République Française – Provisional Government of the French Republic

KDS – Administration of Sicherheistpolizei and Sicherheitsdienst

LFC – Légion français des combattants

LVF, Légion des Volontaires Français contre le Bolshevism – French volunteers in the German Waffen-SS

MBB – Militärbehfelshaber Belgien

MBF – Militärbefehlshaber in Frankreich – the German military administration for occupied France

MOI – Main d'Œuvre Immigrée – Immigrated Labor

PTT – Poste, Téléphone et Télégraphe – French state corporation for post, telephone and telegraph

SAR – Search and Rescue

SD – Sicherheitsdienst – the intelligence agency of the SS and the Nazi Party

Sipo – Sicherhetsdienstpolizei – the police section of the SD

SNCF - Société Nationale des Chemins de Fer – French state rail network

STCRP - Société des Transports en Commun de la Région Parisienne

SOE – Special Operations Executive

SOL, Service d'Ordre Légionnaire – a collaborationist militia which became the Milice

SS – Schutzstaffel – the major German paramilitary organization, tasked with security-related duties
STO – Service de Travail Obligatoire – compulsory labor obligation, under which French citizens were forcibly sent to work in Germany
T.S.F. – télégraphie sans fil – wireless telegraphy

ZONES

Occupied zone, also referred as the North Zone.
Non-occupied zone, also referred as South Zone, zone no-no, free zone, but not Vichy or Vichy France. Journalists and historians coined the expression after the war. It is now officially wrong to use those terms. Pétain government and *État Français* are to be used where appropriate.

Timeline
1936
March 7   Germany occupies the Rhineland
May 5 ‣Italians occupy Addis-Ababa
July 16 ‣Start of Spanish Civil War
November 1 ‣ Declaration of the Rome-Berlin Axis
      25 ‣Germany-Japan anti-komintern pact
1937
November 6 ‣Italy's adherence to anti-komintern pact
1938
March 12 ‣German army in Vienna
      13-15 ‣Anschluss
September 15, 22-24 ‣Chamberlain, Daladier, Hitler meeting
      20-30 ‣Munich conference and accords
November 9-10 ‣Kristallnacht

1939
March 15-22 ‣Germany occupies Czechoslovakia and Memelland
      15 ‣Germany creates Bohemia-Moravia protectorate
April 7 ‣Italy occupies Albania
May 21 ‣Hitler and Mussolini sign the Pact of Steel
August 23 ‣Signing of the German-Soviet non-aggression pact
September 1 ‣Invasion of Poland
      3 ‣**France** and Britain declare war on Germany
      (a) Preparedness
         • Air raid sirens (see Bombings)
         • Art works are evacuated to the country
         • Beaux-Arts director, Mr. Huysman, orders the removal of the
stained glass windows from the Sainte-Chapelle (Paris), Chartres,
Metz, Rouen, Strasbourg, Mulhouse
         • Cafés, restaurants and other venues closed for curfew at
10:00 pm
         • Churches are full. Mass for soldiers
         • Distribution of gas masks to civilians
         • Monuments and buildings are sandbagged
         • Most theaters, cinemas and cafés close
         • General blackout order

- A large number of post offices ceased to operate as postmasters were drafted
    - Animals were evacuated from Vincennes zoo
    - In cities and towns, police on bicycle reprimanded inhabitants whose blackout curtains were letting light through. Quick accusation of collusion with the enemy

(b) Instructions to the population
- Be ready to leave home
- Gas mask to be always at hand. Do not leave home without it
- Have a flashlight or candles at night in case of air raid alert
- Do not stand at the window when there is an alert
- Have food in a tightly closed box
- Do not eat food contaminated by explosion of a gas bomb
- In August 1914 people chanted "To Berlin". In September 1939 they were resigned.

(c) Troops departed from Gare de l'Est
- Hope for peace was sustained as people put their trust in the Maginot Line
- The fear of the Fifth Column was prevalent. Posters recommending silence

(d) Paris Métro stopped running at night

September. 26 ‣French Communist organizations were dissolved

28 ‣German-Soviet treaty partitioned Poland

September-October ‣French military operation in the Saar

November 30-March 12 ‣ Winter War in Finland

1940

March 13 ‣Russo-Finnish Armistice

21 to June 16 ‣Paul Reynaud headed the government

April 8 ‣Invasion of Denmark

10 to June 8 ‣Norwegian campaign

May 10 ‣Holland, Belgium, Luxemburg invaded

‣Winston Churchill appointed British Prime-Minister

10-11 ‣Eben-Emael (Belgium fort) falls

12 ‣Refugees arrived in France. The wealthy first, in bullet-ridden vehicles. Three air raids in the north of France

10-June 25 ‣Campaign for France.

13 ‣Sedan, French front broken. Rotterdam capitulated

18 ‣Philippe Pétain became the vice-president of the Council of Ministers

19 ‣Weygand replaced Gamelin

15-28 ‣Hollande and Belgium capitulated. Narvik fell

26 to June 4 ‣Dunkirk

31 ‣Lille capitulated

June 1 ‣The Wehrmacht (under General Wägner) granted the honors of war to the French defenders of Lille, under the command of General Jean-Baptiste Molinié

3 ‣Paula Operation. Luftwaffe bombed the western suburbs of Paris

5 ‣Battle of the Somme battle. French defeat

8 ‣All schools, lycées, colleges and universities closed

‣Gare Saint-Lazare rail station closed

‣More Parisians left

10 ‣Italy declared war on France

11 ‣Gare Montparnasse closed

13 ‣Paris is declared an 'Open' city (i.e. it will not put up a defence)

14 ‣Paris occupation began.

15 ‣Cafés and restaurants re-opened (Maxim's, Café de Paris, Maxéville, Dôme, Colisée), some movie theaters

15-July 2 ‣USSR occupied the Baltic states

16 ‣Paul Reynaud resigned. Marshal Pétain headed the government. The army continued the combat as the Wehrmacht pushed farther south

17 ‣Pétain asked for an armistice

18 ‣De Gaulle's resistance speech from London

20-25 ‣Battle of the Alps and Italian defeat

22 ‣Pétain signed armistice with Germany

‣France was divided. North zone occupied by Germans. Free zone in the south under Marshal Pétain's government

24 ‣Pétain signed an armistice with Rome

‣Rationing imposed throughout France – both zones (no tickets yet)

25 ‣Armistice imposed throughout France. Soldiers were made prisoners

27 ‣Train service resumed

‣The British government recognized General Charles de Gaulle as head of the France Libre (Free French)

29 ‣Pétain's government temporarily settled in Clermont-Ferrand, in the free zone

July 2 ‣Pétain's government relocated to the town of Vichy, in the Hôtel du Parc. The government accepted Nazi ideology and the persecution of Jews and Romas. Internment camps set up

3-6 ‣Mers-el-Kébir British Navy sunk French fleet

10 ‣Pétain obtained full powers

11 ‣Balls and celebrations of July 14 Bastille Day banned

14 ‣National Day. Cross of Lorraine (opposition) symbols appeared on walls everywhere

15 ‣Compulsory census for everyone in both zones

17 ‣Posters prohibited listening to foreign radio stations under penalty of death

18 ‣Nazi Propaganda Abteilung set up in Paris

19 ‣Official authorization given for refugees to return to the occupied zone

21 ‣USSR annexion of the Baltic states

22 ‣Law removing French nationality from foreigners naturalized after 1927

25 ‣Lists of French soldiers killed or made prisoner made public

August 1 ‣German authorities imposed rules on written and telephone communication within the occupied zone and between the two zones

5 ‣Otto Abetz appointed Reich ambassador to Paris

August 7 ‣Alsace is annexed to the Gau of Baden, and Lorraine (except Moselle department) to the Gau of Saar-Palatinat

13 ‣Pétain's law forbade secret societies

13 ‣Aldertag, Battle of Britain began

19 ‣Dissolution of Freemason organizations

22 ‣The German occupier declared that any French citizen arrested and imprisoned was considered a hostage

26-28 ‣Tchad, Cameroon, Congo, Oubangui-Chari rallied to the Free French

29 ‣Pétain created the Légion Française des Combattants (LFC)

31 ‣Occupiers confiscated shortwave radios

September 5 ‣No communications permitted between France and Moselle and Alsace. The latter two considered foreign countries

7 ‣The Blitz begins over London

10-20 ‣French territories of the South Seas Islands, New-Caledonia rally to the Free French

21 ‣Jews and people of color forbidden to return to the occupied zone

23-24 ‣Dakar attack by and defeat of the Free French Forces

25 ‣Censored mail allowed between the two zones

‣Nazi decree on the status of Jews in the occupied zone

27 ‣Tripartite Pacte (Germany, Japan, Italy)

30 ‣Deadline for return to the occupied zone

October 1 ‣First Jewish Law enacted

2 ‣Start of new school year

3-18 ‣Census of the Jewish population

‣Abrogation of the Crémieux Decree, re. Jews in Algeria

‣General Maxime Weygand appointed general representative of the État Français (unoccupied zone and loyal colonies) in North Africa

‣Hitler-Franco meeting in Hendaye, France

18 ‣Five RAF Spitfires flew over Paris

24 ‣Meeting Hitler-Pétain in Montoire

25 ‣Spitfires returned and sky-wrote *confiance RAF*

November 4 ‣Roosevelt re-elected president of the United States

10 ‣Jacques Bonsergent and German troops incident

November 11 ‣Air raid alert at 0700 hrs. Ends at 0815 hrs (7:00 to 8:15 am)

12 ‣Demonstrations in Paris and country

December 13 ‣Pierre Laval, vice-president of the Council of Ministers, fired from Pétain's government

15 ‣The occupiers brought back the ashes of the Aiglon (son of Napoleon I) to be kept in Les Invalides

December 15 ‣The Musée de l'Homme prints *Résistance* – the first underground newspaper

16 ‣Otto Abetz went to the town of Vichy with an ultimatum and returned to Paris with Pierre Laval

‣Expulsion of 150,000 Alsatians and Lorrains

23 ‣Execution of Jacques Bonsergent

24 ‣Poster announcing Jacques Bonsergent's execution. First of several execution posters

26 ‣De Gaulle asked French people to stay indoors for two hours on January 1

31 ‣Re-activation of the Secours National (National Aid) organization

1941
January 2 ‣Germans ban La Légion des Combattants in the occupied zone
      ‣RAF attack barges on the Channel coast in full daylight
    5 ‣Gestapo arrest Prefect of police Roger Langeron in Paris
    10 ‣First arrest of resistants from Musée de l'Homme, including Geneviève de Gaulle (niece of General de Gaulle)
  March 22 ‣Symbolic opening bars of Beethoven Fifth Symphony heard for the first time over BBC radio.
      ‣Joseph Darnand creates the Service d'Ordre Légionaire (SOL) (Public Order Legion, a paramilitary orgnization)
    29 ‣Xavier Vallat appointed to General Commissionaire to Jewish affairs
      ‣First mention of La Résistance (the entity, the spirit not the actions on the ground) by de Gaulle.
April ‣Foundation of the réseau (network) Alliance
    18 ‣Pierre Laval appointed prime minister on German orders
May 16 ‣Signing of the Paris Protocols
June 2 ‣New law regarding Jews
      ‣No letters allowed. Postcards, one side blank, other side address and five-word message, allowed between the two zones
    10 ‣Foreign diplomatic and consular personnel expelled from occupied zone
    21-22 ‣Germany invades USSR
    30 ‣Pétain breaks off diplomatic relations with Moscow
July ‣Ration tickets for coal
August 3-13 ‣Jews obliged to surrender their radio sets
    14 ‣In free zone, civil servants and military must pledge loyalty to head of state Pétain
    21 ‣First assassination attempt against a German officer in Paris
September ‣Exhibition Le Juif et la France (The Jews and France)
      ‣Henri Chamberlin creates the French Gestapo, rue Lauriston
October 2-3 ‣Bombing of synagogues
    12 ‣Joseph Darnand's SOL changes to Légion des Volontaires Français (LVF). Pledge to Pétain

28 ‣Listening to foreign radio stations banned. Infractions punishable by imprisonment

November 14 ‣Jews banned from public places

20 ‣The Militärbefehlshaber demand that General Weygand in Algeria be dismissed

‣United States inform Pétain they are suspending exports to Algeria

December 11 ‣Attack on Pearl Harbor

1942

January 20 ‣Paris police pledged loyalty to Marshal Pétain

February 23 ‣The Gestapo executed Boris Vildé (Musée de l'Homme réseau) at Fort du Mont-Valérien

March 27 ‣First train to Auschwitz

April-May ‣Allies bombed western outskirts of Paris

18 ‣German authorities (MBF) installed Pierre Laval as head of the government of the État Français in the town of Vichy

May 6 ‣Louis Darquier de Pellepoix appointed head (Commissaire général) of Jewish affairs

28 ‣British raid over Saint-Nazaire

29 ‣MBF obliged Jews to wear the yellow star of David. Pétain refused to do the same in the free zone

‣Jews had the word *Juif* printed on their identity card

June 22 ‣Laval instituted La relève (voluntary workers for Germany)

July 18 ‣Eighty-eight hostages shot at the Fort du Mont-Valérien

16-17‣ Rafle du Vel d'Hiv (roundup)

August 19 ‣Operation Jubilee. Dieppe Raid. Canadian, British, American and Polish troops landed in Dieppe

September 1 ‣Imposition of the STO, Service du Travail Obligatoire – compulsory workers for Germany – in the occupied zone

October 4 ‣Laval imposed the STO in the free zone

7 ‣Jewish decree in occupied zone

October 23 ‣Air raid over Paris. Allied bombing of the western suburbs

November 8 ‣Allied landings in North Africa

‣Admiral Darlan signed the ceasefire

‣Pétain broke off relations with North Africa

9 ‣Hitler-Laval meeting in Berchtesgaden

November 11 ‣Operation Anton. Wehrmacht invaded the non-occupied zone

    ‣The Italian army invaded Corsica and the south-east of France

    27 ‣The French fleet scuttled off Toulon

    29 ‣The armistice army was disbanded

December 1942 ‣Formation of the first large maquis in the Ain region

    24 ‣Admiral Darlan assassinated in Algeria

    31 ‣Allies again bombed western suburbs of Paris

    ‣All police in the former free zone brought under the command of the Milice

1943

January 24 ‣Destruction of Marseille's old district: Le Panier

    27 ‣Pétain banned the Salvation Army

    30 ‣Creation of the Milice

February 16 ‣The STO law was passed

March ‣The demarcation line was abolished

April ‣Creation of the CFLN, Comité Français de Libération National – French National Liberation Committee, with de Gaulle in Algiers

    5 ‣Allies again bombed industrial targets in the western suburbs of Paris

    ‣Allies bombed Antwerp, Belgium

    19 ‣Warsaw ghetto uprising

    29 ‣Hitler-Laval second meeting in Montoire

May 17 ‣Allies bombed Bordeaux

    27 ‣Establishment by Jean Moulin of the Conseil National de la Résistance – National Resistance Council

    29 ‣Allies bombed Rennes

June 9 ‣Gestapo arrested General Delestraint, Secret Army head

    20 ‣Allies bombed Le Creusot (coal mining area)

    21 ‣Jean Moulin arrested in Caluire

July 23 ‣Death of Jean Moulin

August ‣Darnand pledged loyalty to Hitler, and through him the Milice

September 15 ‣Allies again bombed industries in the western suburbs of Paris

November 11 ‣Maquisards of the local maquis paraded in the streets of Oyonnax

    24 ‣Allies bombed Toulon

1944

February ‣Formation of the Forces Françaises de l'Intérieur (FFI) – French Forces of the Interior

2 ‣Pétain's government expanded the age for the STO from 16 to 60 years

8 ‣RAF bombed the Gnome-Rhône factory in Limoges

13 ‣Allies dropped arms to the maquis of des Glières, Haute-Savoie region

21 ‣Appearance of large, red and black placards on the Paris walls announcing execution of twenty-three resistants

March 6 ‣Allies bombed the north of France in advance of Operation Overlord

26 ‣Wehrmacht, Waffen-SS and Milice forces wiped out the des Glières maquis

April 1 ‣SS Das Reich Panzer Division committed the Ascq massacre

19 ‣Allies bombed Rouen

21 ‣Allies bombed La Chapelle district of Paris

23-25 ‣Milice attacked the Vercors maquis

26 ‣Marshal Pétain visited La Chapelle district in Paris

May 1 ‣Allies bombed twenty railroad stations in France and southern Belgium

26 ‣Allies bombed Lyon, Nice, Saint-Étienne and Chambéry

30 ‣Allies intensified bombing of railroad stations, bridges and communication centers

June 1 ‣from 1230 hrs (12:30 pm) to 2100 hrs (9:00 pm) BBC broadcasts coded information bulletin: *Les sanglots longs des violons de l'automne* – the message announcing the imminent landings

3 ‣Comité Français de Libération National (CFLN) renamed Gouvernement Provisoire de la République Française (GPRF) – Provisional Government of the French Republic, with General de Gaulle as president

5 ‣BBC broadcasts second coded information bulletin: *Blessent mon coeur d'une langueur monotone* landings next day

6 ‣Allies landed on Normandy beaches

7-25 ‣Caen liberated – and totally destroyed

8 ‣Bayeux liberated

‣From June 8 to September 27, the Waffen-SS, the Wehrmacht, the Gestapo, SS personnel and the Kriegsmarine committed thirty-five major massacres of more than ten civilians and many more under ten persons.

    23-26 ‣Cherbourg liberated

July 19 ‣Saint-Lô liberated

    20 ‣Assassination attempt on Hitler

    24 ‣August 22 Battle of Falaise

      ‣Milice and Gestapo units committed the Savigny-en-Septaine massacre

    30 ‣U.S. forces entered Avranches

August 1 ‣Warsaw uprising

    8 ‣Le Mans liberated

    15 ‣Allies landed in Provence (Operation Anvil)

    19 ‣Start of the uprising in Paris

    20 ‣Germans took Marshal Pétain to Germany

    25 ‣Paris liberated

    26 ‣Charles de Gaulle in Paris

    28 ‣End of fighting in Marseille and Toulon

September 3 ‣Lyon liberated

    18 ‣Brest liberated

November 19 ‣Metz liberated

    23 ‣Strasbourg liberated

    25 ‣Belfort liberated

1945

January 1 ‣German Operation Nordwind in Alsace

    6 ‣German attack on Strasbourg

    20 ‣Battle for Colmar

    28 ‣End of the Ardennes battle

February 2 ‣U.S. 1st Army crossed the Siegfried Line

  March 8-9 ‣German raid on the port of Granville held by the Allies

    16 ‣Liberation of Bitche (Moselle)

      ‣Lorraine liberated

    19 ‣Alsace liberated

April 15-20 ‣Liberation of Royan and Pointe de Grave (Charente-Inférieure)

    26 ‣Marshal Pétain returned to France and surrendered to the French authorities

    29 April to **May 13** Women voted for the first time in municipal elections

May 7 ‣Germany capitulated

    11 ‣Liberation of Lorient and Saint-Nazaire (Brittany). France was totally liberated

July 23 to August 14 ‣Trial of Marshal Pétain

A Writer's Guide to WWII France

1. Status of France

A. France had a different governmental setup after being occupied by the Wehrmacht in June, 1940 to that of the other occupied countries of Norway, Denmark, Holland, Belgium and the eastern European countries. France was split in two parts, with a French puppet government, headed by Marshal Pétain, in the town of Vichy in the southern, non-occupied zone, called *État Français*, not Vichy France. The Wehrmacht occupied the northern part. French civil administration extended over both zones. Historians are not entirely sure about the reasons the Germans divided the country in this way, but the most likely motives were:

• Hitler wanted direct control of the northern zone, which encompassed the industries and manpower he needed for his war effort.

• Hitler did not trust the French, but respected the highly popular Marshal Pétain. By letting Pétain administer both zones, minus the annexed and forbidden territories, he attempted to ensure there would be no rebellion or agitation among the population in the rear of his army.

• By letting the French administrate the territory rather than install a gauleiter, fewer soldiers and police were required and the Militärbefehlshaber in Frankreich(MBF) did not need to assume the responsibility to keep order. Even after the Wehrmacht invaded the previously non-occupied zone in November, 1942, some rural locations never saw a soldier.

B. All the prefectures in the occupied zone received directives from the Pétain's government. Although, in appearance, the non-occupied zone was totally controlled by the Pétain's government, it took orders from the MBF, except for the restricted zone of Nord-Pas-de-Calais, which was attached to the Militärbehfelshaber Belgien (MBB) in Belgium.

• In the eyes of the occupiers and French citizens, Paris, not Vichy, remained the only true capital of France, occupied and non-occupied parts alike, and the center for all the Reich authorities. The paradox was that the État Français had an embassy in Paris.

C. Parisians and those in urban centers in the occupied zone faced different branches of the occupying authorities and of the État Français. These could range from the Wehrmacht, the Third Reich's political police – the Sichenheitsdienst (SD), Sipo, Schutzpolizei – to the French civilian police.

D. Sicherheitsdienst was the security and intelligence branch of the Schutzstaffel (SS).
   i. The Sicherheitsdienst worked closely with the Geheime Staat Polizei (Gestapo). The SD gathered intelligence to ensure the security of the troops. Their units could arrest and imprison suspects.

   ii. The SD also pursued criminals in parallel with the French police, e.g. black marketers.

   iii. Uniforms. They wore the gray-green SS uniform with SS runes on the left collar and a diamond patch on the sleeve. They used the same ranks as the SS. The Sipo wore a shiny gorgette.

E. Geheimestaat Polizei (Gestapo) were plain-clothed secret police, some of whom were members of the SS but this was not a requirement. They pursued the perceived political and racial enemies of the Reich, i.e. subversive elements, resistants, dissidents, communists and Jews.

F. Schutzstaffel was the dedicated Nazi (National Socialism) party paramilitary organization. The SD and Gestapo were subordinate to the SS. The SS could be compared to an octopus with tentacles in every aspect of life, including Germany's own

25

military units. Members wore gray-green uniforms with the distinctive SS runes on the right collar.

NOTE: The black uniform was phased out in 1937 and only used for ceremonial purposes.

   G. The **Schutzstaffel** and the **Gestapo** were not involved with France's civil administration.

   Caution, the Waffen-SS, the combat branch of the SS, was NOT active in occupied France until 1944 when it saw action against the Allied invasion of Normandy after being transferred from the eastern front.

   H. Hierarchy. Due to tensions and rivalries among the various departments, lines of authority were sometimes blurred.

2. Administration of France
A. French administration
i. Status
• 1939, France had 90 departments (including Algeria and Corsica) distributed over 35 provinces. In modern times some departments have been renamed and the old provinces amalgamated into regions:

ii. Names of the departments that changed after the war:
• Modern maps do not show the names that were in use during the war and until the late twentieth century. When identifying a department from a Google map, use the names in bold letters.
- Charente-Maritime was **Charente-Inférieure**
- Seine-Maritime was **Seine-Inférieure**
- Hauts-de-Seine is made up of the former **Seine** department and **Seine-et-Oise** department
- Loire-Atlantique was **Loire-Inférieure**
- Pyrénées-Atlantiques was **Basses-Pyrénées**
- Alpes-de-Haute-Provence was **Basses-Alpes**
- Côtes-d'Armor was **Côtes-du-Nord**

iii. Names of the historical provinces
• Use:
  - Alsace, Angoumois, Anjou, Aquitaine, Artois, Auvergne
  - Beauce, Beaujolais, Berry, Bourbonnais, Bretagne, Brie, Bourgogne
  - Champagne, Corsica, Dauphiné
  - Flandres, Franche-Comté
  - Gascogne
  - Île-de-France
  - Languedoc, Limousin, Lyonnais, Lorraine
  - Maine, Nivernais, Normandie
  - Orléanais, Picardie, Poitou, Provence

- Roussillon, Saintonge, Savoie, Touraine

iv. Modern regions: do not use the following in your WWII era novel:
- Auvergne-Rhône-Alpes
- Bourgogne-Franche-Comté
- Centre-Val de Loire, Corse
- Grand Est
- Hauts-de-France, Haut-Doubs
- Nouvelle-Aquitaine
- Occitanie
- Pays de la Loire, Provence-Alpes-Côte d'Azur.

• In addition, natural parks or natural areas (nature reserves) were created within the regions. For example, Haut-Doubs is now a natural area in the Franche-Comté province, which is integrated into the Bourgogne-Franche-Comté region, but Doubs is the department, and the Haut-Jura is a natural park, not an administrative area. Jura is the department.

v. Préfet. A prefect is a high-ranking official who headed a department with a general (departmental) council, i.e. a prefecture. Except in Paris, the council nominated the mayor for every town to the smallest village. In Paris, the Ministry of the Interior nominated the administrative prefect and the police prefect.

vi. Public notaries (*notaires*)
• They were not lawyers. They were public officers appointed by the *Garde des Sceaux* (now called justice minister, but the function is identical).
• They dealt with administrative affairs, real estate, wills, legalization of documents.
• They authenticated government's acts where required.

vii. Paris

• Paris was divided in 20 *Arrondissements* (districts). Each one was governed by a municipal council elected by universal suffrage. The prefect of Paris and the prefect of police shared the mayoral responsibilities for the city, i.e. the Prefecture of Paris and the Prefecture of Police. Both had a sub-prefect.

viii. Rural areas
• A mayor was appointed to villages and hamlets by the prefect.

ix. Towns
• A town had an elected municipal council which nominated a mayor.

• The prefect. or the sub-prefect headed the town, i.e. the seat of the prefecture.

x. Status as of August 7, 1940.
• Annexation of Alsace and Lorraine provinces (four departments: Meuse, Meurthe-et-Moselle, Moselle, Vosges). September 15, 1940, the Nord and Pas-de-Calais departments, and three departments of Lorraine – Meuse, Meurthe-et-Moselle, Vosges – were attached to the Brussels, Belgium, military command.

• 85 departments remained under French administration, in both occupied and free zones.

B. German administration.
• Kommandantur only in the occupied zone until November 11, 1942.

i. Structure. Militärbefehlshaber in Frankreich.

• Oberfeldkommandantur oversaw the whole of occupied zone. And after November 1942, the whole of France.

• Feldkommandantur oversaw a department in the occupied zone. And after November 1942, all the departments of France.

• Kreiskommandantur oversaw a municipality in the occupied zone. And after November 1942, municipalities in the formerly non-occupied zone.

• Ortskommandantur oversaw a district in the occupied zone. And after November 1942, the formerly non-occupied zone. In Paris there was an Ortskommandantur for every *arrondissement.*

ii. Militärbefehlshaber in Frankreich commandants:

• October 1940 to February 1942, Otto von Stüpnagel.

• February 1942 to July 1944, Carl-Heinrich von Stüpagnel.

• July 1944 to October 4, 1944, Karl Kitzinger.

• August 7, 1944, Dietrich von Choltitz was appointed military governor of the Groß Paris.

• The Schutzstaffel and the Gestapo were not involved in France's civil administration.

Caution: the Waffen-SS, the combat branch of the SS, was not active in occupied France, until 1944, when it was transferred from the eastern front and saw action against the Allies in Normandy.

NOTE: The Waffen-SS wore the gray-green uniform. The black uniform had been phased out in 1937 and was only used in ceremonies. Do not have your SS characters strutting the streets in their black uniforms as Hollywood would have you to believe.

• The Sicherheitsdienstpolizei (SIPO), with their gorgette on the chest, carried out arrests and occasionally assisted or supervised the French police.

• The Sicherheitsdienst was the security and intelligence branch of the SS and carried arrests.

iii. Annexation

• **Alsace**. October 18, 1940 by an unpublished decree, Hitler declared that Alsace and Moselle were de facto parts of Germany, in violation of the armistice conditions signed June 22, 1940.

• **Alsace** was the only part of French territory to have a Nazi concentration camp, Natzweiler-Struthoff (see Section 28. Interment camps).

• Forced enrolment into the Wehrmacht of young men known as the "*Malgré Nous*" (Against our will).

• French language was forbidden. German language and German curriculum were enforced.

iv. Forbidden areas

• July 1940 the Nord-East line (Nordost Linie, also known as the Führer Line) extended from the Somme River to the Swiss border. It was more difficult to cross this line than the north to south demarcation line.

• **Nord and Pas-de-Calais,** departments were attached to the Bruxelles military command.

v. Territories and departments in the forbidden zone:

• Northern part of the department of Somme, Aisne, Ardennes, Meuse, Meurthe-et-Moselle, Vosges, Territory of Belfort, Doubs, Haute-Saône, northern part of the department of Jura, half of the department of Haute-Marne, Côte d'Or, Pays de Gex and six communes of Haute-Savoie (the latter only until August 24, 1941).

• Those territories were reserved for settlement by German people.

vi. Refugees

• Refugees from Belgium, Holland and Luxembourg were forbidden to return home after the armistice until May 1941, and then only essential workers. After December 18, 1941, other refugees were allowed to return except Jews and persons of color.

vii. Forbidden maritime areas

• As of April 1941, the forbidden coastal zone was a band of territory some twenty to thirty kilometers wide extending from Dunkirk to Hendaye on the Spanish border.
  • It was reserved for the construction of the Atlantic Wall.
  • Only residents were allowed in. Non-residents were only allowed in for funerals, severe illness, birth or wedding of a close relative.

TRIVIA: Considering the population, there were an enormous number of funerals, fatal illnesses, births and weddings, all to benefit the résistance groups outside the zone.

viii. Billboards, placards, posters
(a) Jews. Interdictions Expulsions
  • July 1940. Jews were expelled from Alsace and Moselle.
  • Jews were prohibited from returning to the occupied zone. Their assets were seized.
  • September 27, 1940, first German statute for Jews.
  • Posters with the word Jew in the window of businesses.
  • July 3, 1942, prohibition for Jews to use the telephone.
  • July 8, 1942, prohibition for Jews to take in a show or go to the cinema. (See 32. Jewish Affairs).

(b) Orders to the population
  • No gathering more than three persons
  • Curfew 9:00 pm-6:00 am
  • No dancing (See 8. Art and Entertainment)
  • No badmouthing Germany
  • No showing disrespect to the occupiers
  • Clocks must be advanced to Berlin time
  • No graffiti
  • No listening to foreign radio broadcasts
  • Money: One Reichmark is twenty francs
  • No owning a car without special authorization, such as for doctors
  • No travel after 10:00 pm without special authorization

(c) French posters

• Smaller than the large MBF posters, they tended to depict family and social action.

(d) German posters
• Posters (Bekanntmachung). The yellow poster with a black border to announce the executions of hostages and resistants to warn the population of further reprisals in case of attack against the occupiers.

• Large posters were displayed to persuade the population that the Germans were in France to help and promote the Nazi ideology.

• The entirely red poster appeared in February 21, 1944, to announce executions of resistants (See 39. Propaganda) of 23 members of the FTP and Main d'Œuvre Immigrée(FTP-MOI).

• In Paris, a tract (22 x 26cm) was distributed with a reduced image of the red poster including on the back a commentary blaming the Army of Crime.

CAUTION: Do not have your characters look at the red poster before 1944. Until then they were yellow with a black border.

ix. Fraternization Rules and Reality
• Wehrmacht troops had been given a code of conduct. They were to have a friendly and correct behavior toward the population.

• It was forbidden to enter into a relationship with a Frenchwoman.

• It was forbidden to give a ride to Frenchwomen in a military vehicle.

• From day one, soldiers approached Frenchwomen and were soon having relationships. The rule was ignored by soldiers, from the lowest to the highest ranks of the armed forces.

x. Paris. Capital of the Greater Reich

• Upon arrival, the Reich authorities order the removal of sand bags from the monuments. POWs were assigned to the work.

• Paris was the playground of the German forces. Every soldier was entitled to a leave in Paris. Ordinary soldiers wore a forage cap or field cap. Officers wore a peaked cap.

• There were regular patrols in the streets. They consisted of two men carrying rifles slung over the shoulder.

• After 1941 and the increase of attacks, three or more men, carrying rifles over the shoulder, and a handgun formed the patrols.

• Time change: As the Wehrmacht marched into France it imposed German summer (or daylight saving) time. France was also on summer time from March to October and had to advance the clocks by one hour June 14, 1940 in Paris as Germany was normally one hour ahead of France. The time was now two hours ahead of the Greenwich Mean Time(GMT) – today's UTC(Coordinated Universal Time).

• In October, the time stepped back one hour.

• Paris was considered the cultural capital of the Greater Reich and of the whole of France. In the non-occupied zone, people did not recognize Vichy as being the capital.

• The Wehrmacht came with lists of addresses of buildings that had a front and a back entrance (for security reasons) and of hotels and places of entertainment.

• The lists were made with the help of the pre-war Guide Michelin.

• The population's attitude can be divided in three categories – Collaborators, Résistants, Wait and See.

• With the Occupation came restrictions and rationing. The economy functioned at a slow pace. (see 21. Economy. Industries. Factories. Banks).

xi. Buildings requisitioned
• Building at angle of the rue du 4 Septembre and Avenue de l'Opéra – the Kommandantur headquarters.

- 52 Avenue des Champs-Elysées – Propagandastaffel.
- 31 bis Avenue Foch (nicknamed avenue Boche) – Jewish Affairs.
- 72 Avenue Foch – Headquarters of the Sipo-Sicherheistdienst.
- 84 Avenue Foch – Interrogation of SOE agents and resistants leaders brought from Fresnes prison by Gestapo agents.
- 180 rue de la Pompe – Gestapo offices. Worked with Gestapo of Foch Avenue.
- 93 rue Lauriston – French Gestapo française – La Carlingue. Also annex 3 bis place des États-Unis.
- 11 rue des Saussaies – Administration of Sicherheistpolizei and Sicherheitsdienst, KDS Paris.
- 4 rue d'Anjou – one of the offices of the Feldgendarmerie.
- 12 rue Varenne – Wehrmacht Military tribunal.
- Rond-Point des Champs-Élysées – Oberkommando der Wehrmacht headquarters.
- 27 and 57 Boulevard de Lannes – officers' dwelling at 57 and Sicherheistpolizei offices at 27.
- Porte de la Muette – Kriegsmarine military tribunal.
- Avenue du Maréchal Galliéni – Grand Palais (large covered space for exhibitions). German vehicle storage.

xii. Châteaux requisitioned
- Château de la Muette – Kriesgmarine Staff headquarters.

xiii. Hotels requisitioned
- Ambassador Hotel, 16 Boulevard Haussmann – East sector of the Greater Paris Command.
- Beauharnais Hotel, 78 rue de Lille – German embassy (Otto Abetz ambassador's residence).
- Continental Hotel, 3 rue de Castiglione et rue de Rivoli – exception tribunals.

• Crillon Hotel (place de la Concorde) – Paris military command headquarters.

• George V Hotel, 31 Avenue George V – Wehrmacht headquarters.

• Hotel des Invalides, 129 rue de Grenelle – Staff headquarters.

• Hotel de la Marine (place de la Concorde) – Kriegsmarine headquarters.

• Lutetia Hotel, 43 Boulevard Raspail – Abwehr headquarters.

• Majestic Hotel, 19 rue Kléber (front) 30 rue La Pérouse (back entrance, with bunker in the street) – Militärbefehlshaber in Frankreich headquarters.

• Meurice Hotel, 228 rue de Rivoli – Greater Paris headquarters.

• Orsay Hotel, 93 rue de Lille – South sector of Greater Paris Command.

• Ritz Hotel, Place Vendôme – Luftwaffe headquarters and main entrance for Germans.

• Ritz, rue Cambon – hotel entrance for the public.

• Vernet Hotel, 23-25 rue Vernet Street – North-west sector of the Greater Paris Command.

xiv. Hospitals requisitioned
• Public hospitals were requisitioned first by the French army until the armistice, then some of them by the occupiers.

- Salpêtrière and Lariboisière hospitals.
- Institut Dentaire George-Eastman hospital.

xv. Mansions requisitioned
• Palais Rose (a mansion on Foch Avenue) – General Carl Heinrich Stüpnagel, commandant of Greater Paris).

• Villa Coty, Raphaël Avenue.

xvi. Palais (government buildings) requisitioned

36

- Palais Bourbon, Quai d'Orsay – Greater Paris administration.
    - Palais du Luxembourg – The three armed forces services.

xvii. Troop housing
    - Prince-Eugène barracks, 17 place de la République – for the Wehrmacht.
    - Dufayel warehouses, 26 rue Clignancourt – for the Wehrmacht.
    - Lycée Claude-Bernard, 1 Avenue du Parc des Princes – SS barracks (Germans built a bunker in the basement).
    - Lycée Montaigne, 17 rue Auguste-Comte – Luftwaffe barracks (Germans built a bunker in the basement).
    - Some officers requisitioned houses or apartments in the affluent districts of Paris. Others lodged in requisitioned hotels in the city.
    - Some officers billeted with affluent Parisians (bigger houses and apartments).
    - Some non-commissioned officers housed with local inhabitants. Others lodged in the officers' quarters.

xviii. Billeting in towns
    - As in Paris, the Wehrmacht came with lists of addresses for all the major towns.
    - Hospitals were requisitioned.
    - Officers were housed in luxury hotels wherever they existed or mansions. Châteaux and houses were requisitioned as needed.
    - Officers billeted in private mansions or large houses.
    - Troops housed in boy's schools and community halls.

xix. Repression
    - While still under the non-aggression pact, communists were not the enemy. After June 1941 the invasion of the USSR by the Wehrmacht, the MBF aimed their repression to the Judeo-Bolshevik (Jews and communists).

• Hostages. At the end of the 1941 summer, the MBF changed the hostage policy. Instead of selecting hostages among the notables, they selected them among the prisoners, that is the communists, then the Jews.

• Notice to the population. Suspected authors of attacks will be heavily fined, deported to forced labor in the east and larger deportations will occur if attacks are repeated.
(See 19. Deportation)

xx. Standard Time, 1940

• On arrival in France, time was changed to German time, i.e. one hour ahead. France was on Summer Time (daylight savings time) between March and October. The rest of the year it was on Greenwich Mean Time (GMT – today's UTC). This since 1923.

• In Germany, time was also changed in March and October.

• The non-occupied zone did not align itself to German time. This created problems for the railway – SNCF – and trains crossing the demarcation line.

• The SNCF petitioned the Pétain government to align itself on German time as in the occupied zone. A February 16, 1941 decree announced the south non-occupied zone would be on the same time as the north occupied zone.

3. Allied Landings
A. Allied landings in Corsica
- September 1943

B. Dieppe Raid. Operation Jubilee, Wednesday August 19, 1942.

i. Goal: The stated goal was a raid to destroy the artillery batteries on the east and west side of Dieppe and in the town itself.
- It would test the feasibility of a landing.
- It would boost the morale of the Allies.

ii. Defenses – Wehrmacht.

iii. Location: Between Le Hâvre and Calais, in the department of Seine-Inférieure, in Normandy province.

iv. Popular interpretation: Unnecessary rehearsal for the planned massive amphibian invasion to force the Germans out of Europe.

v. Troops: Canadian commandos to lead the attack. British commandos and American Rangers as support troops.

vi. Weather: Last day of good weather.

vii. Consequences:
- Goal not achieved. The Allies failed to take the town.
- Heavy losses.
- Hitler rewarded the town of Dieppe.
- Lessons learned that later saved thousands of lives on 1944 D-Day.

C. Normandy, D-Day. Operation Overlord, June 6, 1944
i. Goal: To help Stalin's armies on the eastern front by opening a second front in the west.

• To liberate France and other occupied European countries.

ii. German Defenses: Atlantic Wall was reinforced in the northern area.
• Normandy coast had only regular Wehrmacht forces, many young and older recruits.

iii. Location:
• The location was determined because on May 8, 1942, résistant René Duchez stole the plans of the fortifications from the Caen Kommandantur.
• Coast of Normandy province, between Saint-Martin-de-Varengeville and north of the Orne River.
• Landing beaches. Operation names: Utah Beach, Omaha Beach, Pointe-du-Hoc Beach, Gold Beach, Juno Beach, Sword Beach.
• Artificial ports created at Arromanches and Saint-Laurent-sur-Mer.

iv. Troops: American, British with French contingent, Canadian and elements of other occupied countries integrated with the main forces.

v. Role of the French Résistance: to delay the enemy reinforcements on the way to Normandy.
• To sabotage the military materiel and equipment.
• To sabotage infrastructure and communications.

vi. Consequences
• Successful landings.
• Major step in the liberation of occupied countries.
• Defeat of the Nazi regime.
• Mass killings of civilians by the Third Reich troops on their way to the Normandy front.

D. Deception
i. Operation Fortitude, carried out in the Nord and Pas-de-Calais regions, June 6 1944.

ii. Goal: To draw attention to the northern coast as the Nazi military expected that it would take place over the shortest route from England.

iii. Location: North coast of Normandy, between Saint-Martin-de-Varengeville and north of the Orne River.

iv. Defenses: Wehrmacht.

v. Role of the Résistance: To act as if in preparation for an allied landing on the north coast and at the same time sabotage to delay Wehrmacht troops from traveling to the Normandy front.

vi. Consequences
- Destruction of civilian infrastructure.
- Wehrmacht troops successfully delayed.

E. North Africa. Operation Torch, November 8, 1942
i. Goal: Open a second front in North Africa to help divert enemy forces from the eastern front and relieve the Soviet army.

ii. Location: Algeria (Algiers, Oran), French Morocco (Casablanca)

iii. Defenses: Army d'Armistice of the État Français

iv. Troops: American and British troops

v. Role of the French Résistance in North Africa

• Neutralize main personalities and occupy strategic locations.

vi. Expectations
• That the Army d'Armistice, AKA Armée d'Afrique, would immediately join with the American and British forces.

vii. Reality
• Miscalculation by the Americans.
• The landing forces met with stiff resistance.

viii. Victory: Two factors
• Serendipity: Admiral Darlan was visiting his son in Algiers and being the highest ranking officer in Algeria was able to sign the surrender of Algiers.
• The French Résistance actively helping the landing forces.

ix. Consequences
• The Wehrmacht invaded the free zone.
• The French fleet moored in Toulon scuttled.
• The Pétain government remained in place, but basically had no power.

F. Provence. Operation Anvil, renamed **Dragoon**. August 15, 1944
• Winston Churchill against the landing is the reason for the change of name.
• His reasons: to continue through Italy and the Balkans in order to arrive in Berlin before the Soviets.
• Eisenhower and staff prevailed.

i. Goal: Liberate Toulon, Marseille, travel up the Rhône valley and eventually connect with the forces of the Overlord operation.

ii. **Location**: Area of the department of Var, between Toulon and Cannes
  • Three beaches: Alpha Beach, Delta Beach and Camel Beach.

iii. **Defenses**: Wehrmacht.
  • The majority of troops (Waffen-SS, Das Reich Division) had been sent to the Normandy front.
  • Hitler ordered the Wehrmacht to withdraw.

iv. **Troops**: American, British, Free French, and elements of other occupied countries integrated with the main forces.

v. **Role of the French Résistance**
  • Sabotage infrastructure but protect which was necessary for the Allies' progress.
  • Liberate towns ahead of the Allies.

vi. **Consequences**
  • Destruction of the ports of Marseille and Toulon.
  • Hitler now fighting on three fronts.

4. Animals in war: dogs, horses and donkeys, pigeons

• Belligerent countries have used animals to help them and avoid losses of human life. In WWI dogs carried messages from trench to trench to the rear command posts while homing pigeons carried messages back and forth from the front to the Allies. Horses, donkeys. and mules being draught animals were used to pull artillery, often in terrible conditions and suffering. By the time WWII began, cavalry units had been more or less phased out, but the valiant charge of the Polish cavalry must not be forgotten.

• Officers often rode horses.

• In tropical countries, elephants were also used in war.

• Millions of war animals were killed in both world wars.

A. Dogs in war in France
i. Furry four-legged soldiers

• France lagged behind other countries in having four-legged soldiers.

• In WWII, dogs were essentially trained in search and rescue missions, finding wounded soldiers.

• Whereas, during WWI, the French army used numerous dogs in the trenches to carry messages, detect gas and as guards, it was not so when WWII began. France had few army dogs and they were mostly trained as guard dogs and SAR dogs.

• The fast moving war and the advances in telephone and radio communications superseded the need for messenger dogs.

• There were however a number of dogs who became mascots.

• SS-Totenkopf (guards) used dogs in concentration camps, including in Alsace at the Natzwiler-Struthorf camp, and when loading and unloading the deportation trains.

• At the end of the war, France recuperated 600 German dogs (German Shepherds were the breed most used by the Germans).

TRIVIA: After WWI in France, 120 dogs were awarded military honors.

B. Feathered soldiers

• Homing pigeons have been used for communications since antiquity, not always in war. They are an important part of history, which is not well-known.

• Communications by homing pigeons was very efficient in wars, and still did so in WWII despite modern (for the period) radios.

• Messages were written in tiny script on extremely thin paper, rolled into a thin metal tube attached to the pigeon's leg.

• Homing pigeons were used intensively in WWI. In WWII the MBF prohibited anyone to own pigeons. Many were destroyed or were taken by their owners into hiding in the non-occupied zone.

• In WWII, approximately 200,000 pigeons were used by the British and some 45,000 by the Americans.

• The Allied landings in Normandy in June 1944 was greatly helped by the 16,500 homing pigeons parachuted into the Norman forests, recuperated by the résistants and sent back with the location of German positions which the RAF could then bomb with precision.

• The Germans also used some 50,000 pigeons in occupied countries, with 800 men to care and train them.

• After November 1942, pigeon fanciers in the former non-occupied zone went into hiding. They were the ones who received the British pigeons, cared for them and sent them back.

• The feathered soldiers could fly for long distances at speeds up to 70 km/h.

• There is a museum of military pigeons at the Fort du Mont-Valérien where the French military keep up the tradition and train pigeons for competition.

• Pigeons were awarded military honors. Thirty-two of them received the Dickin Medal.

TRIVIA: A pigeon named White Vision was on a Catalina seaplane which had to make an emergency landing on the sea off the Hebrides Islands in the middle of a storm at 8:00 am. Any hope of rescue had to be abandoned. The crew released White Vision who flew 100 km over turbulent seas arriving at his home loft at 5:00 pm, having faced winds up to 40 km/h (25 mph) and poor visibility. Because of his making it home, the navy had a precise location of the distressed Catalina and was able to rescue the crew.

C. Horses and donkeys

• German and Soviet armies maintained horses during WWII.

• Horses in France: 400 000 at the start of WWII. Germany 2,700,000 horses mostly on the eastern front. USSR 3,500,000 horses.

• To create a super-horse was a goal of the Nazi regime. To achieve this end, they stole pure-bred Lipizzan horses.

TRIVIA: Veterinarian Rudolph Lessing was taking care of the Lipizzans some ten kilometers (six miles) from the border between Germany and Czechoslovakia at the end of the war. He feared for the safety of the horses, as the Soviets did not care about this unique breed. He contacted the Americans, and General Patton dispatched Hank Reed (commander of the Second Cavalry in Europe) to help get the horses to safety. They did. "We were so worn out by death and destruction that we wanted to do something beautiful." Hank Reed.

• Over one million horses and mules died during WWI.

D. Metal crickets

• Another animal, albeit an artificial one, was used by the 101th Airborne Division in WWII. It was a small device made of tin which when pressed emitted a perfect imitation of a cricket's chirp. It was a recognition signal for the paratroopers to find other members of their unit and regroup.

5. Architecture. Buildings. Dwellings
A. Architecture

• With resources available online, it is possible to create highly accurate settings for your story. Even so, there are details that may escape even the most meticulous researcher. For instance, having a character *lifting* or *raising* a window is inaccurate. Sash windows are an alien concept to French architecture.

• There were no buzzers and intercoms on buildings. There were, however, some bells powered by electricity. So, no bell when electricity was cut off.

• Houses most often had a small or yard garden in front and a pull bell at the gate.

i. Windows

• In French houses and apartments, windows are in two vertical sections and are hinged on the sides.

• They open inwards and close snugly against each other with a catch in the middle.

• The catch or handle moves a vertical rod, which locks the top and bottom of the window, in a similar fashion to a metal office storage cabinet. The catch is called *espagnolette*.

• In private houses (always detached), windows are all equipped on the outside with two louvered, or partly louvered, shutters, or solid shutters, made of metal or wood.

• They open outward and lie flat against the exterior wall, where they are kept in place by a latch.

• They close together with a small handle.

• All shutters have a device to keep them in the position chosen by the occupant, either half-closed or partly closed.

• In apartment buildings, the windows are recessed and the shutters, usually metal but also wood, fold against the sides of the exterior casement.

• On the outside of the casement, there is a railing, one third or less of the height of the window, acting as a safety bar to prevent anyone from accidentally falling out – an *Appui-bras* or *accoudoir* in French, which could be translated as 'armrest' allows people to lean on the *appui-bras* or *accoudoir* to observe the comings and goings on the street below.

• At the start of the war, no windows were left uncovered. The blackout was enforced. Dark blue cloth had been provided as the war became imminent.

• After the Germans occupied France, the blackout was kept in effect but no longer strictly enforced, i.e. the blackout curtain was compulsory, but depending on the local authorities a crack of light on the edge might be ignored.

• The feldgendarms patrolled.

• Paris. Dimmed lights in certain public places and Métro entrances. (See 17. Daily Life under Utilities)

ii. Apartment buildings and the concierge

• Remember that prior to and during the war limestone buildings, particularly in Paris, were not the natural cream color of the stone but gray due to centuries of coal smoke and later automobile exhaust (containing lead). Not to be confused with towns and villages where local stone is either naturally dark sandstone, blackish or dark blue shale or dark granite. It is only in the 1970s that Paris decided to clean up its monuments and residential and public buildings, as did other cities.

• In Paris and other cities, apartment buildings were old, pre-1920. There was little new construction between the two world wars, except for the wealthy who embraced the art deco style of the 1930s.

• **No buzzer systems**. The majority of apartment buildings were staffed by a concierge. Visitors announced themselves to her (occasionally, him) and were told whether the tenants were in or out.

• There were **no condominiums**. People rented apartments for life. People rarely moved and there was a scarcity of dwellings. An executive with a company that had branches in other parts of the country might relocate, but often, especially in

Paris, would retain the apartment and close it up or sublet it with the concierge's approval.

(a) Apartment buildings of the affluent

• In Paris, many buildings on the grand boulevards and other streets in fashionable districts were built during the Hausmann era. They were spacious and luxurious, and were unique in that the ground floor was occupied by commercial premises, usually stores selling luxury items.

• Cannes, Bordeaux, Marseille and Nice, also had a number of buildings built on the Hausmann principle.

• In Paris and cities, luxury apartment buildings were four- or five-stories high, with an attic divided into rooms. The attic was not considered a story.

• They would have an elevator.

• The attic contained the "mansardes" or garrets, under the roof, reserved for servants.

• There was no running water in the rooms in the attic, only one standpipe and one (Turkish) toilet for the use of all on the landing.

NOTE: A Turkish toilet is a ceramic or cement area with a hole, two pads for the feet, a water reservoir under the ceiling with a chain to release water to flush the toilet. Since the water came down with considerable force, the user had to move away quickly. Public toilets were always Turkish toilets, hence the familiar "les Turques".

• There were back stairs to the attic for the servants and at each floor there was a door to each apartment.

• There was a toilet, always in a separate "closet" or room. Hence the W.C. ("Water Closet").

• While on this topic, toilet paper was considered a luxury. During the Occupation, people resorted to newspapers cut in squares and any scavenged papers. Toilet paper in squares began appearing after the liberation. The softer toilet paper roll appeared in 1960.

• Most of those apartments would have a bath, a sink and a bidet.

49

• The apartments had running water, cooking gas and electricity, but not the attic rooms.

(b) **Average apartment buildings**

• Less bespoke apartment buildings boasted a blue enamel plate on the wall near the entrance door that read *Eau, gaz, électricité à tous les étages* – Water, cooking gas and electricity on all floors. Those apartment buildings were less likely to have an elevator.

• They would have a toilet and a bidet in a separate "W.C."

• Even prior to the war, people were sacrificing space to have a bath installed.

(c) **Apartment buildings in poorer districts**

• Very few had water and gas in the apartments.

• They all had electricity.

• Toilets and standpipe on the landing. They had no W.C. in apartments. There was a communal Turkish toilet on the landing for the tenants on that floor.

• They had coal-burning stoves for heating, which could burn wood by changing the grate, and electric burners to cook on, and sometimes a coal cookstove.

(d) *Meublés*. Those were apartments that were rented complete with furnishings. Tenants could rent long term or short term. Resistants, because they were always on the move, made much use of such accommodation.

• It was not unusual to have a person or a whole family who gone to the free zone, or a friendly country, to put the apartment to the disposal of the résistance.

• They were found in poor and modest areas and advertised as "*Meublés*" and in more affluent areas where a discreet plaque identified them as *Appartements meublés*.

(d) **Role of the concierge**

• Most apartment buildings had a concierge, though some buildings in poorer areas did not.

• The majority of concierges were widowed women or older single women – a consequence of WWI. Exceptionally, a male military veteran, especially one who had been wounded in WWI, might occupy the post.

• Duties:

- Collecting rent, holding it for the owner or sending it by postal money order – women did not have bank accounts.

- Maintenance. In charge of calling and selecting repairmen.

- Vetting tenants. This did not happen often as once someone had secured an apartment, they held on to it.

- Sweeping and washing stairs and hallways.

- Sweeping and washing the sidewalk in front of the building – which was done every day and was an occasion to catch up with local gossip. A concierge would take great pride in having the best swept and washed sidewalk frontage. Competition between concierges was fierce.

• Nicknames for a concierge: Commère, Pipelette.

• The concierge wielded considerable authority.

• She or he accepted mail for the entire building, which was then handed to the tenants.

• Knew everyone's business.

• Usually possessed a telephone paid for by the building's owner.

• Building guardian. A visitor would have to knock on the concierge's door to ask where so-and-so lived. She made sure the newcomer was not an undesirable person. A familiar visitor would make sure to greet the concierge.

• Some wealthier and prominent tenants had a telephone in their apartment, yet this was not widespread in the period under discussion. The concierge would phone to announce a visitor.

• All concierges had a phone, except in the cheapest neighborhoods. If a tenant was expecting a visitor, she or he would mention it to the concierge. Tenants would cultivate their concierge, giving a gift at Christmas and a tip at New Year, and every time they asked for a favor.

• The loge of the concierge always had a W.C. but not usually a bath.

• A glass door with a lace curtain opened onto the living room for her to watch the coming and going of tenants.

• Beside the living room there was a bedroom and a small kitchen. In French apartments, kitchens were small by modern standards.

(e) Elevator

• In more affluent areas, apartment buildings had an elevator.

• Elevator cabins were open cages made of tight wire netting. Luxurious apartment buildings and chic hotels had a cabin made of wood in the lower part and glass in the upper half. They were decorated with gold motifs on the wood frame. A folding metal grill closed the entrance of the cabin and on the landing. Some hotels might have an actual decorated door on the landing.

(f) Heating – central, other types

• Affluent areas

- Central heating with water radiators. Coal fired or oil furnace.

- Kitchens had a gas cookstove.

- Most apartments had a fireplace and a cast iron Godin coal fired stove (the most favored).

• Less affluent areas

- Some buildings had central heating with water radiators. Coal furnace.

- Others had no central heating. Tenants often had a cast iron coal fired Godin stove.

• Every apartment had a chimney flue.

• In poorer districts, apartment buildings did not have any form of central heating.

- People heated the apartment with the coal fired cookstove.

- Where there was a gas cookstove, they had a cast iron coal fired Godin stove.

- Bedrooms were unheated.

• During the war, the lack of coal and oil meant buildings were cool. In buildings with central heating, some heat was produced to prevent pipes and radiators from freezing.

• There was no electric heating, the result of high cost and inadequate technology. Small heaters, called chaufferettes, were available. All you could heat with those were your feet. Electricity was expensive, so they were not used by any but the most affluent.

• When coal and wood became scarce, people soaked newspapers and rolled them into tight balls to make them burn longer.

iii. Private houses and farms

• Bathrooms consisting of a bath and a washbasin were common in private houses. The W.C. and bidet were in their own cubicle. There were no showers.

• Heating. Individual houses in affluent districts might have central heating with water radiators and a coal furnace. A fireplace burning wood in the living room. Sometimes a fireplace in one or more bedrooms.

• Those would also have gas cookstoves.

• In other areas, houses would have a coal fired Godin stove in every room, which could also burn wood.

• Coal fired cookstove or a propane/butane cook top in the kitchen.

• A fireplace burning wood in the living room.

• In the Alsace, Lorraine and Jura, the tiled faïence stove with pipes throughout the house was common, but nowhere else.

• **In rural France**, depending on the area, houses were heated with wood.

• In the Nord department and Pas-de-Calais, coal was readily available, until rationing   came in.

• Farms would have a coal or wood burning cookstove.

• Small towns did not have tall apartment buildings.

• There was no electric heating, the result of high cost and inadequate technology. Small heaters, called chaufferettes, were available. All you could heat with those were your feet. Electricity was expensive, so they were not used by any but the most affluent.

• When coal and wood became scarce, people soaked newspapers and rolled them into tight balls to make them burn longer.

iv. Public and administration buildings
• Government buildings open to the public kept office hours.
• They would have central heating.
(a) National corporations.
• Postes, Téléphone et Télégraphe (PTT) – State mail, and telephone service.
• Société Nationale des Chemins de Fer Français (SNCF) – National rail system.
• Comité de l'Organisation de l'Énergie Électrique (COEE) – National electric grid. Paris had its own system: the Bureau Central d'Exploitation et de Coordination (BCEC).
• Société des Transports en Commun de la Région Parisienne (STCRP) – The Paris transit system, controlled the bus network, while the Compagnie du Chemin de fer Métropolitain(CMP) controlled the underground Métro until January 1942 when CMP controlled both.
NOTE: It was renamed the Régie Autonome des Transports Parisiens (RATP) in September 1944.
(b) Utilities – (See 17. Daily life)
• Electricity was provided to all buildings and houses.
• Gas was an expensive commodity. It was not provided in every apartment building or private houses in poorer districts.
• Water was provided to all buildings and houses. In poorer districts some apartment buildings had water available only on the landings.
• Sewage and wastewater were the responsibility of the municipalities.

• Cities, including Paris, had a network of sewers combined with storm sewers.

• Rural dwellings relied on septic tanks and for many simple outdoor earthen toilets.

6. Armed forces
A. 1939 French Army
• The French army was poorly equipped after years of unstable governments. Despite the efforts of Colonel Charles de Gaulle, there were few tanks.
i. Battles
• **Alps**. 190,000 men against 450,000 Italians. Won by the French Chasseurs Alpins. Much rancor after Armistice when they had to cede the ground they had defended and were holding.

• **Ardennes**. Too much trust in the Maginot line. The Wehrmacht advanced through the Ardennes mountainous and dense forest and pierced the French lines at Sedan.

• **Dunkirk**: 220,000 British and 120,000 French troops embarked in British navy and French navy ships, plus many private vessels. Holding the Wehrmacht out of Dunkirk were 40,000 French soldiers. Heavy casualties.

• **Loire**. Aided by the cadets of the military school of Saumur, soldiers held back the Wehrmacht until given the order to fall back to avoid a massacre.

• **Rhône Valley**, **Chasselay** combats. Fierce fighting, many colonial troops (North African, West and East African). Defeated because of the lack of munitions, the French were taken prisoner. The Germans systematically massacred the Black soldiers. Wounded were bayoneted. Survivors were taken away and shot.

• **Vosges**. Armies (2nd, 4th, 6th) annihilated, 3rd, 5th and 8th are surrounded and taken prisoner.

ii. Demobilization
• After the Armistice is signed, any soldier not taken prisoner went to the nearest military unit or the gendarmerie to be demobilized.

• The special case of Alsace, Lorraine and Moselle, Nord and Pas-de-Calais: Prisoners of those regions were liberated after July 1940 when the regions were annexed or attached to the Brussels' command.

iii. Evaders
• Among the prisoners herded in temporary camps, some escaped. They found local inhabitants sympathetic and got help to travel to the free zone.

• Among those demobilized, some made their way to the free zone.

• Among the evaders, some found their way to England and de Gaulle. Others formed the nucleus of the résistance groups in both occupied and non-occupied zones.

B. Dissolution of the 1939 army
• Soldiers surrendered their arms.

• Planes that were not requisitioned by the Luftwaffe were grounded.

• The fleet was to remain in home ports.

C. Creation of the armistice army in 1940
i. A defeated country is allowed to keep an army – as set out in the terms of armistice convention – to keep order and protect borders.

• Armistice Army, also known as Pétain's Army: Two hundred thousands soldiers and officers formed the armistice army, in the non-occupied zone only.

• Many more troops in the colonies.

• Weapons: They were allowed personal arms and light artillery.

• The remaining Air Force was grounded.

• The armistice agreement allowed the État Français to keep the fleet.

• The armistice agreement prohibited Germany from taking over the French colonies.

ii. Combats of the armistice army, known as Pétain's Army

• Dakar September 23-25, 1940 against the Free French Forces and the British navy.
• Against the American and British in Algeria and French Morocco November 8, 1942.

D. French air force
i. 1939-1940
• Technically advanced.
• Low number of planes compared to the Luftwaffe.

ii. After the armistice June 22, 1940
• Pétain allowed to maintain a small number of planes and pilots, but not allowed to fly unless it was for the defense of the territory.
• A higher number of planes and pilots allowed in the colonies.

E. Navy - French fleet
i. Lighthouses
• Lighthouses were under the jurisdiction of the Maritime Service of the Highways Department (Ponts et Chaussées).
• They had been amended upon declaration of war to reduce the intensity of light and to be camouflaged.
• There were several lightships and lighthouses destroyed during the German invasion.
• During the occupation, lighthouses and lightships came under the Hafenkommandantur, depending on Kriesgmarine staff in Paris.
• The French technicians were retained, but watched by a group of Wehrmacht or Kriesgmarine soldiers or sailors assigned to each lighthouse and lightship.
• Cooperation between the two sides avoided massive destruction when the Germans withdrew
• The fleet to remain intact in their home ports.
• Two lightships refused the Armistice and sailed to Plymouth, England, where they served alongside the Allies until

after the landings, during which they played a major role dropping marker buoys to guide ships and landing craft.

ii. Mers-el-Kébir (Algeria) July 3, 1940. Operation Catapult

• British Vice-Admiral James Sommerville sent an ultimatum to French Admiral Marcel-Bruno Gensoul to surrender and sail to Britain. Admiral Gensoul refused. The British navy opened fire.

• 1,290 sailors killed. Many wounded.

• Destruction of French fleet. Some submarines and smaller ships escaped to England.

• The *Strasbourg* (battleship) escaped and sailed to Toulon.

iii. Consequences

• Anti-British sentiment among the population.

F. Forces Françaises de l'Intérieur (FFI). (See 42. Résistance)

• Only applied to metropolitan France until the 1944 liberation of Paris (except in areas still occupied by the Germans until 1945).

i. Formation

• France divided into sixteen regions, each under its own command.

• From December 19, 1943, progressive gathering of the main Movements of the Résistance (See 42. Résistance. A. Definition), Secret Army, FTP, FTP-MOI, Combat, Organization of the Resistance of the Army. They coalesced in March 1944 under a single command.

G. Free French Army – Forces Françaises Libres (FFL)

• Only applied to the army under General de Gaulle and in theaters of war outside metropolitan France until the Allied landings in Normandy.

• August 28, 1944 (after the liberation of Paris) General de Gaulle disbanded the FFI.

• FFI soldiers were integrated into the Free French Forces (FFL – now, simply, the French Army) or returned to civilian life.

• The French Army joined the Allies to finish the liberation of France, and on to Germany.

7. Armistice, June 22, 1940, with Hitler, June 24 with Mussolini

• An armistice is a temporary cessation of hostilities at the request of one of the opponents and agreed with the other(s). The truce has no time limit. At some point, it is followed by a peace treaty.

• Monday June 17, 1940, Marshal Pétain requested an armistice.

• No peace treaty was even discussed between the État Français and Hitler.

A. Conditions of the armistice

• Immediate cessation of hostilities.

• An agreement was made at the Wiesbaden Commission of Armistice to protect historical monuments, even when occupied, such as Mont Saint-Michel.

• Two zones were created, one occupied (three-fifths of the territory) and one non-occupied.

• Italy occupied a fifty-kilometer strip of territory from Léman Lake to the Mediterranean, as well as the island of Corsica.

• The cost of the occupying power to be paid by the État Français (400 millions francs per day).

• The Germans were not to occupy the French colonies.

• No provisions or mentions of Alsace, Moselle and Lorraine.

B. Consequences
i. General population
(a) **The rejection of the Armistice** was more prevalent among the middle and lower classes. The upper and self-employed (storekeepers, etc.) classes were divided between acceptance and rejection.

• Some accepted that a battle was lost, but not the war. They became fertile ground for recruitment to the Résistance.

61

• Some rejected outright the presence of a foreign power. Nascent resistance groups.

(b) Collaboration. Some embraced Marshall Pétain's Révolution Nationale and the collaboration.

(c) General despondency, fatalism and acceptance of events. Some people were ashamed, but the need to survive is primordial.

ii. Military. Acceptance. Rejection.

• One million eight hundred thousands soldiers and officers were taken prisoner.

• POWs who rejected the armistice escaped to the free zone to be demobilized.

• Soldiers who were in the north zone but not captured, i.e. not with their unit at the time of surrender, were still considered POWs. Many found civilian clothes and went to the gendarmerie to be demobilized to avoid being taken prisoner.

• Gendarmerie was a branch of the military. Most gendarmes were sympathetic to the evaders.

• In the free zone, the attitude was divided. Some military remained and became part of the Armée d'Armistice.

• Some military escaped to join de Gaulle in England.

• Some military returned to civilian life, where they were further divided into Pétain's supporters and de Gaulle's supporters, most of the latter becoming resistants.

• Some essential workers, the sick, veterans of the First World War and fathers of large families were released. However, they were on "captivity furlough" and their status was of a POW. They had to register regularly at the nearest Kommandantur.

• It left one and-a-half million men POWs.

C. Wiesbaden Commission of Armistice
i. Commission d'Armistice seated in Wiesbaden
• It was staffed by German diplomats.
• A delegation represented France's interests.

• Its role was to implement the conditions of the June 1940 armistice.

ii. Pierre Laval
• After the return of Pierre Laval (April, 1942) to the government, the Commission dealt with the Pétain's government directly. The delegation's role lost influence.

iii. French empire
• Overseas countries. Their status was a colony. This term is the one that should be used in your novel as this was the only word used in that period, whether writing about Britain or France or Holland (modern Netherlands).

• Economically, the colonies depended on metropolitan France.

• They were under the administration of the Pétain government.

• The colonies became a source of political and armed conflicts between the Free French (de Gaulle) and the État Français (Pétain).

• Colonies that rejected the armistice and broke away from Pétain's government to join the Free French: Nouvelle-Calédonie (New Caledonia),Tchad (Chad), French Indies, New-Hebrides, French Polynesia, Cameroon, Oubangui-Chari, French Congo, Wallis-et-Futuna, Tahiti, Moorea.

• Colonies and departments that sided with Pétain's government: Algeria (department status), Morocco (protectorate), Tunisia (protectorate), Sénegal, Guinea, Gabon, Indo-China, French Antilles, Guyane (French Guyana), Saint-Pierre-et-Miquelon, Djibouti, Madagascar, Lebanon and Syria (French mandate), French concessions of Kouang-Tchéou-Wan and Shanghai in China.

8. Art & Entertainment & Literature

• The supremacy of French cultural life gave umbrage to the occupiers' homegrown art. The occupiers wish it to continue but to become Germanized.

• To keep the arts in all their forms, including gastronomy, in the face of adversity was both defiance and a challenge.

• Immediately after the invasion, the Einsatzstab Reichslater Rosenberg für die Besentzen Gebiet (ERR) – (Rosenberg Institute for Occupied Territories) – began to function.

• Literary salons, such as that of Françoise Gould, were regularly attended by the literary and artistic elite, both French and German, collaborators and resistants.

• Twice a month, the *Der Deutsche Wegleiter* listing places of entertainment was published for the occupiers.

• Whereas there were restrictions and censorship imposed on the arts and entertainment, they did not apply to official functions.

A. Art Galleries and museums

• The occupying administration (MBF) was very keen to promote cooperation and undertook many exhibitions, notably *Le Juif et la France*, all ideologically biased.

i. Exhibitions venues

• Grand Palais : La France européenne (European France) propaganda exhibition.

• Palais Berlitz: Le Juif et la France (Jewry and France) propaganda exhibition.

• Petit Palais: October 1940: an anti Freemason exhibition.

• Salle Wagram Hall: 1942 exhibition Bolshevism against Europe.

ii. Venues for shows and music

• Large halls: ABC, Salle Gaveau, Salle Pleyel, Mimi Pinson, Bobino, L'Étoile, Olympia, Salle Wagram.

iii. Art Galleries
• Art Market: The major art galleries in Paris were owned and operated by Jews.
• Some paintings were deemed *vernichtet* (to be destroyed) and were burned behind the Jeu de Paume.
• A few were saved by profiteers.
• Some outright looted.
• The lucrative art market attracted every sort of crook and criminal.

iv. Jewish galleries whose owners fled after entrusting their galleries to non-Jewish friends:
• Galerie Pierre Loeb – showed avant-garde works, such as Marc Chagall, Raoul Dufy.
• Galerie Paul Rosenberg – showed avant-garde and classical works.
• Galerie Zak – showed avant-garde and classical works.
• Galerie B. Weill – avant-garde.

v. Others
• Galerie Wildenstein, Paris – a controversial gallery, with an owner who was later accused of collaboration by the Americans. Many legal battles ensued after the war.
• René Gimpel closed his Paris gallery.

v. Auction Houses
• Hôtel des Ventes, public auction, rue Drouot (11th Arrondissement). Admission forbidden to Jews.
• On the Riviera, Nice in particular, brisk art business also restricted for the Jews.

vi. Sculptures and Statues
• A few statues were actually destroyed because of ideology. Notable ones: Edith Cavell (English nurse even though she also nursed German soldiers in WWI) by the occupiers.
• General Mangin, by Pétain's government.

• Sculptures in art galleries were sold at auctions or looted. Those deemed degenerate were broken up.

• In the occupied zone, metal statues except war memorials, statues of saints, kings, queens and funeral monuments were collected and melted down – for the benefit of Nazi industry.

• In the non-occupied zone, metal statues except war memorials, statues of saints, kings, queens and funeral monuments were collected and melted down – for the benefit of Pétain's regime.

• A number of statues were taken away and hidden by resistants.

• Bells. They were spared by arrangement between the État Français and the MBF. The État Français had to supply an equivalent tonnage of metal to the Nazi industry.

B. Art Pillage
i. Wehrmacht role

• As early as July 1, 1940, the Wehrmacht declined to remove works of art from private galleries and collectors as per the Hague Convention (October 18, 1907).

ii. Otto Abetz with the help of the Feldpolizei from July 27, 1940 to August 4, 1940, was able to make a considerable strike against private Jewish collections.

Some major collectors

• Rothschild, at Hôtel Pontalba, rue du Faubourg-Saint-Honoré.

• Jacques and André Seligman, collectors and dealers.
• Georges Wildenstein, gallery 57 rue de la Boétie.
• Paul Rosenberg, gallery rue de la Boétie.
• Bernheim, collector and dealer.
• Alphonse Kann, collector.

iii. Einsatzstab Reichsleiter Rosenberg (ERR) Paris

• Systematic removal of artworks to be stored in three emptied rooms at the Louvre and at the Musée du Jeu de Paume. Each piece was documented on lists and an index card for each, most of them with a photo.
   • April, 1941, first shipment of looted art works to Germany.
   • 1942, ERR ordered all Jewish furnishing and domestic assets to be seized. 38,000 dwellings totally emptied.
   • Three warehouses. 600 prisoners to sort the loot.

iv. Outside Paris
   • Château de Sourches (Sarthe department) Collection David Weill. Unfortunately, there were also pieces stored there by the Louvre.
   • Château de Chambord (Loire department).
   • Château de Brissac (Maine-et-Loire department).
   • 1942, ERR ordered all Jewish furnishing and domestic assets to be seized. 31,916 dwellings totally emptied.
   • Assets crated and sent to Germany.

C. Actors, Artists, Dancers, Singers, Writers
   i. Dilemma: continue working to a German audience, resigned or flee to the non-occupied zone
   • Performing arts depend on an audience. Performers were faced with an audience which was mostly German. Some were enthusiastic about performing for the occupiers. Others rejected it outright and quit. The majority of performers hid their feelings.
   • They needed the work, so quitting was not an option as any other work was still working for the occupiers. It was not long before resistance cells were formed. They were in a good position to gather intelligence and pass on hidden messages.
   • Some songs had double meaning: *Ça fait d'excellents Français* (This makes excellent Frenchmen) and *Paris sera toujours Paris* (Paris always Paris) sung by Maurice Chevalier. The barbs were so fast that the censor on duty never caught

them, but the anti-Nazi audience had a more receptive mind and did not miss them.

ii. Survival
• There were already those performers and artists whose "collaboration" fed and sheltered Jews who had been expelled from their positions. It was a matter of survival. This was the reasoning after the Liberation.

• Most helped the résistance. Theaters were great places to hide.

• Some made their way to the non-occupied zone. The majority later joined the résistance or the FFL in London.   .

• There was a subtle resistance among many performers by poking digs at the occupiers which only the French in the audience understood and laughed at. This led the occupiers to laugh too to hide the fact they did not understand.

• Performers had a special Ausweis to allow them to circulate after curfew.

• Those performers who actively promoted the Nazi ideology and maintained close ties with the État Français were viewed differently by the population and the Free French provisional government. Those were hunted down at the Liberation.

• The *Train de la honte* (Train of Shame) designated the artists, performers and intellectuals who went to Weimar by train, as organized by the Göbbels to promote Franco-German collaboration in October 1941.

NOTE: The expression was applied to the deportation trains ONLY after the war. Only use it in the above context.

iii. Artists and intellectuals
• Whether painting or sculpting in a studio or employed by theaters for stage sets, they faced the dilemma of working for the occupiers.

• Behind the scene technicians, costumes makers and designers provided hiding places.

• Some behind the scene workers had a special Ausweis to allow them to circulate after curfew.
• Some accommodating or outright resistant artists: Braque; Bonnard, (Matisse, Picasso both became recluses), André Fougeron.
• Some accommodating or outright resistant intellectuals: Jean Cocteau (unproven), Jean-Paul Sartre, Albert Camus, Paul Eluard, Robert Desnos.
• Some accommodating performers: Danielle Darieux, Louis Jouvet.
• Active resistant performers: Jean Marais, Jean Gabin (left for England), Michelle Morgan (left for the U.S.).

iv. Collaborating artists and intellectuals
• Songs commissioned by the État Français: *Sous les plis du drapeau* (Under the Flag), *Être maman, c'est être plus jolie* (Being a Mom is More Beautiful).
• Literary works by Céline were hardened anti-Semitic.
• Intellectuals: Céline, Brasillach, Drieu de la Rochelle, Jean Giono.
• Performers: Sacha Guitry, Arletty, Édith Piaf, Mistinguette, Corinne Luchaire, Serge Lifar, Suzy Solidor, Charles Trenet, Fernandel.
• Derain (artist).

v. Cabarets
• Plenty of champagne.
• Some owners sided with resistance.
• Others with collaboration.

vi. Clientele
• Occupiers and collaborators.
• Resistant spies.
• Upper-class elite (the *Tout-Paris*) who refused to be denied their usual pleasures.

vii. Montmartre, most with naked dancers. Favored by the occupiers:
* Alcazar (show exclusively reserved for the occupiers), Bagatelle (20 rue de Clichy), Cabaret Bal Tabarin, l'Écrin (bilingual show), l'Étincelle (bilingual show), Moulin Rouge, Moulin de la Galette, Les Folies Bergères, Les Préludes, Savoy, Le Parnasse, Le Jockey.

viii. Champs-Élysées refined enternainment
* Boeuf sur le Toit - *Das Berühmte Pariser Kabaret: Eine Grosses Attraktions mit den reisenden, Tanzerinnen des Wronska-Ballets.*
* Cabarets: Lido, Le Nid, Villa d'Este, Le Paris Paris, Le Don Juan, L'Heure Bleue.
* Performers: Django Reinhardt, Stéphane Grappelli.

ix. Grand Boulevards: La Vie Parisienne (Suzy Solidor sang Lily Marlene every night – the irony being it was the unofficial anthem of both the German Afrika Corps and the British desert troops), The *Sheherazade.*
* **Performers**: Joséphine Baker, Maurice Chevalier, Damia, Fernandel (actor-singer), Sacha Guitry, Mistinguett, Edith Piaf, Suzy Solidor, Charles Trenet.

x. Théâtre des Deux Ânes
* **Les chansonniers** (satire): Raymond Souplex, Jeanne Souza, Michel Blanc, Jean Rigaux.

xi. Casinos. Casinos were strictly regulated and only allowed in resorts.
* Deauville: The Normandy Barrière, taken over by the Germans.
* Dieppe: destroyed by bombing 1942.
* Enghien-les-Bains.

• Pier and Crystal Casino, Nice. In 1942, it was stripped of all valuable metals (copper, brass, bronze,electric wiring) by the occupiers. The Pétain's government ordered its destruction.
• Saint-Malo, destroyed by bombing in 1944.

D. Movie Theaters in Paris

i. They were reopened after June 14. Except for those reserved for the occupiers, the others welcomed both civilians and occupiers.

ii. The majority of cinemas were located on the Grands Boulevards. Bicycles and cars were prohibited on the Grands Boulevards without a special authorization from the Opéra Garnier to the place de la République (Boulevards Haussman, Montmartre, Poissonnière and Saint-Martin).
• Normandie (Avenue des Champs-Élysées) requisitioned for the Wehrmacht troops.
• Gaumont Palace (rue Caulincourt), Maillot Palace (Avenue de la GrandeArmée) were opened to all.

iii. In 1943, venues were obliged to close one day per week in addition to the regular non-performance day.

iv. From March 1944, venues were closed four days a week.

v. Censorship
• American and British films were banned.
• Others were scrutinized, censored or amended.

vi. Content
• In the occupied zone: Newsreel geared to the Third Reich's victories and propaganda (*Les Actualités globales*). Audience booed and whistled. Threats from the management (under MBF control) to leave the lights on or to evacuate the cinema if the disturbance continued.

• French produced films complied with censorship. Some contained subtle hidden messages, which the occupiers missed, but the majority of the audience understood.

• In the non-occupied zone: the État Français applied the same (MBF) rules as in the occupied zone.

vii. Public. Increased attendance
• The need to escape grim daily life.
• To keep warm. Cinemas were heated in winter.
• A morale booster.
• Middle and lower-class clientele.
• The idle occupiers.

E. Circus
• Permanent circus: Cirque d'Hiver in Paris.
• Traveling circus: Cirque Amar, which operated under a different name, Cirque des Alliés, which had to change its name to Cirque National.
• Cirque Pinder refused to perform in front of the occupier. Animals were sent to Spain for safekeeping, the props hidden.

F. Dances, public balls
NOTE: Playing music was not banned as long as it was not one of the prohibited songs. Accordionists often played in cafés.

i. Dancing
• Dancing was the favorite pastime of all classes. In the interwar years, new dances from America gained popularity, foxtrot, samba, charleston, tango. There was a long dance tradition on the national day (July 14), any celebrated days, weddings, any pretext for a celebration such as achievement, award, etc.

ii. Escapism
• Dancing was an escape from the war. For some young people, it was to defy parents and the Pétain's regime.

iii. Bans
• For Pétain dancing means bodies in close contact and goes against his ideal of pure and healthy life. Public balls were banned in both zones.

• Secret dances venues appeared everywhere.

iv. Cities and towns.
• Dances sprang up in various locations, in apartments (where neighbors approved), private houses, cellars, stores, backrooms of cafés to 78 rpm records or musicians, usually an accordionist or two.

• Attendees wore their Sunday-best clothes.

• No État Français or German music or songs were played.

v. Rural areas locations
• Youths braved the bans by holding dances in clearings, barns, isolated farmyards, with an accordionist or two or a record player. The accordion dominated.

• Attendees wore their best clothes. They walked or bicycled and might have to carry their dance shoes in a bag.

• As in the cities, no Pétain government or German music or songs were played.

• Lookouts kept watch for approaching gendarmes. Dancers dispersed in the many hiding places in the country.

• Most gendarmes did not look too hard.

vi. Favorite songs
• *La java bleue*, *Le petit vin blanc*.

vii. Repression: When a clandestine dance was denounced, the gendarmes issued a fine. Sometimes the music got too loud and gave them away. Dancers fled the best they could to hide.

viii. Guinguettes
• Outside cities and close to towns, the guinguettes were small establishments favored by the less affluent classes, where

they could drink, have a meal and dance. The accordion was the most popular instrument. Some guinguettes provided a covered stage or outside patio for dancing. Lookouts kept watch for approaching gendarmes.

G. Dance schools
i. Strictly regulated, dance schools became de facto places where people could dance to their heart's content. A lookout was always posted to watch for approaching gendarmes, in which case the *students* resumed the learning stance. Enrolment was high.

• Clientele: Anyone under the pretense of learning, many young people.

H. Embassies
i Embassy parties
• Until the Wehrmacht marched into Paris, there were regular cultural parties at the embassies, well-attended by spies.

ii. German embassy and its quirky status in France
• Hôtel Beauharnais, 78 rue de Lille.
• An odd situation as it was most unusual for a victorious state to appoint an ambassador to a country it occupied. The Germans occupied three-fifths of the country. Moreover, the ambassador was accredited to the Militärbefehlshaber, not to the État Français, this enabled him to deal with the Pétain government and influence politics.
• The Pétain government being in the free zone, État Français, Pétain appointed an ambassador to the occupied zone, which, being under German control, had become a "foreign country".
• As early as the fall of 1940, the Tout-Paris and collaborators frequented the German embassy. Champagne flowed freely.
• December 22, 1940 Christmas party. Suzanne Abetz hostess. Only French was to be spoken.

• May 15, 1942. Sumptuous evening to celebrate the grand opening of Arno Breker sculpture exhibition.

iii. Neutral countries and countries allied with Germany had embassies in Paris. They also held parties.
• American embassy until December 1941.
• From a *non-involved* country, the U.S. embassy was allowed by the MBF to remain open. However, President Roosevelt ordered Ambassador Bullitt to move to Vichy. Bullitt did not obey until mid-July 1940. He remained in office in Vichy until November 18, 1940, when he was replaced by Admiral Leahy.
• As of December 1941, the U.S. became an enemy of Germany and therefore of the État Français, and the ambassador was recalled.

iv. Role of diplomats
• Inform their government of the political situation, trends, events in the country to which they are posted.
• Diplomats in post in Germany were aware of the rise of Nazism, and the anti-Semitic trend which eventually led to the Holocaust.
• Some sounded the alarm at the international level. Others obeyed the rules and regulations of their government, i.e. not to reveal what could become detrimental to their country.
• They sifted the propaganda to inform their government of their perceived reality.
• As intermediaries, they had influence and opportunities to act, as did Swedish diplomat Raoul Wallenberg.

I. Exhibitions
i. Primary role was Nazi propaganda

ii. État Français' goals
• To bolster Pétain's Révolution Nationale.
• To promote collaboration.

J. Literature
• The power of the written word was never more evident and more influential than during the Occupation. The Germans also understood that concept. Writers supporting the Nazi ideology were readily published.

i. Fall of 1940
• Publishing resumed. Pétain wanted the literature to be esthetic and moral to reflect the ideology of the Révolution Nationale.

• The occupiers wanted to control literature by promoting only that favorable to their ideology. They did this by establishing lists:

(a) The first was the Bernhardt list, published in August 1940, to remove books from libraries and bookstores. The occupiers were helped by the French police and gendarmes who were often sluggish in their search.

(b) The second Otto list, published in September 1940, increased the number of titles to be removed and was expanded again in July 1942. The same teams went again to remove additional books. Better prepared, booksellers and librarians succeeded in hiding many books.

• Publishers cooperated by pledging not to republish those books.

• The occupiers put collaborators in charge of publishing houses.

• Clandestine publishers appeared, such as the Éditions de Minuit, that published the first resistance novel *Le silence de la mer* (Silence of the Sea).

• The Pétain government, in conjunction with the German Propaganda Abteilung, published the Mathias list of recommended books. The list contained titles that glorified the Révolution Nationale, morality, motherhood and supported Nazism.

ii. Salons littéraires (Literary salons)

• Writers met at the *salons littéraires* of the Tout-Paris. Literary salons, such as that of Florence Gould (American), were regularly attended by the literary and artistic elite, both French and German, collaborators and resistants. The latter gathered much useful information.

• Florence Gould's salon, every Thursday, frequent guests at her salon included:

(a) French writers Marcel Jouhandeau, Jean Paulhan, Paul Léautaud.

(b) German writers Ernst Jünger, Gerhardt Heller, Ludwig Vogel (Luftwaffe pilot and American spy).

• Marie-Louise Bousquet's salon. She was not related to René Bousquet, the chief of police.

iii. Some writers during the Occupation

• Collaboration writers included Lucien Rebatet, Louis-Ferdinand Céline, Pierre Drieu de la Rochelle.

• Neutral writers included Jean Anouilh, Henry de Montherlant, Jean Cocteau, Paul Morand, Colette.

• Writers possibly leaning to resistance as they did not write propaganda style included Simone de Beauvoir, Jean-Paul Sartre, Jean Guéhénno.

iv. Poetry

• Poetry blossomed anew. Since the censors were automatically cutting what they did not understand, the long complicated passages gave way to an easy-to-understand language, which poets manipulated to serve the résistance, rather than necessarily criticize the occupiers or collaborators.

• Aragon, poet, communist and engaged resistant.

• Paul Éluard. poet and engaged resistant. He published the clandestine *Le livre ouvert* in 1940. The RAF dropped copies of his anti-Nazi propaganda poem *Liberté* in occupied countries.

K. Museums

• Musée du Jeu de Paume. In the Tuileries Gardens.

• Musée du Louvre. Adjacent to the Tuileries Gardens.
• Musée Grévin. Wax museum of personalities.
• Musée d'Orsay. In a former train station, rue de Lille.
• Musée Carnavalet. 23, rue de Sévigné.
• Le Petit Palais. Avenue Nicolas II (post-war Avenue Winston Churchill).
• Musée de l'Orangerie, west corner of the Tuileries Gardens. Frequently used for art exhibitions. In 1942, the exhibition of Arno Breker, the official Reich artist who studied in France.

L. Music
• The Institut Culturel Allemand, established in Paris, soon opened branches in the major cities and towns in the occupied zone and after November 1942 in the former non-occupied zone.
• Music is a universal language. It was at the heart of the Nazi cultural policy. It was familiar to the French with Bach, Beethoven, Brahms, Mendelssohn, Mozart, Schumann.
• German classical music was promoted to reach the socio-economic elite. This bourgeoisie was vital to the Third Reich to ensure political submission.
• French music was tolerated except for those composers labeled *degenerate* and Jews.
• In the non-occupied zone, the État Français commissioned new works from winners of the Prix de Rome.
• Right after the Armistice, the music scene resumed. Musicians and singers went on recording. People kept buying records (78 rpm).
• There were street musicians in the cities, in the early days of the Occupation. Then they were banned due to the edict forbidding the gathering of more than three persons on the street.
• Musicians found ways to resist. They would slip a few bars of patriotic songs, such as *Non, vous n'aurez pas l'Alsace et la Lorraine* (You won't have the Alsace and Lorraine) into a composition. The occupiers were totally oblivious, all the French

spectators recognizing it. They would also play music by Jewish colleagues under another name.

i. Concerts venues
• Salle Pleyel (hall).
• Salle Gaveau (hall).
• Théâtre des Champs-Élysées, Avenue Montaigne, re-opened early in 1941 with Orchestre de Radio-Paris (MBF controlled radio station) under the baton of the Dutch (of German origin) conductor Willem Mengelberg.

TRIVIA: At the Liberation, he was banished for five years because of his collaboration, yet he had protected the Jewish musicians in his orchestra and defied the authorities by playing banned music in the evening when the audience was almost entirely French. The audience was sensitive to his interpretations, such as of Tchaikovsky's *Pathétique* or Beethoven's Ninth Symphony, and the message he was sending was his hatred of Nazism. This became clear when recordings were found years after the Liberation.

ii. Music Conservatory. Administration
• Jews first statute, October 3, 1940, applied to all Jewish teachers. They were expelled December 18, 1940. The director (Rabaud) was zealous in contacting the Propagandastaffel and writing to Pétain regarding the Jewish students. Until 1942, according to French law, which made a distinction between a full Jew and a half-Jew (only one or two grandparents being Jewish), nothing prevented Jewish students from continuing their education, but they could not be granted awards. This director was replaced shortly afterwards by Claude Delvincour, a veteran of the First World War, strongly anti-Nazi. Students who are only half-Jewish were allowed to compete for awards.
• As of September 1942, all students of Jewish origin were excluded.

79

• The Orchestre des Cadets du Conservatoire (Conservatory Junior Orchestra) was created to keep young people from being enrolled in compulsory work service (STO).

iii. Opera
• There was a nest of artistic resistance at the Opéra throughout the Occupation. Musicians inserted fragments of banned songs or of the *Marseillaise*, the national anthem, in the works they were playing. In the ballet *les Animaux modèles* they inserted the chorus from *Non vous n'aurez pas l'Alsace et la Lorraine* (No, you will not have Alsace and Lorraine) performed August 1942. In *Carmen*, a fragment of the *Marseillaise* was inserted. These subversive additions were recognized by French audiences but not by the Germans, or if they did, they remained quiet.
• All English and American operas were banned.
• German opera imports – Capriccio (Richard Strauss), *The Ring of the Nibelung, Tanhäuser, Lohengrin* (Richard Wagner), *Der Freischütz* (Carl Maria von Weber).
• New works – *L'enfant et les sortilèges* (Maurice Ravel); *L'enlèvement au sérail* (Wolfang Amadeus Mozart).
• Traditional – *Damnation de Faust* (Hector Berlioz) performed at the re-opening in July 1940, *Lakmé* (Léo Delibes), *Lucia di Lammermoor* (Gaetano Donizetti).
• The Orchestre des Cadets of the Opéra de Paris was also created to keep young people from being enrolled in the compulsory work service (STO).
• Ballet was an integral part of operas. Ballets were also performed on their own. The Diaghilev ballet company performed at the Opéra (until June 1941). The Paris opera operated the École nationale de danse. (National School of Dance).
• Ballet banned as of 1940 – *Les Sylphides* (Frederic Chopin). Ballets banned after June 1941– All Tchaikovsky ballets.

• Classic ballets – *Giselle* (Adolphe Adam), *Coppélia* (Léo Delibes).

• New works – French *les Animaux modèles* (Francis Poulenc), *Carmen* (Georges Bizet). German *Joan von Zarissa* (Werner Egk).

iv. Opéra Comique
• A separate organization before the war, it came under the direction of the national theaters headed by Rouché, director of the Palais Garnier – Paris Opera. Opera and ballets that required less scenery were presented there.

v. Popular singing
• **Major singers**
- Joséphine Baker, Maurice Chevalier, Damia, Fernandel (actor-singer), Sacha Guitry, Mistinguett, Édith Piaf, Tino Rossi, Charles Trenet.
• **Major songs**
- *J'ai deux amours* (Joséphine Baker), *Ma pomme* (Maurice Chevalier), *Parlez-moi d'amour* (Lucienne Boyer), *La chapelle au clair de lune* (Léo Marjanne), *Mon homme* (Mistinguett), *Lily Marlene* (Suzy Solidor), *Y'a d'la joie* (Charles Trenet), *Je suis seule ce soir*; *J'attendrai*, *Le p'tit vin blanc*; *L'accordéoniste* (Édith Piaf).

• Forbidden songs such as *Vive la terre de France*, *Ça sent si bon la France*, were sung in clandestine venues.

vi. Music stores
• Music stores sold instruments and sheet music.
• Scores from banned musicians were destroyed. Many storekeepers hid banned scores.
• Music teachers worked from home.

M. Reading. Libraries
i. Book buying

• French of all classes were avid readers and bought books. They resented the censorship.

• Comics grew in popularity as cartoonists mocked the rationing and the new foods like rutabaga, Jerusalem artichokes and ersatz coffee.

ii. Censorship

(a) **Bernhardt list**, established in Berlin: 143 books. Teams of two Sipo police agents plus one French gendarme, went to libraries and bookstores to remove the books on the list, August 27-31, 1940. 700,000 copies seized and destroyed.

• English-language authors – Franz Boas, Louis Fischer, H. R. Knickerbocker, James Joyce, D.H. Lawrence.

• French authors – Louis Aragon, André Malraux, Georges Duhamel.

• German authors opposing Nazism – Heinrich Mann and Otto Strasser.

(b) **Otto list** was established by the Abteilung Propaganda with French publishers that were requisitioned to help, namely Hachette, which already had a distribution network for books.

• For publishers to continue working, they had to pledge not to publish books by the proscribed authors. It was expanded from the Bernhardt list.

iii. Libraries in Paris

• There were public libraries run by the municipal council in every arrondissement.

• If libraries were caught short in August 1940, they were better prepared in September and October. Books were hidden. Some loyal users took books to hide.

• The library-bookstore Shakespeare and Company. The United States being a non-combatant country, owner Sylvia Beach was allowed to keep operating. After December 1941, she was able to continue – after briefly closing – under the protection of the Countess of Chambrun whose connections with

Pierre Laval and Pétain gave a special status to the store, though proscribed books were not overtly available.

• Libraries in cities and towns, in both zones, were subjected to the same regulations with the Bernhardt and Otto list.

N. Hotels
• The person who greeted and saw to the comfort of the clients was the concierge d'hôtel – no abbreviation – and can be written simply as the concierge. It was a profession for which a person had to study at the Institut de Conciergerie, a superior graduate school for hotel management staff. Not to be confused with the apartment building concierge who were mostly war widows or veterans, or retired public service persons in need, and required no training.

i. Hotel categories
(a) Café-hôtel
• A modest establishment with a café on the ground floor. It rented rooms to travelers by the day but also by the month or longer.

• The café served sandwiches.

(b) Hôtel de passe
• A hotel that rented rooms by the hour. It often had a café on the ground floor and a separate exit.

(c) Luxury hotels or palaces
• Those would be listed in the Guide Michelin. They had a restaurant and private dining rooms.

• Clients were tourists and businessmen.

(d) Travelers' hotels
• Usually located near a rail station, clients stayed while waiting for a connection or to avoid being caught out by the curfew. The most common name was Hôtel de la Gare.

ii. Some hotels in Paris
(a) Requisitioned (see 2. Administration of France for a list)
(b) Some other hotels

• Bristol hotel. Although luxurious, it was not requisitioned. It housed many American diplomats until December 1941. It was also the refuge of the Jewish architect Léo Lehrman (room 106) who only came out at night to plan renovation of the palace. His secret was well kept by the 210 employees.
  • Vendôme hotel.
  • Hôtel de L'Abbaye (Saint-Germain-des-Prés district).
  • Vernet hotel.
  • Napoléon hotel.

iii. Some hotels outside Paris
(a) Bordeaux
  • Splendid Hotel.
  • Hôtel de la Gare.
(b) Lyon
  • Helder Hotel.
  • Mercure hotel.
  • Hôtel de la Gare.
(c) Marseille
• The hotels Bompart, du Levant and Terminus were requisitioned by the Pétain administration to house Jewish women and children as an annexe of camp des Milles.
• Splendide Hotel, where Varian Fry took up residence. After the Werhmacht invaded the non-occupied zone, the Germans requisitioned the hotel.
• Belle-Vue hotel and Caravelle hotel. The Germans bombed the Vieux-Port May 27, 1944. The hotels were still standing but could not function.
(d) Nice
• Hôtel Excelsior. After November 1942, it became the occupier's headquarters and place of torture and death.
(e) Vichy
  • Les Princes.
  • Le Parc – Pétain's office on the third floor (fourth floor in North America parlance).

• Majestic Plazza.

• Hotel du Portugal. In November 1942 became HQ of the Gestapo.

• Le Thermal Palace. Housed the War Department.

O. Restaurants
i. Maître d'

• *Maître d'* is the English abbreviation of *maître d'hôtel*. It is not abbreviated in French. Writing in English, one would describe characters speaking French or a French person going to the restaurant and saying *maître d'hôtel*. Despite the title, *maître d'hôtel* only applies to restaurants not hotels. Hotels have a *concierge d'hôtel*, not abbreviated, though sometimes shortened to *concierge*.

ii. Food scarcity

• As early as the fall of 1940, food was scarce. Some small and averaged-size restaurants closed, some amended their menus, others used the black market.

• Some ordinary restaurants flourished as they obtained supplies through the black market. Many others struggled, in particular family owned, offering homemade meals with or without the help of paid staff. Those tended to be respectful of the law, asked for ration tickets and did not use the black market extensively.

• Most restaurants complied with the law and asked for ration tickets, but would discreetly serve someone who had no tickets. Resistants knew the restaurants that did not ask for ration tickets. Occupiers did not patronize the smaller, more ordinary restaurants or family-owned restaurants.

iii. Menus

• Pétain's government banned *à la carte* menus in both zones. Restaurants must only offer the Menu of the Day. It had to be on display at 10:00 am. It had to show how many ration tickets were necessary. Fish, butter, sugar and eggs were not allowed to figure on the menus.

• Although the exclusive restaurants, including those reserved for the occupiers, obtained all the ingredients they needed, they paid lip service to the rationing by making dishes where the meat was hidden under a leaf of lettuce.

iv. Fruit and names of dishes

• Fruit and other dishes were not allowed to be visible from outside the restaurant.

v. Definitions of restaurants and cafés and salons de thé

• **Auberge** – small hotel restaurant in villages and small towns.

• **Bistro(t)** – familiar name for a café. Modest drinking establishment. Can serve limited food, such as sandwiches. Sandwiches were a length of long loaf or baguette, cut down the length, buttered and filled with *saucisson sec* or garlic sausage or cooked ham slice – *jambon*, less often another cold cut, such as *jambon cru* – uncooked cured ham.

(**a**) It might also serve homemade soup at the request of known clients.

(**b**) Clients frequently played a card game called *belote*. There might be a pool table. There might also be a table where customers played checkers.

• **Brasserie** – restaurant where the favored drink is beer. Usually elegant settings and clientele. They were requisitioned during the Occupation.

• **Buvette** – a small restaurant in train stations, serving sandwiches and basic food, such as plain omelet, vegetable soup, cheese – depending on the supply. Wine by the glass and ersatz coffee. For children, water with a drop of mint, grenadine or strawberry syrup, while the supplies lasted. Buvettes in theaters and cinemas sold candies, peanuts and ice cream on a stick or between wafers while supplies lasted. The Pétain's government had banned ice cream and candies, except in venues reserved for the occupiers.

• **Buffet** – establishment similar to *buvette*, mostly in train stations, where the choice and time to serve was limited. Mostly found in cities and larger towns. Small stations would not have a buvette or buffet and travelers would go to the *Hôtel de la Gare*, usually opposite the station.

• **Café** – name most commonly used. It's a place where one can drink anything from water or café to wine and spirits and buy sandwiches (see Bistrot above).

(**a**) Sandwiches were a length of long loaf or baguette, cut down the length, buttered and filled with *saucisson sec* or garlic sausage or cooked ham slice – *jambon*. Less often, another cold cut, such as *jambon cru* – uncooked cured ham.

(**b**) It might also serve homemade soup on request from known clients.

(**c**) Clients frequently played a card game called *belote*. There might be a pool table. There might also be a table where customers played checkers.

• **Café-bar**: They had the word bar on their signage. A café-bar usually did not serve food. People simply called them *cafés*.

• **Café-hôtel** – operated a hotel for travelers as well as renting rooms on a long-term basis. Functioned like a café.

• **Café-restaurant** – operated a full-service restaurant, but a person could order just a drink or a coffee without having a meal. There might be a section reserved for the restaurant or meals could be served at any table. Many served home-cooked meals. Meals were usually modest. A customer would not expect exotic dishes or lavish desserts.

• **Café-tabac** – the only establishment where one could purchase tobacco and tobacco-related products and lottery tickets. They also sold postage stamps. Not all of them served food or sandwiches. They all served drinks.

• **Estaminet** – term mostly used in the northern region of France. Same as a café.

• **Gargote** – a familiar name for a cheap restaurant serving basic food, nothing fancy. Students and down on their luck persons were its main clients.

• **Restaurant** – mostly high end establishments that served food and drinks with meals. It might be simple bourgeois like La mère Catherine or more exclusive like Maxim's, Le Fouquet.

• **Rôtisserie** – elegant restaurant where meat and poultry were roasted in the traditional manner on a spit.

• **Salon de thé** – a chic venue where tea and non-alcoholic beverages were served with pastries, cakes – *viennoiseries* – and exotic candies.

• *Taverne* – old-fashioned nineteenth century name for a small drinking establishment often of ill repute. No longer in use by the time the war started.

NOTE: Do *not* use in your WWII novel.

• *Troquet* – a familiar name for a small café or bistrot. No longer in use by the time the war started. **NOTE**: Do *not* use in your WWII novel.

vi. Cafés in Paris
• Café de la Paix (5, place de l'Opéra) – closed during the Occupation. Re-opened after the liberation and served its first meal to General de Gaulle.

(**a**) Popular cafés
   • Le Dôme – Boulevard Montparnasse.
   • Les Deux Magots – 6 place Saint-Germain-des-Prés, favored by writers.
   • Café du Cadran – rue Louis-le-Grand, favored by journalists.
   • Pam-Pam, Souflot, Grand Cluny, Petit Cluny.
   • Colisée – on the Champs-Élysées.

(**b**) Bistrots. Inexpensive restaurants
   • Bouillon Chartier – 7 Rue du Faubourg Montmartre.
   • Café du commerce – 51 rue du Commerce.

(**c**) Café-restaurant la Mère Catherine – 6 place du Tertre, much favored by the occupiers.

• La Rotonde – rue de la Roquette – being in the predominantly Jewish 11th Arrondissement, it rarely saw any occupiers.

vii. Restaurants requisitioned in Paris
• On his arrival, Hermann Göring tried to enforce a rule that French people would not be permitted in restaurants. It did not work from day one and the ruling was never heard of again.
• No civilians were allowed in requisitioned establishments. It did not take long before the rule broke down. Only the upper class would patronize those establishments.
• La Tour d'Argent – no civilians unless in the company of a German military. The rule was enforced.
TRIVIA: Before the arrival of the Germans, Claude Terrail, the owner's son, walled up the famous wine reserve containing thousands of bottles. The occupiers never discovered the ruse.
• La Chope Latine – no civilians unless in the company of German personnel. Rule enforced.
• All the Brasseries alsaciennes – no civilians unless in the company of German personnel. •
Some brasseries that relaxed the rules.
- Brasserie Lipp – 151 boulevard Saint-Germain.
- La Brune – 42 avenue de la Motte-Picquet. Banner on the canopy read *Wehrmachtspeiselokal*
- Brasserie Wepler – 14 Place Clichy.
- Brasserie Elsass Lorthringen – Boulevard Parmentier.
- Deutsch Gasthaus – Boulevard Saint-Germain (no longer exists).
- La Coupole – Boulevard Montparnasse, welcomed artists and writers for meals.
- La Rotonde – 105 Boulevard Montparnasse.

viii. Higher end restaurants open to all
• Lasserre – Avenue Emmanuel III by the Champs-Élysées (modern Franklin Delano Roosevelt). The restaurant became a hub of résistance.

- Lapérouse – obtained an exemption to serve all clientele.
- Maxim's – 3 rue Royale.
- The Ritz – Place de la Concorde.
- La Reine Pédauque – 6 rue de la Pépinière.
- À la Marée – 1 rue Daru.
- Le Fouquet – 99 avenue des Champs-Élysées.
- Carrère – rue Pierre-Charron (no longer exists).
- Châtaigner – rue du Cherche-Midi. (no longer exists).
- La Closerie des Lilas.
- Pavillon Ledoyen – in the Champs-Élysées gardens.
- Drouant – 18 rue Gaillon. Famous for private salons and literary gatherings.
- Buffet de la Gare de Lyon – located in the Gare de Lyon. Despite being called a buffet, it was very elegant – long like a train with a central passage, large windows, paintings on the ceiling and separating walls, recreated train fine dining with banquettes, lots of gilded decor, chandeliers.
- Pavillon d'Armenonville – in the Bois de Boulogne.
- L'aiglon.
- Bagatelle.
- Le Pré Catalan.

ix. Restaurants serving other clientele
- Le Tyrol – 146 avenue des Champs-Élysées. French Nazi party, collaborators, French Gestapo.
- Brasserie Mollard – opposite Saint-Lazare station. French Gestapo, collaborators.

x. Restaurants in towns in the non-occupied zone.
- The more rural the town, the fewer requisitioned restaurants and other pleasure venues for the occupiers. All towns had small restaurants and bistrots. A village might only have one café which might or might not serve meals.
- Bordeaux – L'Empire (elegant).
- Lyon – Brasserie Georges AKA La Georges (elegant).
- Marseille – Le Petit Nice (high end).

• Nantes – Brasserie La Cigale (high end).
• Vichy – Le Cintra. Rendezvous for the Who's Who of the town of Vichy (luxurious).

xi. Salons de thé in Paris
• Angelina – rue de Rivoli.
• Carette – Place du Trocadéro.
• Ladurée – rue Royale.
• Ruc – 59 rue Saint-Honoré, opposite la Comédie Française.

P. Sports
i. Sports and the État Français
• Sporting activities were encouraged by the État Français. It was a big part of the Révolution Nationale, which promoted healthy living. A powerful ideological influence for youth.
• Nine hours of sport per week were made compulsory in schools.
• Sporting participants had to pledge to be the best possible for the country.
• The occupiers facilitated travel for French teams. Encouraged by the occupiers, sporting activities resumed right after the occupation of the country. They wanted life to be *normal* to prove they had won the war.
• Matches were well attended. It was a form of escapism, survival, as well as defiance.
• Creation of the Chantiers de Jeunesse for young men of twenty in the summer of 1940. Eight months long. Fitness and sports occupied a large part of the day with themes of back to nature.
• There was a running battle between the Catholic Church and the sport associations, both accusing the other of wanting to rule the youth.
• Displays and competitions were held, both in the zones as well as between the two zones.

• Many young people joined teams, not necessarily out of love of sport but because after a match or competition they were provided with a meal.

• Sports were gradually forbidden to Jews.

• Pétain was a proponent of amateur sports and wanted to abolish professionalism.

• Under the influence of État Français propaganda, sports were held in the many stadiums in cities, towns and villages throughout the country.

• Resistants could distribute tracts, meet and could melt away in the anonymity of the mass of spectators.

ii. Boxing. For men only.

iii. Cycling

• Tour de France – Suspended during the occupation.

• In Paris, the Vélodrome d'Hiver, known as Vel d'Hiv, venue for cycling, roller-skating, soccer and boxing, became infamous in the roundup of Paris' Jews in July 1942.

• Unwittingly, most of the population became sportive as the bicycle became the number one mode of transport.

iv. Gymnastics

• Artistic for men: beam, parallel bars, vaulting horse, rings.

• *Gymnastique artistique* for women: beam, parallel bars, vaulting horse, floor displays.

v. Shooting – suspended during the occupation.

vi. Skiing – Skiing in the Alps, and to some extent, the Pyrénées, was popular with the occupiers, the collaborators and anyone who could afford it.

• Ski resorts were not highly developed. There were few hotels. Many locals rented rooms to skiers.

• Ski lifts were not sophisticated, mostly just a perch to drag the skier up the slope.
• There were few cable-cars.

vii. Swimming
• **Paris – swimming pools** reopened immediately after the occupation.

- Molitor pool – swimming pool reserved for the occupiers, men and women.
- La Butte-aux-Cailles pool – open to all. Built over an artesian well with warm water.
- Deligny pool.
- Tourelles pool.
- Bois de Boulogne pool.

(a) Outside Paris and reserved for the occupiers
• Saint-Fiacre – Morbihan, Brittany. The occupiers built a pool behind their bunker at the edge of the woods.
• Martinvast – close to Cherbourg. A large pool with diving area.

viii. Tennis – canceled September 3, 1939, resumed in 1941, for French citizens only. The championship, the French Open, was renamed *Le Tournoi de France*. Women's titles of the French Tournament during the Occupation were not recognized after the war, but the men's were (!).
• Men wore a tunic or blazer and long pants. Women wore a dress mid-calf and a cardigan – for modesty (!).

xix. Track and Field
• For the occupiers – competitions between military units.
• The French championship was canceled in 1940 and 1944. It took place in Bordeaux in 1942, 1943.

x. Weight lifting. For men only.

xi. Paris stadiums

(a) Stade Parc des Princes – part of it was requisitioned by the occupiers and used for military training and sports for the troops housed in the Lycée Claude-Bernard.

• Tournaments organized among French teams from the occupied, non-occupied and the forbidden zones.

• It was damaged by the bombing of nearby industrial areas.

(b) Roland-Garros tennis stadium. From September 3, 1939 to spring 1941, the stadium was used as a transit camp for undesirable foreigners.

(c) Stade de Colombes – soccer and rugby. Also used as a transit camp for undesirables from September-October 1939.

• Foreign males, in particular those of German origin, aged 17 to 50 had to report to the stadium where they were searched, held and either freed or directed to another camp.

• It was damaged during the bombing of nearby industrial areas.

(d) Stade Pierre-de-Coubertin – volleyball, basketball, handball, athletics.

• Some damage during nearby bombing.

xii. Rural towns and villages

Most towns had an outdoor stadium. Villages improvised space in a field.

xiii. Team sports

• Basketball, handball, rugby, soccer, volleyball. Matches between French teams.

• Soccer (called football in France) and rugby. Men only.

- Organized matches between Third Reich units such as Luftwaffe against Panzers.

- Organized matches between French teams.

xiv. *Pétanque*. Boules

• Although not officially listed as a sport, the game of *boules* or *pétanque* in the south of France was played with steel balls by two teams. It was also played in the occupied zone.

 • It demanded skill and was played outdoors.

 • It was tolerated by the occupiers, who occasionally would join in.

Q. Theaters

 • While the performing arts resumed after the armistice of June 1940, censorship was brutal. Any and all expressions of free thinking were banned. Scripts were cut or re-written.

 • Some playwrights produced plays that could be interpreted differently according to one's political opinion, such as *Antigone* by Marcel Anouilh.

 • Some theaters were obliged to change names. For example, Théâtre Sarah Bernhardt became Théâtre de la Cité.

 • In 1943, venues were obliged to close one day per week in addition to the regular non-performance day, traditionally Tuesdays.

 • From March 1944, venues were closed four days per week.

 • Translations of Shakespeare's plays were tolerated by the occupiers until 1944 when they were banned.

 • Increased French theater attendance. One reason was the need to escape the grimness of daily life. Another was the theaters were heated in winter – occupiers also patronized theaters.

 • Hours of performances were adjusted for curfew.

 • Theaters were obliged to reserve seats for the Propaganda-Staffel.

 • Increasingly, plays were replaced by German anti-Semitic and propaganda plays. Some written by French playwrights or amended to fit the new order.

 • Mixed clientele. French and cultivated Germans.

i. Traditional theaters

• The Comédie Française theater received subsidies from the État Français. Always the leading national theater, it thrived in a collaborationist way.
• Théâtre des Champs-Élysées, l'Empire et la Salle du Palais de Chaillot were requisitioned, though French playwrights could present their work by permission of the occupiers.

ii. Vaudeville and music-hall
• Châtelet theater, Place du Châtelet. Performing arts – music-hall acts and ballet.

9. Black market
• The black market was **not a physical place**. The term designated the flaunting of the imposed economic legislation by an individual or company.

i. Anyone with a surplus of an item in demand – especially as far as food was concerned – who would sell at an inflated price became a black marketer.

B. Development of the black market
• Urban families went to forage in the countryside, trying to buy food, then on return playing cat and mouse with the authorities at the train station or if on bicycle at the checkpoints.

• Both the occupiers and the gendarmes were concerned about people buying food in the rural areas to resell at inflated prices in the city.

• Those who had just enough for an average family usually were let go. Though later in the war, they sometimes saw their meagre booty confiscated.

i. As early as November-December 1940, the parallel economy of the black market began to flourish, in particular for meat. Most people were against it, especially the poorer classes, who could not afford black market prices.

• People learned by word of mouth where items could be obtained. Many storekeepers indulged in black marketing. Rations up front, back room without tickets.

• In classifieds advertisements, the wording never mentioned money but an exchange. For example, *Will exchange an almost-new suit for a ham*. It was understood that sometimes money would also change hands, but never specified.

ii. Black market in books
• Bookstores and librarians had hidden banned books which they sold under the counter.

• Publishers who had hidden banned books sold them under the counter.

• Some publishers succeeded in obtaining paper and clandestinely published banned authors'manuscripts and sold them to bookstores under the counter.

• The black market in books was not primarily for profit but to defy the authorities.

iii. Denunciations

• Denunciations were frequent.

• The black market became a major preoccupation of the population, especially in cities and towns.

• As early as November-December 1940, the parallel economy of the black market began to flourish, in particular for meat. Most people were against it, especially the poorer classes who could not afford black market prices.

• Early in 1941, suppression of the black market became the government's priority. A number of repressive services were given the means to crack down on black marketeering. They were especially harsh on the small black marketers, as they were the only ones that did not have the means to hide their illicit commerce. For example, a man who takes the train to the country, buys some produce, cheese and eggs and is stopped by the control at the train station.

• Pétain's repressive measures touched the working class and Pétain became aware of the critics, that the Révolution Nationale was failing.

• In a speech in August 1941, he promised to take drastic measures against those who were *building a fortune on the backs of the general misery.*

iv. Laws March 15, 1942

• Pétain's government finally came to the realization that the small black marketer ought not to receive the same punishment as one who operated on a larger scale strictly for profit. The law was not amended, but gendarmes and inspectors were instructed to be lenient.

v. By the end of 1941
• The official calorie count had been reduced to 1,100. The government failed to curb the black market. They then authorized *family parcels* – food parcels, which could not contain meat unless dried in the form of saucisson or cured ham, and were sent directly from the farmer or family gardener.
• Parcels were sometimes stolen in transit.

vi. Occupying forces
• Despite the rules imposed by the Feldkommandantur, officers and private soldiers dealt directly with farmers or their intermediaries. In 1943, the occupiers *supposedly* ceased to use the black market because the État Français, in the name of collaboration, provided everything the MBF asked for. The reality was different.

vii. Causes and consequences
• As early as the fall of 1940, many foodstuffs became unavailable, because the occupying forces had requisitioned the harvest. Hunger and food insecurity, especially among the poorer and middle classes, pushed people to resort to the black market, despite the penalties if caught.
• Soldiers had no hesitation in selling at a price the food they had pillaged.
• On a higher level, the MBF authorities created the Bureaux d'Achat – Buying Bureau – where traffickers built fortunes, and made food pillage systematic.
• German Buying Bureau – the gang *Bonny-Laffont* made up of former convicts who later became the French Gestapo, had a network of crooks to supply the Buying Bureau.
• Petty opportunists such as an individual stealing a bicycle and reselling it for a hefty price.
• Anybody who had something valuable to sell and needed money became a black marketer in the eye of the law since the sold items were mostly overpriced.

• Rationing was the underlying cause of the development of the black market. Food rations were inadequate and had to be supplemented for survival.

• Requisitions at the source – producers and growers were given quotas to fill, which did not leave enough for them to supply the regular market.

• The consequences for those who had no discretionary income or rural contacts were slow starvation, especially those in the cities and older people without family.

• Among the poorer classes children suffered most as they had less resistance to tuberculosis and other childhood diseases. Their growth was impaired.

viii. Food suppliers

• Farmers found ways to deliver the least possible to the authorities in order to sell above the fixed price, but below the black market rates. Some out of patriotism, others to increase their well-being.

• Profiteers – men who circulated in the more affluent classes and the collaborator class driven by greed.

ix. Public opinion
(a) French

• Psychologically against the black market. It began to change as the extremely cold winter set in.

• A new idea took form in 1943, the "patriotic black market". The résistance groups and maquis reinforced the concept with the producers that any clandestine products sold to the resistants and maquisards were proof of solidarity against the occupiers and Pétain's government.

(b) German

• With their Deutschmarks, the occupiers were only concerned with getting what they wanted. However, they strongly condemned the black market while using it both as customers and suppliers.

• In early 1943, the occupying authorities closed the Buying Bureau and employed the traffickers as police or intelligence agents. The État Français and the occupying authorities were now working together for the repression of the black market but with little success. Prison sentences were handed out. Only the small fry was caught, as they had no way to hide.

10. Bombing
A. Air-Raid Shelters
i. Cities and towns were divided into areas each with a leader and volunteers to direct people to shelters where wardens helped them.

• Sirens on tall buildings sounded a rising and falling blast for three minutes when aircraft were approaching. To signal the end of danger, the sirens emitted a prolonged sound, at the same pitch. It could be heard far away. There were numerous sirens in urban areas.

• Shelters in basements of houses and apartment buildings. Additional shelters were built in 1939.

• In 1939, there was a general fear of gas attacks. Since 1920, the authorities equipped some buildings, including hospitals, and several métro stations with hermetic doors and a system to purify the air.

• Public building shelters would have a sign which read *Abri, 20 places* – Shelter, 20 places or whatever number of persons it accommodated. They were equipped with shovels and other tools as well as food and water.

• In all the cities and towns air-raid shelters were built specifically in case of war, or in places the natural irregularities of the terrain were converted into shelters.

• In Paris and other cities, apartment buildings were most often in rows with adjoining walls. They had basements and it was not unusual to have connecting basements. In Paris, some basements had an exit into ancient underground quarries.

• The basements of apartment buildings over four stories also served as public shelters.

• Some shelters had a nursing station. Some shelters under hospitals were fully equipped to treat casualties and infectious disease. L'Hôtel-Dieu had a gas-proof bunker underneath the hospital.

• Private houses usually had basements.

• A large bunker under Gare de l'Est in Paris was built prior to the start of the war from which train traffic could be controlled.

• In Paris the deepest métro stations were used as shelters, particularly in the poorer districts where buildings were ancient and less secure.

• In wine country, winemakers let people shelter in the cellars.

• In addition, in Paris, after June 1940, the occupiers built tunnels to join stations and their requisitioned buildings and hotels.

ii. 1940
• The air raid sirens created an intense fear in people. There was an unspoken knowledge that after the bombs, the troops would march in.

iii. 1942. Beginning of the allied bombing
• When allied bombing began, the mood changed. The citizenry still had the fear that a stray bomb might obliterate homes and lives. For the majority of people this fear was mitigated by the hope that the occupiers would bear the brunt of the bombing and they would survive.

B. Allied bombing
i. Objectives
(a) Civilian
• Destruction of the rail and road system.
(b) Military
• Destruction of factories serving the enemy.
• Destruction of munitions depots.
• Destruction of barracks or troop concentrations.

ii. 1941-1944
• Allied bombing, although very destructive was, if not welcome, accepted as a necessary evil. Adults discussed where

the bombs would fall and how much damage they would inflict, with a few words of sorrow for the civilians that would lose home or life. Morale remained high despite losses. The occupiers were blamed.

• Young people were excited and wished they could tell the pilots where to drop their payload. Young people were quick to volunteer their help.

• Sabotage achieved 99% of its objectives. Repression over the civilians was comparatively less than losses inflicted by stray bombs.

• Bombing achieved only 20% target accuracy, though it improved somewhat by 1944.

iii. Role of the Résistance

• The résistance groups communicated the location of many targets but were concerned about the impact of the air raids on civilians. In some cases, they refused to indicate a target. They made offers of sabotage to important factories to avoid bombings.

• The Citroën factories (Suresnes, Boulogne-Billancourt) – sabotaged the trucks they were forced to produce by moving the *Full* line lower on the engine dipstick. Hence, the vehicles would quickly run out of oil and damage the engine.

• Peugeot – Sochaux. The family was involved in the résistance and helped sabotage their production.

• The Berliet factories – Lyon. The Pétainist management refused to sabotage. Consequently the factory was bombed.

• Dunlop – Montluçon. The Pétainist management refused to sabotage. Consequently the factory was bombed.

• Gnôme et Rhône – Gennevilliers. The Pétainist management refused to sabotage. Consequently the factory was bombed.

• Michelin – Clermont-Ferrand. The management refused to sabotage. Consequently the factory was bombed repeatedly by the RAF and the USAF. However, the whole family was heavily committed in the local résistance. The family and workers quietly made sufficient defects into the tires which after a while and especially in the cold of the eastern front were rendered useless.

• Renault factories – Boulogne-Billancourt. Louis Renault, a pro-Nazi who visited Hitler, refused to allow sabotage. The factory was bombed repeatedly by the RAF and the USAF.

• March 1, 1942. RAF took risks to drop warning leaflets for the workers of the Renault factories. Bombing took place on March 3 and April 4, 1943, USAF bombing in daylight. September 1943, RAF at night, USAF in daylight.

• Villacoublay aviation factories. Taken over by the Luftwaffe. Heavily bombed from 1943 onward.

iv. 1943
• Intensification of strategic bombing throughout France.

v. 1944.
• Transportation Plan began in May. In coordination with the résistance groups, rail and road networks were bombed and sabotaged. Lacking precision, the bombing caused innumerable casualties. Towns, such as some in Normandy, were razed to the ground.

• The bombing only achieved 40% of its objectives. Civilian casualties and building destruction were high.

C. Enemy bombing
i. 1940. As the German forces advanced heavy, indiscriminate bombing.

• 1940 (May-June) – German bombing spread fear among the population, spurred anger against the occupiers for hitting civilian infrastructure and refugees on roads. It created a thirst for revenge.

• Operation Paula (Unternehmen) June 3. Paris and suburbs. Objective was to destroy armament and aviation factories as well as the airfields west of Paris. Intelligence received in time avoided the planned massive destruction.

• Renault and Citroën were also to be destroyed as they manufactured armaments.

ii. 1944
• October 4, a V2 Rocket was launched from the Saar region and fell on Deuil-la-Barre, department of the Seine-et-Oise (now called Val-d'Oise 95).
• August 26-27 at midnight. Paris has just been liberated. Von Choltitz had signed the surrender of the troops. There were still people dancing in the streets. The Luftwaffe, more than 100 bombers, took off from Belgium, Holland and Germany, toward Paris, turned to fly from the south toward the north and north-east and dropped incendiary bombs over Paris and the suburbs in a V shape, starting in the south of Paris (Sceaux district), toward Saint-Denis for the west branch and Noisy-le-Sec for the east branch.
- Damage consisted of 189 killed, 890 wounded, 431 destroyed buildings, 1600 damaged buildings.
• Indiscriminate bombing during troops movements and near the front after the 1944 D-Day landings.

D) Public opinion
i. 1940 German bombing
• During bombing by the German advance in 1940, people were angry, calling the Germans assassins and worse.

ii. 1942-1943 Allied bombing.
Regret over the destruction, empathy for the victims, acceptance as a necessary evil before liberation, solidarity.
• A general wish the Allies would speed up.

iii. 1944
• With the intensification of allied bombing new hope emerged. The end was near, the sacrifices were worth it. Renewed energy to help the victims.

• Allied bombing also brought retaliation from the occupying forces and indiscriminate bombing.

• Enemy bombing and other forms of retaliation by enemy troops brought on a deep hatred and a thirst for revenge among the population. Hatred that lasted into the 1960s, when people began to talk about Nazis instead of boches, and other pejorative names, or Germans, (see 33. Language).

11. Brothels - *Maisons closes*
A. General
• During the Occupation there were the requisitioned brothels for the occupying troops and brothels for Frenchmen.

• Especially in Paris, Parisians made use of those establishments for other reasons than sex. It was heated and there was an abundance of food. They could meet in a private room to discuss politics between men.

• Resistants made good use of the facilities to hide and pass on messages.

• Brothels were almost never raided, especially those receiving German officers, who shunned the requisitioned brothels, and collaborators.

• Brothels were mostly an urban phenomenon. The arrival of occupying troops in rural areas and the lack of procurer-hotels (*maisons de passe*) led soldiers and women to conduct business in various places including the woods.

i. Public opinion
• Tolerance since the beginning of the nineteenth century. A monthly health check for prostitutes was made compulsory by decree. Still applied during the war.

• Public opinion: Prostitution was hidden behind walls, therefore did not affect the ordinary citizen. However, society as a whole condemned prostitution.

• Even a village could have a woman earning a living by prostitution. Everyone knew, but ignored it as long as it remained discreet.

B. Prostitution
i. French regulations
• Prostitutes had to register with the *préfecture* then with a *maison close* (brothel). A debate during the interwar years discussed closing brothels, but nothing happened and the declaration of war put an end to such talk, at least temporarily.

• The reason was a question of health and hygiene and spread of venereal diseases.

- It was illegal to solicit clients. A woman could be punished, including prison, if caught.
- Clandestine prostitutes were those not registered with the Préfecture and who did not undergo health checks. Police pursued them and the women were punished.
- Brothels were controlled by the *Brigade des Mœurs* (Decency brigade).

ii. German regulations

- The authorities were most concerned with the health of the troops. Upon arrival in France, they requisitioned brothels for the exclusive use of officers and troops. There were over two-hundred brothels in the occupied zone and over sixty in Paris alone.
- As this was not sufficient, the Wehrmacht health services requisitioned apartment buildings, or hotels, and placed a madame of their choice in charge of running the place.
- All prostitutes were registered with the prefecture.
- Prostitutes were subjected to regular bi-weekly health checks by the health services attached to the Feldkommandanturen, spurred on by the German phobia of disease and contagion.
- A woman soliciting a member of the German Forces on the street could face internment in a camp if caught.
- Women of Jewish, or of an origin considered undesirable, were removed from the requisitioned brothels.
- If a soldier was found to have contracted a venereal disease, he had to indicate which woman he had sex with. She was immediately arrested.
- The occupiers made huge use of the brothels.
- Three reasons behind the tight control by the health services were prevention of disease, control of relationships between the occupiers and Frenchwomen (there were a list of restrictions, which were largely ignored, such as not to offer one's arm to a Frenchwoman in the street, not to give her a ride

in an official vehicle, not to have marital relations) and to allow the soldiers to share in the victory.

• Another reason which appeared in the winter 1941-42 was the rise of resistance, particularly communist, and the fear that a serviceman could divulge information. All women, including legal prostitutes, were potential spies.

• Proof that the regulations did not work was the thousands of children born of a German father and a non-prostitute Frenchwoman.

• Where the military was billeted in private houses, especially in rural areas, relationships developed. The Germans, whether officers or troops, were eager for relationships.

iii. Pétain's government
• Brothels were so prosperous that the Pétain's government passed a law on December 31, 1941 that the owners had to pay a tax of 8 to 18 percent. Owners were happy to pay as it sanctioned their legitimacy as *honest merchants.*

C. Requisitioned brothels
i. Short list
• One-Two-Two – 122 rue de Provence, 8th Arrondissement.
• Le Chabanais – 12 rue Chabanais.
• Soldatenkaffe Madeleine –place de la Madeleine.
• Le Sphynx – 31 Bd Edgar Quinet.
• La Fleur Blanche – 6 rue des Moulins, 1st Arrondissement.
• Raspoutine – 58 rue Bassano.
• Hôtel Marigny (Homosexual brothel) – 11 rue de l'Arcade, 2nd Arrondissement.
• The Abbey – rue Saint-Sulpice (disguised as a church).
• Chez Christiane (BDSM dungeon) – 9 rue Navarin.
• The Medieval – 32 rue Navarin.

ii. Requisitioned but resistant brothels

• L'Étoile de Kléber (forwarded messages to Résistance, hid Jews and downed airmen) – 4 rue Paul Valéry, 16th Arrondissement .

• Aux Belles Poules, 32 rue Blondel.

TRIVIA: It was famous for its erotic mosaics. Now a heritage protected building.

12. Clothing and Fashion.
A. Beauty, personal appearance
i. Beauty
• Beauty (makeup, nails) and hairdressing salons each had a storefront.

• Their clients came from all classes of society as long as they could afford the prices.

• In poorer districts, there were only hairdressers.

• They declined in numbers during the Occupation.

NOTE: At the time, no one used the term hair stylists. It was *hairdressers*.

In French, the term is *salon de coiffure* and more commonly, especially in poorer districts, *coiffeur*.

• A favorite hair style was rolls at the back of the head, the sides and sometimes above the forehead.

• Since women often rode a bicycle, rolled curls were not practical and rather than lose precious hairpins and the horsehair supports, they tied their hair back with a ribbon. Young women often let their hair fall loose on the shoulders, unless they had to perform a formal errand.

• Few women cut their hair short as this required a visit to the hairdresser. For most, the expense was not justified and could be better spent on black market food.

• Makeup became unavailable as early as 1941. What a woman had was jealously guarded for special occasions. Women soon showed their ingenuity (the *Système D* – débrouillardise: using ingenuity and resourcefulness). If they were able to obtain beetroot to eat, some of the water in which they were cooked was saved and applied on lips, and so on.

• L'Oréal among its hair and makeup products manufactured *Ambresoie* a liquid silk stocking.

ii. Barbers
• They had a storefront, usually smaller than a hairdresser.

• Their clients were men and boys. The barber was always a man.

• They offered shaves, done with a straight-razor.

iii. Evolution of the barber trade.
• Before the First World War, Gillette invented the safety razor. This allowed men to take care of shaving at home. However, it was not a total abandonment of visits to the barber. Barber shops were social gathering places for men, and the new razor was costly.

• Men's haircuts remain the prerogative of the barbers.

• During the wartime period, men were generally clean-shaven, though some older men might sport a mustache. Beards were not in fashion.

• Men and boys wore their hair short.

• Maquisards (resistance fighters) due to lack of facilities, were often unshaven. However, they did not take a stroll in town without shaving first. A scruffy man would immediately be arrested. The occupiers believed all scruffy men were *terrorists*.

B. Clothing stores
i. Standard wardrobe
• According to the Pétain's government, a woman's standard wardrobe consisted of two dresses or two skirts, three shirts, two slips, two aprons or shifts, one waterproof coat, one winter coat, two pairs of winter gloves, three panties, six handkerchiefs.

• The list also included six pairs of silk stockings but those quickly became unavailable by the end of 1940. Women carefully kept any they had from before the war. Stockings became valuable trade items for food on the black market.

• Almost all the available stock of silk, wool and leather was requisitioned and sent to Germany.

Note: There was no mention of a standard wardrobe for men (!).

ii. Custom made

• Seamstresses and tailors worked from home. It was a thriving business until the war. It declined in the occupied zone but flourished in the non-occupied zone as women who used to go to Paris to buy dresses, now had them made by the local seamstresses.

• Even in the non-occupied zone, fabrics and other notions were hard to get. Basting thread was carefully removed and saved.

• Affluent classes used to have all their outer garments custom made by a seamstress.

• Affluent men went to a tailor who also made shirts and ties.

• Poorer classes had only custom made garments for special occasions – weddings, christenings.

• Men in poorer classes rarely saw the necessity of spending money for a special occasion if they owned a good suit.

• All were affected by the restrictions and lack of fabric. Seamstresses and tailors made new with old and put their ingenuity to work.

• Men in executive positions wore a three-piece suit and tie. The Germans were favorably impressed by well-dressed people.

• Much sewing was also done at home. Women, especially with growing children, were on the constant lookout for what could be used. The Marché aux Puces – flea market – was a source of secondhand clothing that could be altered.

• Affluent households had curtains to the floor, usually velvet or heavy drapery. Women cut them to cover just the window and used the cut off fabric to make coats or dresses.

• Decorative bedspreads also found their way into garments.

• In the occupied zone, women got tips from fashion magazines – *Le Petit Echo de la Mode, Modes et Travaux.*

• The magazines *Marie-Claire* and *l'Officiel de la Mode* had moved to Lyon in the non-occupied zone. They were not available in the occupied zone.

• Importance was attached to simplicity, back to nature. Floral fabrics favored by Pétain were a symbol of the Révolution Nationale.

• Divergent fashion. The zazous. Mainly boys and young men going against the grain by wearing wide pants, extravagant jackets, scarves, sleek hairstyles and any variations on that theme. Young girls were less outlandish and less noticeable, with wider skirts than authorized and slightly shorter hair usually worn loose.

iv. Fashion establishments

• *Grands couturiers* – haute couture. They occupied whole buildings in Paris.

• The MBF was determined to transfer all the fashion establishment to Berlin, which was to become the center of fashion of the new Europe and Vienna. Facing the strong refusal of the couturiers and of Lucien Lelong, director of the Chambre syndicale de la haute couture (Trade Union of the haute couture), the MBF agreed for the haute couture to remain independent. They, however, had to work with them.

• The occupiers, with their advantageous currency exchange, became the most faithful customers of fashion houses.

(a) The main fashion houses were Hubert de Givenchy, Jeanne Lanvin, Jean Patou, Nina Ricci.

• Alix – refused to obey restrictions and taunted the occupiers by creating blue, white and red models. The exasperated occupiers finally closed her fashion house in 1944.

• Cristobal Balenciaga, Spanish refugee, was obliged to close toward the end of 1943.

• Jacques Heim (whose enterprise had been aryanized and personally was a resistant).

• Coco Channel had closed her fashion establishment but kept the perfume store open.

• Jacques Fath, Maggy Rouff and Marcel Rochas were eager collaborators.

• All the garments were hand sewn, with the help of sewing machines.

• The MBF's demands, lack of fabrics and more, spurred the *grands couturiers* to be more creative and use new synthetic material like rayon and viscose, but many of the less prominent had to close their doors.

(b) In 1941, the annual collection was limited to one hundred garments per fashion house.

(c) Since the whole of France was administratively the responsibility of the État Français, edicts from Pétain's government applied in the occupied zone. Therefore, when the rule about banning wide and pleated skirts was made, women in the occupied zone were to amend their wardrobe. Some did. Most ignored it. Pant cuffs were banned, the length of dresses measured and restrictions were imposed on the width of hems. Economy of material was the new mantra.

• The edict spurred *grands couturiers* to create a new fashion of narrow skirts and short jackets.

(d) Dismantling a worn garment and turning it inside out to make a new one was embraced by fashion houses as much as seamstresses, tailors and housewives.

• The couturiers in Paris were no longer able to obtain fabrics from the mills in the north like Lille, Roubaix, nor from the free zone like Lyon.

• Women bicycling daily shunned the narrow skirts and instead those who could afford it adopt the split skirt.

• Shortages and regulations affected mainly the couturiers in Paris, as the capital was the center of fashion. Other cities and towns in the rest of the country did not have the setup fashion houses had in Paris. Fashion was made locally after travel restrictions were imposed.

• Basting thread was carefully removed to be re-used.

• Some fashion houses fled to the non-occupied zone.

v. Corset store

• In 1939, older women still wore corsets with whalebone stays. The younger generation wore an elasticized *gaine* (girdle). Gabrielle (Coco) Channel played a major role in women's emancipation from the restrictive corset.

• The bra had made its appearance after WWI.

• Girls were introduced to wearing a corset as early as age six.

• 1941, the importation of rubber ceased and the Germans, having taken all the available stocks, young women in particular, stopped wearing corsets and girdles. It was replaced by a garter belt to hold up the stockings.

• After the war, as industries began to cater to the French market, the fashion soared again and the full girdle came back, but by 1960, young women had abandoned it.

• There were stores that catered exclusively to selling ready-made corsets, girdles and bras.

vi. Corset maker

• Corset making was a thriving home business. It offered privacy and discretion.

• It was made to measure.

vii. Footwear stores, Bootmakers, Shoemaker, Cobbler

• In normal times, France manufactured some ten million shoes, boots, sandals and slippers per year. The MBF demanded six millions shoes to be delivered immediately to be sent to Germany. This did not leave enough footwear for the French population.

• Main manufacturers were Les Chaussures Marco, located at Pont de l'Arche (Eure) and Fanien located at Lillers (Pas-de-Calais).

• The decree of October 29, 1940 by the *Comité général de l'organisation du cuir*, (General Committee for Leather Management) made strict rules about leather use. High boots and ankle boots were forbidden.

• November 1940, the sale of leather shoes was banned, except to the occupiers.

• All leather had been requisitioned except for a small allowance.

• Ingenuity in footwear led to using other materials. Shoemakers became creative making tops with the customer's unwanted shoes, canvas or a combination of both. Rafia was used for slippers and sandals, including the sole. Bullrushes and braided straw on fabric were quite decorative. Rabbit skin, with the fur inside, was also used, but it was not very strong and tore easily.

(a) Cobbler, shoe repair stores thrived. The majority of people could not afford to have shoes made for them nor could they afford the newer fashion in footwear, which required tickets and was expensive. People had their shoes and boots repaired. They brought anything that could be turned into a top, old purses, old boots, pieces of canvas, and so on. Since boots were forbidden, cobblers were skilled at cutting off tops to make a shoe, and reusing the leather.

• Soles were the biggest challenge. People walked many miles or bicycled. The creation of the wooden sole was a solution. Some soles were articulated at the ball of the foot. Heels were hollowed out wood.

• The wedge heel elevated the foot and enhanced the leg.

(b) Shoes. From this point on, when a person needed a pair of shoes, they had to make a written request to their mayor and explain why they need a pair of shoes. There were priorities:

• Children over six who could not use older siblings' hand-me-downs.

• Workers who had to walk long distances, such as letter carriers, providing they did not already possess two good, or repairable, pairs.

• For rural areas, Pétain promoted the simplicity of the land and encouraged workers and women to use the traditional wooden *sabot* or *galoche* – clog – worn with felt slippers or, if not available, stuffed straw.

• The Pétain's government also tried to impose, with minimal success, a standard shoe to shoe manufacturers.

(c) *Bottier* (shoemaker) A shoemaker only custom-made shoes and boots. He might repair his own-made boots or shoes.

• His only customers were the occupiers and collaborators. Other footwear was repaired by the *cordonnier* (repairer, cobbler).

viii. **Milliner** (hat maker)

• Men, women and children wore hats.

• Milliners had a storefront, such as Maison Caroline Leboux, Maria Guy, Paulette.

• They made custom made hats to match an outfit.

• Milliners tried to stay ahead of fashion with ready-made hats and to show their creativity.

• They used any materials from straw to dog hair. Buyers were advised to avoid being caught in the rain. Some materials disintegrated or smelled of wet dog.

• At the start of the war, the *bibi* was king, a small hat, perched forward with a decoration, feather or ribbon. As the Occupation continued, the *bibi* grew in size and decoration. It was regarded as a defiance of the almost universal restrictions – there were none on hats.

• The woman's turban was popular, especially among the more affluent. It was perfect to hide the hair until the next visit to the hairdresser.

• In the non-occupied zone, the triangular (or square folded in two) headscarf reflected Pétain's ideal of simplicity.

ix. **Ready-made clothing stores**

• Besides department stores, there were ready-made clothing stores, particularly in towns that did not have a department store.

• Those stores also offered alterations and repairs.

• A woman might buy a ready-made garment and have it adjusted by her seamstress.

x. Undergarments, Lingerie stores
• Ready-made silk undergarments. Due to restrictions, manufacturers began experimenting with synthetic materials, mostly rayon and viscose.

• The store sold terry towelettes for periods and a belt to hold it. Two ends were thin cotton so it would fold without bulk over the loops of the belt. As part of customer service, the store also offered two safety pins. Safety pins could be bought by the box at a sewing notions (haberdashery) store.

• **No nylon stockings** were available until after American forces arrived in France after the landings in 1944. Only silk and thin wool stockings were sold before and during the war.

• When silk stockings became unavailable, the store sold liquid stockings – a stain that could be painted on the legs to imitate silk stockings, and a black wax pencil to draw the seam at the back, available from Elizabeth Arden.

• The occupiers were the largest group of customers.

iii. Wool stores
• A wool store sold skeins of wool or cotton and necessary accessories to knit, crochet or weave.

• It often sold ready-made sweaters, scarves, gloves, mittens and socks.

• As stocks diminished, knitters were unraveling old garments to re-knit. They would buy one skein of new wool to give the re-knitted garment some allure.

• Women who did not knit would take their old woolen garments to a knitter or to the store and get in return a new garment for a fee.

• Woolen mills began to experiment with synthetic materials.

C) Department stores
i. Paris

• Galeries Lafayette – Jewish department store, placed under the État Français administration until 1944. On the Boulevard Haussmann.

• À la Belle Jardinière – Quai de la Mégisserie.

• Le Printemps – Boulevard Haussmann.

NOTE: Employees were requisitioned for the STO. Women replaced them. A large ornate staircase stood in the vast octagonal hall and was removed in the late 1950s to increase sales area.

• Brummell – a smaller location of Le Printemps catered exclusively to fashion-conscious men. Also, a branch in Deauville.

• Prisunic – Not in the same category as the more exclusive stores. Fixed low prices for usual items. Owned by Le Printemps. Well-patronized during the Occupation.

• La Samaritaine – rue de la Monnaie.

• Bon Marché – rue de Sèvres.

• Bazar de l'Hôtel de Ville – rue de Rivoli.

• Grands Magasins du Louvre – rue Marengo and Rivoli.

TRIVIA: On the night of September 23, 1943, a RAF bomber crashed on the roof. Crater in the middle, but part of the building and the outside walls were still standing.

ii. Marché aux Puces

• Not a department store, but needs to be mentioned. Le Marché aux Puces de Saint-Ouen – Porte de Clignancourt. An open-air, with covered stalls, market of secondhand items.

iii. Towns and cities

• Except for Le Printemps store, which had a branch in Deauville, towns usually had a relatively large store run by a local businessman.

• There were many smaller, specialized stores.

D) Fashion accessories. Luxury items
i. Clocks and watches

• Everything ran on clockwork. There were no battery operated watches or clocks.

• Timepieces had to be rewound at regular intervals.

• Watches were usually rewound at bedtime, occasionally, in the morning, by means of a small winding knob on the side of the watch. To adjust the time, the knob was pulled out and turned, then pushed back in place.

• Artisan-clockmakers ran a small store that doubled as a workshop. They made clocks, from elaborate grandfather clocks to utilitarian kitchen clocks. During the Occupation, due to the lack of materials, they only repaired watches and clocks.

• Artisan-watchmakers and watch factories made watches for the French army that included compasses and altimeters until the armistice of June 1940.

• The largest manufacture of watches and clocks was the family-owned Lip company. The main factory was located in Besançon, La Mouillère suburb, and was immediately requisitioned to manufacture watches and dashboard clocks for the Luftwaffe and the Wehrmacht. The aviator watches included compass, altimeter and anemometer. They also manufactured chronometers.

• Ernest Lipmann (created the wristwatch) remained in Besançon to keep an eye on his factory. As restrictions on Jews became more intense, Ernest and his wife fled south. Arrested in Aix-les-Bains in November 1943, they were deported to Drancy, then onto Auschwitz where they were murdered.

TRIVIA: Meanwhile, Ernest's son, Frédéric, fled the occupied zone and, along with most of the factory engineers, went to the secondary factory at Issoudin, Indre, in the non-occupied zone. This plant had been producing shell heads and timers for the war effort. He moved the factory, materials and machinery, to Valence, Drôme. The convoy was strafed by the Luftwaffe suffering minor damage.

Within a year, Frédéric Lipmann had developed an entirely new clockwork mechanism using aluminum despite restrictions, material requisitions, lack of adequate machinery and the lack of specialized personnel. Frédéric Lipmann was stubborn and wanted to make sure his family would still have a factory after the war.

• November 1942. Invasion of the non-occupied zone. Frédéric Lipmann and his factory were declared *enemies of the Reich*. To avoid deportation, he joined a resistance cell in the mountains. The factory closed until the liberation in 1944.

ii. Jewelry.

• All imports having stopped, there was a shortage of precious gems. Jewels were considered important to a woman's elegance. Affluent classes would have custom-made jewelry and inherited jewels could be reset.

• Gold and silver were imported. With imports at a standstill, jewelers were eager to buy gold jewelry from individuals.

• Engagement rings were a must no matter the income level, as were wedding rings.

• All married men wore a wedding ring. Frenchmen wore a wedding band on the left hand. Germans on the right.

• During the Occupation, the occupiers and collaborators were the main customers.

• Jewelers made replicas of expensive jewelry which were kept in a home safe or bank deposit box.

• Line Vautrin, a jewelry designer, launched patriotic themes – *plat comme une galette* (flat as a pancake), *maigre comme un clou* (as thin as a nail), *long comme un cou de giraffe* (long as a giraffe's neck), all referring to how emaciated women were. She also created buttons in the shape of a rooster, the French national emblem, and used the national colors blue, white and red in her designs.

• Jewelers also sold an attractive range of fake jewels and trinkets.

• An unexpected source of gems came from the anti-Semitic measures. Jews sold jewels to get money to flee or hide.

iii. Leather goods store – *maroquinerie*
• Leather items only, no garments except gloves and matching purses.
• Leather had been requisitioned. The allowance was too small to make accessories, so leather was reserved to repair soccer balls.
• New purses and handbags were made with synthetic materials. The shoulder bag gained popularity, as it was more practical for bicycling.
• The bag became larger in order to hold any foodstuffs a woman might come across.
• Wallets, traditionally made of leather, were now made of synthetic materials. People got their aging leather wallets repaired.

iv. Luxury items
• Silk, furs and luxury items were out of reach of most French people other than collaborators. It was possible to obtain such items on the black market if one had money and connections.
• Fur being imported, the supply ceased.
• Handmade lace was produced in the Nord and Pas-de-Calais departments or imported from Belgium – dentelle de Calais-Caudry, dentelle d'Alençon. Those two departments being in the restricted zone, they were unable to trade as usual.
• High quality machine-made lace was manufactured in the Lyon area.
• Even before the war, women would detach lace from a garment that was no longer being used to decorate another one.

v. Perfume and makeup
• Women had always used perfumes, even more so during the Occupation. Perfumes were available, but expensive. Haute couture and perfume were strongly associated.

• Most perfumes were manufactured in Provence, in particular in Grasse

• *Channel No 5* by Coco Channel. Guerlain with its elegant bottles. Coty, directed to the masses. Bourjois, with its *Soir de Paris* and its range of makeup products, including nail varnish. Houbigant. Roger et Gallet. Lancôme. Lanvin. L'Oréal, innovator of makeup and hair care and *Ambresoie* the liquid stockings.

• The occupiers and the affluent classes were the main market.

• Less affluent classes bought perfume only for special occasions as a gift.

vi. Porcelain, ceramics, china

• Two principal manufacturers for fine porcelain were Limoges and Sèvres.

• Fine *faïence* – ceramics – in Gien and in Moustier-Sainte-Marie.

• Other local manufacturers made everyday china of earthenware, bone china, fired and glazed terra-cotta.

vii. Silver cutlery (See also 16. Culture, Traditions)

• Households would have two complete sets of cutlery, one less expensive for everyday use and one more expensive reserved for special occasions.

• Less affluent households had plated silverware, with perhaps a couple of individual pieces in silver.

13. Collaboration
A) Collaboration *horizontale*
i. Causes

• Some women, particularly of the haute-bourgeoisie class, had embraced the national socialist ideology and supported the Pétain regime. They formed liaisons with officers.

• Women whose husbands might be prisoner or in the FFL and had children saw a liaison with a soldier as a practical means to obtain extra food. Feelings were of no concern.

• Some single women who did not see much prospect for their future and were attracted to the good-looking soldiers actually fell in love.

ii. Consequences

• The higher class women had the means to escape France until the after liberation chaos calmed down. Some were publicly denounced with little consequences.

• Among the performers and artists, the division was quite severe. Some were pardoned and continued working after the liberation, while for others it was the end of their career.

• Ordinary women, whatever their motives, took the brunt of people's anger after the liberation.

• Husbands who returned to learn their wife had consorted with a German, often divorced. Those divorces were promptly expedited by the courts, whereas other divorces for French couples took years.

• Some husbands accepted their wife's liaison and sometimes a child, especially when they themselves had had a liaison and sometimes a child with a German woman. These were mostly prisoners who had not been held in camps but worked on farms and other needed trades.

• Some ordinary women found themselves abandoned, more often than not with a child, and were frequently ostracized. The child, often blond and blue-eyed, suffered taunts and isolation in school after the war.

B. Government
i. Compliance
• For the Pétain regime, compliance with the occupiers was a means to improve the life of French people by obtaining concessions and thus consolidating its position.

• For some individuals, it was a means to gain political power.

ii. Resistance
• Some administrators remained in post in order to counteract the collaboration measures, while appearing to support Pétain's government.

• Among those, some took risks by providing blank documents and rubber stamps.

C. Individual
i. Ideology
• There were French people who embraced collaboration for ideological reasons while at the same time getting rich. Such people were particularly ruthless.

ii. Opportunists
• The majority of the population saw little alternative and collaborating offered some advantages. At the same time, they were wishing the Germans out of the country.

iii. Résistance
• A fraction of the population also wished to see the Germans out but *rejected* collaboration. Activities might involve active participation in a résistance group, engaging in minor and individual acts of resistance, which could be as little as keeping quiet about what they saw.

D. Manufacturing sector
i. Social conscience

• Many French companies were German-owned through investment during the previous interwar years or under joint Franco-German ownership. The industrial and banking elite were faced with the dilemma of collaborating or rejecting. Three categories of industry leader emerged.

• Those who believed in Germany's invincibility and Nazi ideology. They actively supported Pétain's government and had no hesitation in handing over their Jewish employees. They were also driven by profit.

• Those who rejected the armistice, did not believe in Nazism, felt responsible for sometimes thousands of employees, but realized the Germans would simply take over if they did not obey. They also obeyed the Pétain's government, but were hesitant about the Jewish question. They protected their Jewish employees as much as they could without taking undue risks. Profits were less important than staying afloat.

• Those who rejected the armistice and Nazism and believed that their employees would follow their lead, but they could not close factories knowing the Germans would simply take over. With their employees, they engaged in subtle sabotage and, later, major sabotage. They protected their Jewish employees and their families. This group sometimes paid with their lives for resisting. Profits were not important.

ii. In the non-occupied zone

• The Pétain's government's collaboration policy was imposed on various factories to supply the German industry. Some collaborated readily.

• The policy was not always well received everywhere, but there was a great deal of passivity. When the industrialists objected, their German counterparts cynically remarked that they were only manufacturing parts, not whole tanks.

• Some, however, complied, all the while hiding stocks and slowing production.

• Except for the collaborators, the industrialists objected to having German inspectors come to their factories.

• Negotiations had to go through the Wiesbaden Armistice Commission.

• German industrialists came in person to negotiate contracts which had to be ratified by the Wiesbaden Armistice Commission. This caused major delays.

iii. Profiteers

• The Berliet case. After the war, Marius Berliet claimed to have been forced by the Pétain government to operate the factory for the Germans. The factory made no effort to sabotage the production.

• The Renault case. The factory was family-owned. The president, Louis Renault, adopted collaboration with enthusiasm. He made visits to Berlin and received German industrialists. He was a supporter of the Pétain.

iv. Resistant industrialists
(a) Occupied zone

• Citroën's president, Pierre-Jules Boulanger, encouraged his employees to work without haste. It is not known whether he or someone else made the simple suggestion of lowering the notch on the oil dipstick gauge, but Boulanger implemented the idea. Later, after being put into service, the truck engines suffered from insufficient oil and seized up. The factory being so far away could not be held responsible.

• Peugeot, a family-owned factory in Sochaux. In the summer of 1940, they were assigned a controller, von Guillaume. From the floor workers to the president, they found ingenious ways to lower the production by as much as 80% less than prewar through subtle sabotage, which caused vehicles and later planes to break down but far away from the factory so it could not be faulted.

TRIVIA: Jean-Pierre Peugeot made contact with the local résistance to ask that the English avoid bombing the factory. Once, in July 1943, due to a series of series of errors and poor weather, the RAF bombed Sochaux, severely damaging the town and a part of the factory. Although there were regrets over the loss of life and damage to the factory, Jean-Pierre used the incident to prove to the occupiers that Peugeot was totally innocent of résistance.

• In the early 1943, Ferdinand Porsche of the Porsche industry took over. Peugeot continued to find ways to delay production and undermine the quality of parts.

(b) Non-occupied zone

• Michelin, a family-owned business, while appearing to collaborate, made tires with synthetic rubber which had defects. They would fail in the cold of the eastern front. Elsewhere, their poor quality caused delays to the troops. In the meantime, members of the family were active in the local resistance.

TRIVIA: Of note, they allowed the Americans to photocopy all their maps and guides prior to the landings to hand to the Allies troops. Remember, all direction signs had been either removed or altered.

• Pastis Ricard, a family-owned alcoholic beverage business. The Pétain's government, for moral reasons, forbade Paul Ricard to manufacture the alcoholic drinks. Undaunted, he made fruit juices instead.

TRIVIA: Paul Ricard gave the alcohol normally used for the pastis to the local résistance to use as fuel. He bought property in the Camargue and sent most of his workers there, especially those that needed to remain out of sight, to cultivate rice.

E. Légion Française des Combattants(LFC), Service d'Ordre Légionnaire(SOL) and the Milice
i. Formation

• Marshal Pétain ordered Joseph Darnand, a decorated lieutenant and WWI veteran, to create the Légion Française des Combattants (veterans legion) in July 1940. It was made up of veterans of WWI and its mission was to regenerate the nation by their example of sacrifice in 1914-18. Despite other veteran associations being disbanded, few veterans joined the LFC.

• Only existed in the free zone.

• Their role was mostly ceremonial. They had no uniforms but were smartly dressed.

    • They did social work mostly for prisoners.

    • They pledged loyalty to Marshal Pétain.

ii. Evolution

    • Although some of the LFC members joined the Service d'Ordre Légionnaire, created in 1941, the SOL was a separate organization created to fight bolshevism.

    • Recruitment was less successful than what Darnand had expected. He bolstered the ranks of his new organization by obtaining the release of men imprisoned under criminal law.

    • He claimed a force of 30,000 men and some women. This number has never been verified and is contested as being a lot less. What they lacked in numbers, they made up in violence.

    •Their uniform was khaki shirt, black tie, a badge and beret, a dark jacket and armband, and dark trousers. Members supplied their own uniform, which led to variations in color.

    • They pledged loyalty to Pétain.

iii. Finalization

    • The SOL attracted the attention of the SS. On January 1, 1943, Darnand transformed the SOL into the Milice (Militia), under his direction. Later that year, he and his men pledged allegiance to Hitler and the SOL was converted into a Waffen-SS unit.

    • Joseph Darnand was made *Untersturmführer* (equivalent to Second Lieutenant).

    • As a paramilitary organization, they trained like the military.

    • They only had light arms – rifles and sidearms.

    • They operated solely in the south zone, previously the non-occupied zone.

    • In February 1944, Darnand obtained permission from the Germans to operate in the north zone, the previously occupied zone.

• He obtained other arms, though not heavy armament.

• The Milice worked closely with the Scherheitsdients(SD). For the civilian population, there was no difference between the Nazi Germans and the Milice.

F. Revenge. Epuration.

i. After the 1944 liberation of France, political and social *épuration* (cleansing) took place.

• Collaborators, other than the Milice, who took up arms against the Allies, were tried in court, as were collaborators who promoted Nazism in commerce, industry and government.

• Other individuals who had had dealings with the occupiers (see 13. A. Collaboration horizontale) were also tried.

• When captured, members of the Milice were tried. 15% of Milice members were women. No distinction was made between male and female members.

ii. Illegal tribunals

• Illegal tribunals were composed of what became known as *résistants de la dernière heure* – resistants of the last hour – meaning individuals whose own past was not exactly pure and took measures to eliminate any collaborators who could denounce them.

• After a farcical trial, victims were taken behind the building and shot.

iii. Traitors

• The gendarmerie and police cracked down on the illegal tribunals and jailed the self-appointed judges.

• Once identified, collaborators were imprisoned and eventually were brought to regular trials.

• Milice officials were arrested.

• Members of the Charlemagne division, considered traitors since they fought with the Germans against the French, were traitors to the nation and were arrested.

• 1945. Trials took place of higher level of collaborators, such as government officials, heads of industry.

• The public was reeling from the violence of the Milice and was thirsting for revenge.

iv. **Summary justice**

• In the case of shaved women, justice was dispensed mostly by the resistants of the last hour, eager to show their new allegiance.

• Resistants, who were not part of a maquis, eliminated collaborators considered traitors, such as those who denounced them and miliciens.

• Less disciplined maquis members pursued traitors from the Milice.

• Maquisards eliminated armed collaborators, including members of the Charlemagne division.

• There were a few cases of Wehrmacht soldiers, SS in particular, who, when taken prisoner, were summarily executed. In one case, at least by members of the public.

14. Communication

• In these days of instant phone and internet service, it is necessary to emphasize the lack and the difficulty of communication during the war years. Radio communication with London is idealized in fiction. In reality, it was disorganized, difficult and dangerous (See 43. Resistance).

• No individual, or company, could correspond with an inmate of a concentration camp, or internment camp.

• This also was the case for prisoners in regular prisons. There, bribery was sometimes successful in passing letters or parcels.

• As of June 22, 1940, the armistice, all communication by letter, telegram or telephone was forbidden by the MBF within France. This ban lasted until August 11, 1940.

• Correspondence with POWs was via the Red Cross. Initially, this was by postcard. Later, letters were allowed but only in an unsealed envelope, and were censored.

• There was absolutely no communication between individuals in France and a foreign country whether neutral or belligerent.

• Until December 1941, Americans in the non-occupied zone were able to communicate with the U.S.A. via a neutral country, usually Spain and Portugal, as well as Switzerland, and by diplomatic channels. Letters were subjected to French censorship. In the occupied zone, Americans could only communicate with the embassy and consulates. Letters were subjected to MBF censorship.

• When the U.S.A. entered the war, Americans in France, in both zones, were treated as enemy and interned.

A) Pneumatique – compressed air post
i. Paris
• Places that were equipped with compressed air communications.
(a) Banks.
(b) Department stores were connected to this postal service but also had an internal independent circuit which was not subject to censorship, being out of reach of the inspectors.

(c) Government buildings were connected to the *Pneumatique* service, but also had an internal independent circuit which was not subject to censorship, being out of reach of the inspectors.

(d) Some large industries were connected to the *Pneumatique* but also had an internal independent circuit which was not subject to censorship, being out of reach of the inspectors.

ii. Towns and cities
• Government buildings were equipped with *Pneumatique* service in Algiers, Lyon and Marseille.

B) Postal service: Poste, Téléphone et Télégraph (PTT)
i. Interzones
• June 22, 1940 (armistice) – all letter mail, cable telegrams and telephone were forbidden by the MBF.

• August 11, 1940 – interzonal, official pre-printed postcards fill-in-the-blank spaces were allowed.

• May 5, 1941 – interzonal, pre-printed postcards no longer had the pre-printed lines. The thirteen lines, now blank space, were reserved for family matters. No commerce allowed.

• August 27, 1941 – ordinary (tourist but without picture) postcards replaced the official pre-printed postcards.

• All these postcards rankled with everybody in all levels of French society.

• June 16, 1943 – letters, parcels, vaccines and serum were permitted to be sent between the two zones as the demarcation line had been abolished. Mail was still controlled and censored by the *Prüschtelle* (the inspectorate) and the PTT.

ii. Non-occupied zone
• Letters from the occupied zone to the non-occupied zone were smuggled (and vice versa). At the demarcation line, the German border guards might search a traveler if they suspected him of concealing letters. Women were not searched as often.

• Once in the non-occupied zone, letters could be sent abroad via consulates or embassies. Thousands of letters reached the BBC in this way.

• Censorship – Service de Contrôle Technique (SCT).

• The Red Cross took charge of letters and parcels for POWs.

• Stamps. Tax stamps were added to regular postage.

• Telegrams were submitted to the same censorship as postcards.

iii. Occupied zone

• All the correspondence was examined by the Prüfstelle (the inspectorate).

• Pre-stamped postcards printed with fill-in-the-blank spaces were allowed from September 26, 1940. A card would be sent back if it had a word outside the space or a non-authorized word.

• June 2, 1941. Postcards, no picture, could be bought and sent. They came with the warning that text took longer at the censor.

• There was no correspondence allowed between individuals and companies in the occupied zone and a foreign country, including the annexed territory of Alsace-Lorraine as this was defined as part of Germany.

• All the correspondence was examined by the Prüfstelle which supervised the French censors. Correspondence with POWs was allowed via the Red Cross from January 1941, and consisted of pre-printed cards. Later, letters were allowed in unsealed envelopes.

• Commercial correspondence was all sent to Paris in a sealed envelope to be examined and stamped by the Ministry of Production and Work before being allowed into the non-occupied zone.

• In a few cases, the International Red Cross facilitated the transmission of telegrams and letters from individuals to another belligerent country. After the war, they were criticized for not doing more.

C. Telegrams
• Telegrams were also subject to censorship.

i. Cities had telegram delivery service – usually a boy on a bicycle.

ii. Rural towns and villages. Wherever there was a train station, there was a telegraph. The station master arranged for the telegram delivery.

D. Telephone
• Prewar and through the war, very few individuals had the telephone. The network was limited. The MBF monitored the calls. There was an MBF inspector watching the switchboard in every post office and approving or rejecting calls.

i. Paris – those who had the telephone
• Administration buildings – concierges, industry, factories, many merchants (small stores and artisans did not as it was expensive).
• Doctors, lawyers, pharmacists.
• Post offices had telephone booths.
• Public telephone booths could be found in train stations, cafés, hotels, public places, restaurants. There were no phone booths in the street.

ii. Rural areas
• Public telephones in cafés.
• Some merchants had the telephone.
• Prominent citizens had the telephone.
• Villages may have had a public telephone booth located in the Place de la Mairie (main square), opposite the town hall.
• Town halls had the telephone.

iii. Large towns and cities

• Similar to Paris.

iv. Wireless (radio) – T.S.F.
(a) The set
• Most of the sets in that era had short-wave capabilities. This is why the MBF authorities, especially in Paris, ordered anyone with a set to exchange it for the approved Pétain's government set without short-wave capacity. Many households had an extra set, sometimes a non-functioning one, and would exchange this set while hiding the good one with its short-wave function. The wireless functioned with vacuum tube bulbs and they had a limited life. It was cheaper to buy a new set.
(b) Broadcasting
• The T.S.F. provided news and entertainment programs.
• Radio-Paris, formerly a private station, was taken over by the occupiers and became the official broadcasting station in the occupied zone.
• Radio-Stuggart was the German broadcasting station in the French language.
• The Großdeutscher Rundfunk could be heard daily from 12:30 pm until sometime in the evening.
• There were other local broadcasting stations in the non-occupied zone, which had to obey Pétain's government regulations and their subtle propaganda. Many songs exalted the landscape and healthy pursuits.
• On short-wave, the BBC broadcasted programs between messages, *Les Français parlent aux Français*. A favorite program was humorist and satirist Pierre Dac (real name Isaac) who succeeded in reaching England in October 1943.

v. Television in France
• The PTT were in charge of the technical aspect of television.
• There was a race for producing television that started in 1897. First black and white images were produced in 1927. First moving pictures produced in 1931.

• Television was not commercially available until 1950-1951. In fact, during the war, few people even knew about such a thing called television.

TRIVIA: In the early fifties, transmission used telephone lines and few people had a telephone. Screens (a cathodic tube) were curved and showed lines, the pictures being distorted and grainy but recognizable. Only the very rich with a large house owned a cathode ray tube, itself being 30cm(24in) long, contained in a large boxy cabinet. The viewing screen was small – 20cm(8in) by 25cm(10in) and one was even smaller, the size of a postcard. It was recommended to sit a *good distance* from the screen. There were perhaps less than twenty sets in the whole of Paris in the early fifties.

(a) 1938

• Paris inaugurated one television channel broadcasting on air waves from the top of the Eiffel Tower. The transmitter was powerful enough to broadcast up to 80 kilometers (50 miles) from the Tour Eiffel to a receiver, which transferred the content to a telephone line.

• Cathode ray tube receivers were installed in a few public venues. They were a very large piece of furniture with a small screen, about the size of a postcard at first, and attracted the curious.

• Broadcasts took place at 5:00 pm and consisted of an actor reading poetry or a text in front of the camera.

(b) September 1, 1939 – broadcasts ceased.

• June 6, 1940 – the main transmitter was sabotaged. All other transmitters were sabotaged so that the enemy could not use them.

(c) May 1941

• The MBF had shown no interest in rehabilitating the Eiffel Tower transmitter until an order from Berlin arrived to recuperate all useful material from it for the war effort.

• Kurt Hinzmann, formerly with the television in Berlin and drafted as a simple soldier, opposed to the dismantling of the transmitter and proposed to restore it to broadcast programs to

139

the wounded soldiers in the Kriegslazaretts (field hospitals) in Paris. He also suggested it would open the French market to the German electric industry.

(d) **May 20**, 1942

• The Oberkommando der Werhmacht ordered the PTT (who had been in charge of the transmitter before the war) to repair the transmitter.

• Fehrensehsender Paris(transmitting station) set up a studio in a disused ballroom – the Magic City.

• It transmitted only by telecinema, meaning restricted transmission to the Kriegslazaretts hospitals, to a select few German private receivers, as well as a few privileged French persons – namely, high-powered collaborators.

(e) **September 30**, 1943 – first live broadcast.

(f) **August 1944**

• One week before the liberation of Paris(August 25), Berlin ordered the destruction of the transmitter. Kurt Hinzmann refused and instead handed everything, except the cameras, over to the PTT.

TRIVIA: To obey orders, Kurt Hinzmann shot a bullet or two into inconsequential equipment.

(g) September 1, 1945 – broadcasts with actors reading resumed as in 1938. The U.S. authorities had banned the general use of the transmitter beyond a limited area in Paris until the war was totally over.

15. Law Courts under French jurisdiction

• The Law Courts were under French jurisdiction.

• Courts were located in separate buildings in cities and towns. In villages, court would be held in the 'town hall' which might simply be a dedicated space at the rear of the café.

• The Palais de Justice in Paris, located on the Île de la Cité, Boulevard du Palais, housed the four courts of the judicial system.

• In Paris, lawyers rented an office on the ground floor of a Hausmann building, a large apartment building with commercial space on the ground floor. Or they could have an office in their home if it was large enough. In cities such as Bordeaux, Marseille, Nice, which had Hausmann buildings, they rented a ground floor office. Where there were no buildings designed with ground floor offices, they would rent a former store, without a storefront, or a first-floor apartment.

• *Notaires* – public notaries – usually rented a small store, without a storefront, unless they were in a city, town, with a Hausmann building. Notaries were not lawyers but public officers appointed by the *Garde des Sceaux* – now called justice minister.

• Notaries dealt with administrative affairs, real estate, wills, legalization of documents.

• Notaries authenticated government acts where required.

i. Law of September 11, 1940

• The law banned lawyers who are not of French origin from practicing.

• Whether in the courts of law under the État Français or the MBF administration, the legal proceedings lasted less than one hour. Verdict and sentence were rendered immediately.

• Very few black market offences were prosecuted.

• There were two types of tribunals run by the department of justice, depending on the État Français – correctional and special.

ii. Correctional courts

• Criminal courts judged petty crime from possessing a firearm to stealing parcels destined for POWs.

• They were also supposed to enforce anti-Semitic and repression laws. A judge could deal with four cases in one hour. The defense lawyer had ten minutes to make his case. No appeal. Verdict and sentence rendered immediately. Press and public not usually allowed to attend the proceedings.

iii. Judges, Lawyers and Prosecutors

• The majority of the judiciary being anti-Pétain, they tended to expedite the court proceedings.

• As soon as 1940, but increasing in the summer 1941, the État Français added special courts.

iv. Special courts.

• The special sections operated from September 1941 to March 1944 in the occupied zone. After November 1942, the whole of France. They judged communists, attempts against the security of the state, subversive and terrorist activities.

• After February 1943, infraction to the law of February 1943 regarding the Service du Travail Obligatoire (Forced Labor to Germany). The defense lawyer had ten minutes to make his case. Later, when résistants were being judged, he was not even present the courtroom. No appeal. Verdict and sentence handed out immediately.

• No press and no public admitted in the courtroom.

v. German courts

• All the acts against German troops or acts of resistance, even merely carrying a clandestine newspaper, were judged by the Militärbefehlshaber in Frankreich (MBF) courts operating on the German system. The accused were labeled terrorists. Verdicts were quickly arrived at and sentences handed out at the same time. The defense lawyer was not present. He received the file after the judgement. No appeal.

• No press and no public admitted in the courtroom.

• The résistants had already been in prison for some time. They may be taken back to prison waiting for execution or deportation. Depending where the court was held, the death sentence could be carried out immediately in the prison yard.

• In Paris, resistants imprisoned in Fresnes, which had its own courtroom, and those sentenced to death were housed in a section of cells (death row) and executed in the courtyard, though mostly in 1941 and 1942 they would be taken to Fort du Mont-Valérien or Fort de Vincennes.

vi. June 1942

• A Höherer SS und Polizeiführer was appointed and all legal proceedings were dealt with by the Sicherheitsdienst and résistants could be executed without trial.

16. Culture

• It has to be understood that manners and customs described below did not change during the occupation, but food and beverages did. Manners and customs applied equally to the cities and the rural areas.

• Pourboire – tipping for service

The *pourboire* was an institution in France. Before and during the war and for a long time after, tipping was not only accepted but expected. Anyone who provided a service received a tip. No amount was ever specified. If customers were pleased with the service, they would give more than if the service was lackluster. There were no door to door couriers (such as Fedex, etc). People kept some loose change by the door. Anyone delivering an item to the door, such as flowers or laundry, received a tip. Department stores and smaller stores usually offered delivery (after a purchase was made in the store) and kept a roster of youths with bicycles and tricycles for small items and vans and trucks for large deliveries. It was a must to tip the boys on bicycles delivering telegrams, the concierges of apartment buildings and letter carriers. Taxi drivers would often be handed money and told to keep the change. For waiters in cafés and restaurants, the custom was to pay the bill – *l'addition* – and leave an appropriate tip on the table or hand it to him.

Trivia: The *garçons de café* – waiters—received no salary and relied solely on tips. It was reputed that many made for money that way than if they if they received a fixed wage.

A) Addressing people

i. Capitalizing. Formal and informal terms of address of madame, monsieur, mademoiselle, mesdames, messieurs, mesdemoiselles.

(a) In written text, *Madame Durand, Monsieur Durand, Mademoiselle Durand*. A capital letter because it was used as a title.

• Abbreviated forms –*Mme Durand, M. Durand, Mlle Durand*.

• In dialogue – *"Good morning, madame." "Good morning, monsieur." "Good morning, mademoiselle."*
• More familiar – *"Good morning, Madame Yvonne." Good morning, Monsieur Gaston." Good morning, Mademoiselle Arlette."* No abbreviation in dialogue. Only the first name was used, never the last name.

ii. Other capitals
• In English *Mother, Father* are always capitalized. If you want to keep the French flavor by using French words, such as maman, papa, grand-mère, mémé, grand-maman, grand-père, pépère, grand-papa, do not use capitals.

iii. Among the more affluent classes, before two strangers were on a first-name terms, they had to have known each other for a long time, perhaps one year at least, or had lived through some drama together.
• When there was a difference in age, the younger would always address the older using the *vous* form.
• If they were of the same age, but had not known each other since childhood, they would use the *vous* form. They may, or not, progress to the *"tu"* form.

iv. Among the less affluent classes, strangers would dispense with much of the formality and use the *tu* form after a year or so of acquaintance.
• When there was a difference in age, the formality remained from the younger to the older person, but the older person would quickly adopt the more familiar *tu* form to address the younger one.

v. Handshaking and kissing hands (*baisemain*)
• Among all classes, men shook hands when meeting. In some circumstances, men might shake with the right hand while giving a hug with the left.

• In higher society, a man on meeting a woman would bow over the *gloved* fingers of the lady's hand and give a pretend kiss.

• Among other classes, a man would shake a woman's hand if she offered it first while giving a slight incline of the head. If the woman did not offer her hand, the man simply inclined his head.

• When women were closely acquainted, they kissed three times. Otherwise, they nodded and smiled. They never shook hands.

B) Etiquette
i. Men

• Always allowed the woman to enter a room first. A man would allow men of superior status to enter first, while holding open the door.

• A man gave up his seat on crowded public transport to a woman or an old man. On Métro trains, some seats were reserved. It was obligatory to relinquish one of these seats if for the use of a pregnant woman, an older woman, or man, or a war veteran.

• A father was expected to correct an unruly child. The mother would have warned the child and reported the misdemeanor to the father upon his return from work.

• In French society of the period, a man was considered the undisputed head of the household and possessed what was known as *autorité paternel* – paternal authority. His word was final. This applied to all levels of society. Even among the liberals and educated, rare were the families that did not conform to this unspoken rule.

• The husband would read the newspaper while his wife finished preparing the meal.

• A man expected his wife to cook, clean, raise the children, all the time looking her best (!).

• Men held doors open for women.

• Out of courtesy, a man would step off the sidewalk when meeting on-coming pedestrians with a woman or older man present.

• Men tipped their hat when meeting or passing acquaintances.

ii. Women.
• The majority of women expected to become housewives, even during the Occupation.

• They could not have their own bank account (Not until the mid-1960s).

• They could voice an opinion, but the husband made the decisions.

• They did not have the vote (granted by de Gaulle in 1946).

• They received housekeeping money from the husband.

• Women who found themselves alone during the Occupation had to adjust and take responsibilities. For some, it was liberating. For others, it was a difficult time.

C) Customs and conventions
i. Adolescents
• They ate with the parents.

• They did not hold a part-time job.

• They were aiming at higher education.

• Boys were expected to take on responsibilities in the absence of the father, such as keeping younger siblings in order, helping the mother.

• Affluent families gave their adolescents pocket money.

• Less affluent families did not give their adolescents pocket money. An adolescent might leave school at fourteen and learn a trade for two years. Once employed, he would hand over his wages to the father, who would let him have some money to take care of his personal needs. Some families made sacrifices to ensure their adolescents stayed in school and went on to higher education.

• Working-class families had no money to spare. Children left school at fourteen and went straight to work. Occasionally, an adolescent would get a bursary.

ii. Children
• Affluent classes – children under twelve ate before the parents did, in the kitchen under the supervision of a maid, if there was one, and especially if guests were present. They often received pocket money.
• Less affluent classes made no distinction. If there were guests and not enough room, then the children would eat first and be sent to their rooms or outside to play. They did not automatically receive pocket money, but it was not denied if they requested some.
• Children in poorer classes ate with the parents. If there were guests and not enough room, they ate before or after and went to play in the street. They were not given pocket money but would receive some money on New Year and on birthdays. They were encouraged, when not coerced, to put it in a *Livret de Caisse d'épargne* – a savings account at the post-office.

iii. School students were expected to do homework daily.

iv. Summer break
• Elementary students were expected to study with a summer copybook every morning.
• Secondary students did not get a summer job. They studied a self-directed program. Some, of course, being teenagers, did nothing.

D) Manners (home, in public, restaurants, table)
• People kept both hands above the table at all times. No elbows were permitted on the table. Among the pooer classes, men often put both elbows on the table.
• Farmers (males) more often than not, leaned their elbows on the table while eating.

• Family meals – The meal started only when everyone was seated.

• Maids – if the household employed a maid, she would serve each diner from the left.

• Among the affluent classes, the dining table was always covered with a tablecloth. The less affluent classes not too often.

i. In the home

• Among the more affluent, meals, even family meals, were still somewhat formal occasions, with a strictly adhered to seating arrangement. The father, as the man of the house, sat at the head of the table. His wife sat to his right and the children were usually placed in age order down the table. For a more formal dinner, with guests, the younger children might eat separately. The father sat at the head of the table. To his right sat the senior, in age or rank, female guest. His wife now would be seated to her husband's left. Other guests and family members would be seated according to age and rank down the table.

(a) Dishes

• The serving dish was not placed in the middle of the table but put to the right of the most important female, seated to the right of the man of the house. She would serve herself and pass the serving plate to the person immediately to her right. When it was only family present, the mother would serve and pass the plates of food down the table.

• Only one food item at a time was placed on the plate, unlike the British and North American custom of heaping the plate with both meat and vegetables.

• Eating with fingers, particularly poultry with fingers, was not done in affluent society – except by children eating in the kitchen under a maid's supervision. The only exceptions to this rule was with asparagus and artichoke. The diner would lift the asparagus or artichoke off the plate with the fingers and dip it into a small bowl of sauce. All other food was eaten with the appropriate knife, fork and spoon.

• Asparagus and artichokes were not served to guests.

149

• Among the less affluent classes, poultry would be served only on Sundays. Here, the use of fingers was mostly the norm.

• Knives used to cut meat, or fish, were placed, when not in use, on a *porte-couteau* – a knife holder (usually made of china or crystal) – to the right of the plate. Rarely used among the less affluent classes.

• Affluent classes – meat was cut off the bone with a knife and fork.

• Less affluent classes – the meat was first cut off the bone, then the host or hostess gave the signal that fingers can be could be used to clean the bones. If fish was not fileted, the flesh was extracted with knife and fork and whatever did not come off stayed on the plate. The less affluent would lift the bones with fingers and shake the flesh onto the plate.

(b) *Serviettes*, napkins

• There were no paper napkins at the time.

• A linen serviette or napkin was, as today, a square of cloth which must be opened and placed on the lap before the first dish was put on the table or served if there was a maid or at the restaurant. It was used to dab the mouth before drinking, and discreetly wipe fingers.

(c) Soup

• Soup was not served in a bowl but in a plate with a curved edge. Only served at the evening meal.

• The soup was scooped up with the spoon from the far edge of the plate toward the eater, the opposite of British polite society custom, where it was scooped up with a forward motion, away from the eater.

• The French soup spoon was larger than most North American spoons and the soup was eaten from the side of the spoon, not the tip. It was poor table etiquette to drink while eating soup.

• Bread was not eaten with soup.

• On farms, it was not unusual to break pieces of bread into the soup.

• The lips were then wiped before drinking.

ii. Home table manners

• Conversation at the table was permitted only between dishes, except moderate comments about the food and compliments to the hostess.

• Family meals – the meal only started when everyone was seated.

• Hands were always kept above the table.

• Among the affluent classes, when a dish had been eaten, the fork or spoon was placed on the plate, not on the table, and the plate removed for the next course.

• The less affluent classes put their fork on the table and used the same plate for the next course. During the Occupation, there was only one course, anyway.

• If there were several forks, spoons, knives by a plate, it meant plates and cutlery would be removed between dishes by the maid, the hostess, or the waiter in a restaurant. The order of use of knives and forks and spoons was from the outside in.

(a) Bread was either the long two-pound loaf or the long, thin half-pound loaf (See 17. Daily life, Bread) and placed in an oval (usually) basket on the table. Each person broke a piece and put it directly on the table to the left of the plate.

• It was never buttered.

• In high-end restaurant dining, a bread plate was provided.

• If the bread arrived cut in slices on the table, each person took a slice. The Pétain's government strongly recommended cutting the day old bread into very thin slices.

TRIVIA: Pétain believed people would eat less bread if it was stale.

• Mopping the plate with a morsel of bread was not something done by higher status members of society.

• Among the less affluent classes, the practice became common during the Occupation so as not to waste any of the little food they had.

    • Poorer classes always mopped up their plates with bread.

    • The less affluent classes would have only one set of cutlery and one plate per person. On special occasions, when dessert was on the menu, there would be a dessert plate and dessert spoon, fork or knife.

    • Children of all classes licked their plates. In upper-class families, they were savvy enough to do so when no one was looking. Otherwise, people tolerated it. There was no point in depriving the children of the little food they were allowed.

    • At a larger restaurant, the plate would not clean up with bread, but at a café or bistrot in a working-class district, people invariably cleaned up their plates with a piece of bread. Any deviation would be spotted immediately.

NOTE: Small gestures like the above were sometimes the downfall of a downed Allied airman trying to make his way back to safety.

    (b) Cheese. At that time, camembert and emmental were more or less available with ration tickets. Good manners demanded that the person cut the piece of camembert on her plate and use a fork to place it on a piece of bread.

    • Cheese was always cut and a piece placed on a piece of bread. Fingers never touched the cheese. It was a breach of etiquette to pick up cheese with the fingers.

    • A less cultivated person might slice the cheese with the knife, and holding the piece of cheese on the knife with the thumb, put it straight into the mouth. This practice was not unusual on farms too.

    • Lettuce and pasta were never cut with a knife.

iii. Restaurant manners

    • The no-elbows-on-the-table rule applied to restaurant dining.

• Children would accompany their parents to the restaurant only if it was a full family outing.

• Lower income classes generally made an effort of good manners when in public.

iv. Picnics

• There were no tables provided in parks and other picnic areas. People spread a cloth on the grass and laid out the food. Most items were eaten with fingers.

E) Guests
i. In the home

• Only close friends, or by necessity, colleagues, were invited to a meal at home. A guest was indicated where to sit and would remain there. He or she would not be invited to tour the rest of the house.

ii. At the restaurant

• Acquaintances and lesser colleagues might be invited to a meal at a restaurant – until they graduated to a closer relationship and be invited at home.

iii. Etiquette
(a) Upper classes

• Guests sent expensive flowers to the hostess, preferably to be delivered the day before.

(b) Middle classes

• Guests brought modest flowers – no roses – for the hostess and or a bottle of French wine.

• It was an etiquette blunder to bring foreign wine or cheese.

(c) Poorer classes

• A guest brought a bottle of wine or a cake. Children ate with the adults.

• Saccharine was a common sugar substitute. Guests brought their own saccharine.

• Children over twelve ate with the parents, including if there were guests, unless there was not enough room around the table, in which case they ate in the kitchen or at a small side table in the dining room.

• Liqueur or liquor was always offered at the end of the meal after coffee had been served. Poorer classes offered liquor.

(d) Coffee

• During the Occupation when real coffee became unavailable, French people used the German word *ersatz* or the French *succédané* – *ersatz* being more common for coffee substitutes. There was no such thing in France as *national coffee*.

• There was no such concept in France of a *National Coffee*. The expression came into use under British influence only after the war by writers, journalists and filmmakers, partly due to a lack of research. During the war, people used the German term *ersatz* for coffee substitutes. The French equivalent is *succédané*. There is one mention of *café national* in a Pétain government document in the archives of the État Français alluding to the proportions of one third coffee, one third chicory and one third barley. Had Pétain intended this blend to become the model for a *Café national,* the term never caught on, not in Pétain's non-occupied zone, nor in the occupied zone. In the latter there was no coffee available at all – except on the black market – and people drank various concoctions of acorns, chickpeas, roots or grains, roasted and ground. They certainly had no notion of a *national* coffee.

• French people drank coffee, not tea. For an intimate gathering or significant dinner with mostly women in attendance, some upper class hostesses would offer tea as well as coffee. It was considered snobbish or pretentious by the rest of the population. Neither was available during the war, except on the black market and only until stocks lasted.

• In the home, most coffee was made using a *cafetière*, an enamel, later aluminum, pot with a detachable top having a perforated base to hold the ground coffee. Boiling water was added and passed through the grains and into the lower pot. The top was then detached or left in place and the hot coffee poured into cups. Electric coffee makers, so common today, did not exist in the period.

NOTE – Do not have your characters *dying for a cup of tea* and drinking it all day, as seen in many novels.

• In normal times in a café, it was frequent to ask for *un crème* or a *café-crème* – coffee with milk or cream. This was an absolute no-no during the Occupation and the downfall of some Allied escapees. Milk and cream were not available except in rationed quantities for children. The occupiers always drank black coffee and sometimes had to put up with chicory ersatz when supplies did not get through the Allied blockade.

• Women of the affluent classes entertaining women friends would serve black market coffee and apologize they could not get tea. They may also go to a *salon de thé*, such as Ruc in Paris, which managed to have a reserve supply, usually reserved for the occupiers and special customers.

• In normal times, a meal would finish with a cup of coffee. Milk was not offered by the hostess. If requested, it was poured in after the coffee, not before – there was no milk substitute during the Occupation. Customers asking for milk or cream in a restaurant immediately labelled themselves as foreigners, an act that often led to the downfall of escapees.

• Sugar cubes would be on the table in normal times. During the Occupation saccharine, an ersatz, replaced sugar. Guests brought their own saccharine ration.

• Upper classes retired to the salon (parlor) to drink coffee/ersatz and smoke.

• Less affluent classes remained at the table if the living room was combined with the dining room, as in an apartment.

• In poorer households, the family ate in the kitchen. They were less likely to have a separate dining room.

• Coffee disappeared in the occupied zone, except on the black market and German supplies. Ersatz was made of chicory and roots or grains or acorn.

• In normal times, people bought coffee beans and ground it at home in a manual mill - *moulin à café*. There is no record of ground coffee being sold in stores during the Occupation. Coffee beans disappeared in 1940 and people used their coffee mill to grind replacement products, such as rye, chicory, seeds or other grains they may have found.

• In the non-occupied zone, the government decreed that coffee was to contain one third coffee, one third barley or rye and one third chicory. When stocks of coffee beans ran out, it was only ersatz.

F) Smoking
• Smoking took place in the *salon* – parlor in affluent classes.

i. Men
• Smoking was widespread among men. Tobacco and cigarettes were rationed.

• Men had an allocation of tobacco.

• It was customary to hold the cigarette between the thumb and index finger.

ii. Women
• Before women's allocation of tobacco was removed toward the end of 1941, most traded their cigarettes for food.

• Those who smoked bought cigarettes on the black market.

• A woman might smoke at home but generally not in public. An exception might be in the back room of a café, but this was not usual. This did not apply to women in the résistance who freely smoked with their resistant companions, though not in public.

• Women usually held the cigarette between the index and middle finger.

• Women of the upper levels of society might smoke at a party but never in the street or public. They held the cigarette between the index and middle finger and often would use an elegant cigarette holder.

• In small towns and rural settings, women smoked at home, but the practice was less common than in the cities, and never in public.

G) Social norms

i. The affluent classes employed maids and other domestic servants. Women took care of the home and were not expected to work. This changed for many households during the Occupation, but women did not always work for an income.

ii. The less affluent classes – despite women not being expected to work, according to the Pétain government propaganda, many women found employment when an income was desperately needed. Widows or women whose husbands were prisoners of war had to work to supplement the meager pension they received. It could take a year before the paperwork was ratified.

iii. Unmarried pregnant girls – such girls were blamed by parents, church and society and carried the most shame. The father was forced to marry the girl. When it was not possible, either by his running away or the girl refusing to name him, there were few options.

• An affluent family would send the girl to either a willing family member or to Switzerland so that acquaintances would not stumble upon her, and the baby put up for adoption. Should the girl refuse to give up the baby, she would be cut off from the family, who would nonetheless set up a fund for her in most cases.

• Less affluent families were more tolerant, but the girl still had to marry the father whenever possible or go away before the pregnancy showed. If going away, work was arranged to pay for her keep with a willing family, which might be a relative or otherwise.

157

• Rural girls in a village or on the farm had little chance of getting away. People knew too much of everyone else's business. Rural folk were not so rigid about pre-marital sex. Marriage was the solution in the majority of cases. Situations worthy of novels did happen, like the girl's mother taking the baby as her own. The parish priest still gave the blessing and baptized the baby, though there were exceptions with inflexible priests.

H) Traditions
• Despite restrictions and costs during the Occupation, most people endeavored to respect traditions.

(a) **A complete set of silver** table cutlery would be given to newly weds by both sets of parents, hence why most couples received two sets.

(b) **A new baby** received a silver tumbler and a silver spoon with a matching fork.

(c) **At a christening**, a silver christening medal and a gold chain were given.

(d) **A solemn first communion** took place when the child was aged twelve.

• A girl received a jewel (often a chain with a gold cross) or a bracelet with her name and birthdate, together with a missal (prayer book) bound in fine leather. She also received a rosary, which could be simple wooden beads or real pearls.

• A boy received a missal bound in fine leather, a book and a small chest. He also received a rosary, which could be simple wooden beads, coral or tortoiseshell beads but never pearls.

i. Flowers – there was a longstanding tradition of giving flowers, and florists never went out of business in normal times.
• The majority of flowers came from Provence in the south of France. During the Occupation, commerce was interrupted with the non-occupied zone for a lengthy period. There were flowers cultivated in the occupied zone, especially near Paris.

There were also greenhouses, though soon they were not producing due to the lack of fuel or electricity to heat the greenhouses.

• The occupiers also wanted flowers and exemptions were finally granted for the floral trade.

• Florists also relied on locally grown flowers. Even in winter, there were snowdrops, hellebores – also known as Christmas rose – winter jasmine, which can survive down to minus 15° C (5° F), winter viburnum. In Paris, the Jardin des Plantes provided orchids.

• May 1 was Labor Day. At the beginning of the twentieth century, the Parisian grand couturiers offered a small bouquet of Lily of the Valley to their seamstresses. This became a general tradition.

• People gave Lily of the Valley to persons they liked for good luck.

• Lily of the Valley was a cheap and abundant flower, growing practically everywhere and came into blossom at the end of April, beginning of May.

• In the rural areas of the occupied zone, children collected Lily of the Valley in the woods

• May was the month of the Virgin Mary. Since the beginning of the twentieth century, some communities had designated May 25, to honor mothers of large families of nine or more children. After WWI, it was extended to widowed mothers of six or more children.

• Soon after taking power, Marshal Pétain instituted an official celebration – Mother's Day, to be held on May 25 to celebrate all mothers regardless of the number of children. But a medal was given to the mothers of large families.

NOTE – Marshal Pétain was very dismissive of childless married women, this from a childless man who did not marry until age 60, had had numerous mistresses and visited brothels.

• A husband and the children bought flowers for the mother.

159

• Every celebration was accompanied by flowers –
birthdays, christenings, first communion (white lilies were
given), weddings and funerals.
   • Guests brought flowers to the hostess.
   • Men in affluent families had flowers delivered to their
wives every Sunday after mass or presented the flowers
themselves.
   • In less affluent families, bringing flowers home on
Sunday after mass was less frequent and more often consisted of
only one or two flowers. During the Occupation, this became
episodic then ceased as money was diverted to buying food.
   • Besides Lily of the Valley, which was only available in
season, greenhouse carnations or those from Provence were the
cheapest and were available year round.

ii. Birthdays
   • The age of majority was twenty-one. There were no
celebrations at sixteen as there were in the United States.
   • The patron saint's day was important.
   • Average families saved sugar rations for two or three
months to make a cake for a child's birthday.
   • Affluent families and collaborators provided a more
lavish meal and gift.
   • A birthday was a family occasion.
   • A gift, depending on the child's age, would be something
practical. Only the very young received a toy, and during the
Occupation presents consisted of more useful items, like
clothing.
   • Lower-income families with several children rarely
celebrated birthdays during the Occupation. To mark the day, the
child might be exempted of chores and given a larger portion at
supper. Whenever possible, a cake was made.

iii. Engagements

• In normal times, the young man brought his girl to meet his parents and shortly after, she took him to meet her parents. In that order.

• The young man and his father met the girl's father to seek permission to marry his daughter.

NOTE: During the Occupation, this social ritual was interrupted as often only the girl's mother would be at home and the young man's father also absent. At such times, the young man would speak to the mother on his own.

• A date was set to celebrate the engagement, which usually took place at the young man's home.

• Announcements were sent out.

• The young man put a single diamond engagement ring on the finger of his fiancée. Often a family jewel handed down through the generations, which meant that sometimes it was not a diamond, but some precious gem and a more elaborate mount.

• In less affluent families, the tradition was respected even if the ring may not be a diamond.

• The war put a dent in traditions, except in the upper level of society. Many engagements were shortened if not altogether skipped.

iv. Funerals and mortuaries

• Mortuaries were administered by the municipalities as were the cemeteries, including those next to churches.

• A section was blessed by the priest and reserved for Catholics. Priests could refuse to bury someone judged to have been of low morals, died by suicide or of a different religion, in the consecrated ground.

• Burial plots had to be paid for. There was, however, a provision by the municipality for the burial of destitute persons.

• When a death occurred, the entrance of the deceased's dwelling was draped with black cloth.

• After the body was prepared at the mortuary, it was brought to its residence.

• The deceased was laid in wake. The funeral took place the following day.

• In poorer classes the body was washed at home, dressed, and laid in wake the same day, with funeral the following day.

• The casket was carried on an open hearse pulled by one or more horses, depending on what the family was prepared to pay, from the home to the church, then to the cemetery.

• After a church mass the hearse carried the deseased to the cemetery for burial, followed on foot by the mourners.

• The hearse was decorated with black drapery with white accents and silver braid. Flowers were laid alongside of the casket.

• How much decoration depended on the price that was paid.

• For a non-religious funeral, the hearse went straight to the cemetery.

(a) In the occupied zone, church bells remained silent.

(b) In the non-occupied zone, bells tolled as normal.

(c) Other religions followed their own rituals.

• In 1941, Jews no longer could proceed with their burial rituals due to security concerns.

v. The mailman's calendar – called Almanach des Postes et des Télégraphes

• Between Christmas and New Year, or sometimes before Christmas, the mailman did an extra round with a bag full of calendars, the Almanach des Postes et des Télégraphes, issued by the post office. He bought a number of them at cost.

• He gave a calendar to each of the people to whom he delivered mail. He never asked to be paid for it. It was understood that people would give what they could. Unlike the relationship with one's concierge, which was often, if not always, tainted with bribery, the relationship with one's mailman was strong and friendly. People usually gave generously. The calendar was a single stiff card, usually about 30x20cm (12x8in) with a picture in the middle and the months arranged around it. The patron Saint was printed for each day. The back could have a map of France or a map of the department. People could choose the picture they liked.

TRIVIA: The calendars for the years 1941 to 1944 were government propaganda, with a picture of Marshal Pétain. In 1945, the Almanach des Postes et des Télégraphes depicted innocuous pictures. In 1946, the favorite picture was the military presenting arms to a tall officer – no one doubted it was General de Gaulle.

vi. Weddings

• Although limited during the Occupation because of the law about gatherings of more than three people, single friends of the groom found ways to gather one last time. The bride might have lunch or dinner at a close friend's home, possibly with a couple of other friends.

• A wedding, with everyone in their best clothes, started at the town hall, no matter what their religion was. The mayor married the couple. They, along with their witnesses, signed the register and could request a marriage certificate.

• The mayor gave the couple the *Livret de famille*, a booklet recording their wedding and in which the birth of each child would be registered.

• The *Livret de famille* was the only valid official document needed to prove they were married.

• Only family members attended the civil ceremony.

• For Catholic couples, the majority, the town hall ceremony was followed by the church ceremony, either the same day or more often on a different day, and was considered to be the *real* wedding. Couples signed the church register.

• Everyone dressed as smartly as possible. The bride wore a long white dress and a veil. Though during the Occupation, she was not always able to afford the traditional dress and wore something simple if no one in the family could lend her a traditional wedding dress.

• The bride, however, always wore something new, something blue, something old, something borrowed. This tradition had been borrowed from the English at the end of the nineteenth century.

• She also wore a garter which a male guest had to remove.

• The church wedding could be lavish for the affluent classes or modest for the less affluent, but family, friends and neighbors attended the church ceremony.

• Only family and guests attended the banquet and dance.

• In rural areas, the whole village attended.

• The bride threw her bouquet over her shoulder to the women in attendance.

• Weddings did not take place during the month of May (month of the Virgin Mary), and never on a Friday because of the superstition of bad luck.

• Gifts to the newlyweds were optional and usually only given by the family, while guests brought flowers and wine.

• One complete serving of silverware was given to newly weds by both sets of parents, hence why most couples received two sets.

• A china set usually given by one of the godparents and a coffee set by the other.

vii. **New Year**, January 1 – New Year's Day, a public holiday

• A gift of money was given to children, to the concierge and to the servants.

vii. **January 6. Epiphany**, *Épiphanie* – Twelfth Night. *Jour des Rois* – Day of the Three Kings

• At Epiphany, following an ancient tradition, households bought or made a flat, round pastry filled with almond paste, a *galette des rois*, about 22cm (9in) in diameter. A small figurine, *la fève,* was baked inside and the person who found it in his or her portion was given a cardboard crown to wear. This tradition was known as *tirer les rois* – draw the king. In some families, a child sat under the table while the pastry was being served and called out who should receive each portion.

• During the Occupation, only the more affluent were able to buy or make a *galette*.

viii. Easter – *Pâques*. Variable date
• Good Friday was a working day with procession along the Stations of the Cross in the late afternoon. In normal times, the bells stopped ringing on Good Friday and rang again on Easter Sunday. The children had been told the story that the bells went to Rome on Good Friday and came back on Easter Sunday.
• Bells were not ringing in the occupied zone. Children missed out on that legend.
• A tradition adopted in the nineteenth century was the children's chocolate Easter egg hunt. Originally, the bells had brought the Easter eggs. The less religious families or those with no religion told the children that a rabbit had hidden chocolate eggs outside. During the Occupation, with rationing and an absence of chocolate, families improvised.
• Forty days after Easter, on a Thursday, was the *Ascension*, a religious day and public holiday.

ix. Whitsunday and Monday. *Pentecôte*. Fifty days after Easter. A religious day. This public holiday was canceled during the war.

x. Bastille Day, July 14. National Day. Public holiday. Banned during the Occupation. In normal times, there were parades, fanfares, public balls and fireworks.

xi. Assumption Day. August 15. Public holiday.
• Procession carrying a statue of the Virgin Mary, flowers.
• Everybody dressed up.
NOTE: The MBF did not dare ban this holiday.

xii. All Saints, *La Toussaint*. November 1 – public holiday
• Families went to the cemetery and placed flowers on the graves of departed family members.

• The previous evening, Halloween, with its trick-or-treat concept, did not exist in France.

xiii. Armistice Day – November 11 commemorating the cessation of hostilities of the 1914-18 war. Banned in the occupied zone.
  • Defiance. Flowers were seen around the war memorials. The authorities removed them promptly or, in some places, very slowly.
  • Mass was said in most churches.
  • In the non-occupied zone, ceremonies were held as usual.

xiv. Christmas, 1940-1943
  • December 25. *Noël* – public holiday.
  • On Christmas Eve Catholics went to midnight mass.
  • It was more important than the actual Christmas day and families ate a banquet either before the midnight mass when there were small children or after the mass. Due to the curfew, the midnight mass was held early in the evening.
  • Children and parents put a shoe in front of the chimney – many dwellings had a fireplace. When they did not, the shoes were placed near the coal stove.
  • Presents were opened on Christmas day.
  • Adults took great care to make the children believe in Father Christmas, the *Père Noël*.
  • There were no Boxing Day activities as in England. The next day was a workday.
(a) Christmas 1940. The Secours National prepared packages with food and clothes, and collected toys to distribute to impoverished families and children refugees.
  • The stores did not have chocolate, candies or the traditional Christmas log cake – *la bûche de Noël*. Like for everything else, they improvised. Pâtisseries catering to the occupiers were able to make the *bûche* and diverted some to sell under the counter.

(b) Christmas 1941. Marshal Pétain planned a day of recreation for the children, followed by a lunch. It did not materialize, though some communities may have tried. There simply was not enough food to go round.

(c) Christmas 1942. In Vichy, several students from various communities were selected for a visit and lunch with the Minister of Education. Marshal Pétain appeared afterwards and talked to the young people.

• The lunch the children eagerly awaited turned out to be bread with jam and a biscuit with added vitamins. Some disappointment.

• As for the previous year, Christmas was characterized by the lack of toys and food.

(d) Christmas 1943. Toys made of wood (said to have been made by POWs) could be found in stores, but too expensive for most families.

• Many Frenchmen working in Germany had spent their spare time to make wooden toys for their families.

• There were no Christmas trees commercially available. Communities near pine forests put up a Christmas tree for the children at the town hall.

• Decorations were made of pieces of cotton wool, small pieces of thread, cut out children's drawings.

• In towns and cities, if a family had been able to go and cut a small tree, it was cut up for firewood after Christmas.

(e) Christmas 1944. It was celebrated with mass, more food than previously, but subdued as the war was not over. It was geared to the children, inexpensive presents and cookies. Rationing was still in effect. Foodstuff was still limited due to the destruction of the infrastructure.

17. Daily life
A. June 14, 1940

• As the Wehrmacht marched into France, it imposed German daylight savings time on France, which itself was also on daylight savings time, one hour behind Germany. France had to advance the clocks by one hour, making it two hours ahead of French standard time.

• In October, the clocks went back one hour.

• Curfew was initially from 9:00 p.m. to 5:00 a.m. It varied throughout the Occupation and in various locations.

• German technicians' supervision teams were implanted in the PTT and all its services.

• Radio stations were shut down except Radio-Paris, on the Champs-Éysées, which came under the control of the Propaganda Abteilung.

• In Paris, the Eiffel Tower was decked, as was the Chambre des députés, with a large banner which proclaimed *DEUTSCHLAND SIEGT AUF ALLEN FRONTEN* – *Germany, victorious on all fronts.*

• The Palais Bourbon, seat of the National Assembly, was also decked with this banner.

• At 10:20 a.m., Place du Châtelet, a Wehrmacht officer told the crowd how badly France had been governed and how good it was going to be under the New Order.

• A café offered free drinks to Wehrmacht soldiers, and some old men offered their services to guide the Germans.

• At the end of the afternoon of June 14, the first parade took place on Avenue Foch for the benefit of the German press to film and photograph.

• In the afternoon, news got around that fifteen Parisians committed suicide, among them the well-respected Dr. Thierry Martel, head of the neuro-surgery at the American Hospital.

• Some people saw their apartments or houses requisitioned and had to pack quickly or accept to share if the dwelling was suitable.

B. June 15, 1940

• June 15, 1940. First military parade on the Champs-Élysées at 11:00 am.

• There were still battles going on in the rest of the country until June 25, when the cease-fire was announced and the armistice was fully operational.

• Paris was quiet. The few cars on the streets all belonged to the occupiers, with the exception of some commercial vehicles and the occasional doctor's car. French vehicles quickly converted to gazogène, because of the scarcity of gasoline.

• A vehicle equipped with a gazogène gas generator burned coal or charcoal to produce a gas that powered the engine. The gazogène engine was not highly efficient.

• August 28, 1940. Ban of public meetings, processions or demonstations.

i. Blackout

• Since no authority issued a ruling about the blackout, people kept using the blackout curtains, but were less strict about them being tightly closed.

• In Paris, street lights were usually shut off in the less affluent districts and were dimmed in areas where there were occupiers present, such as Montmartre, 16th and 7th Arrondissements. There were dimmed lights at Métro entrances.

• All street lighting was shut off after midnight.

• Curfew was imposed.

• In rural areas of the occupied zone, lighting was dimmed and shut off at curfew.

• With the beginning of allied bombings, blackout was strictly enforced everywhere.

ii. Street safety

• Streets were relatively safe from thieves and other criminals.

• Paris. French gendarmes and the Sicherheitsdienstspolizei(SIPO) kept order. The Paris police was in charge of criminal matters.

• Rural areas. French gendarmes, and where there were troops stationed, the Feldgendarms kept order.

B. Society
i. Aristocracy
• The 1789 Révolution did away with titles. Later, Napoléon bestowed titles, won by merit, to the new aristocracy. Descendants of the old aristocracy formed a small society, where their titles were respected. They were disdainful of the Napoleonian aristocracy. After the Occupation, many sided with Nazism.

• Society was divided along the lines of wealth and employment. The Occupation blurred those lines to some degree.

ii. Regionalism
• Among the population, there was a strong attachment to a region. People did not relocate unless they were forced to. They worked and socialized locally.

iii. Urban life
(a) **Non-occupied zone** – there were difficulties in obtaining food and coal or wood, but not impossible until November 1942.

• Rationing was in effect. Hunger and cold were commonplace and increased dramatically after 1942.

• Curfew was enforced.

• Blackout was in effect but not strictly enforced until 1942, when it was enforced.

(b) **Occupied zone** – hunger and cold already felt during the winter 1940-41, progressively worsened as time went on.

• Allied bombings intensified in 1942.

• Curfew strictly enforced in early 1943.

• Blackout in effect. Enforced everywhere.
• Journeys in the country to buy farm products became increasingly difficult.

iv. Rural life
(a) **Non-occupied zone** – supplies of food, coal and wood were adequate.
• After 1942, it became increasingly difficult to avoid the German controllers.
• Curfew was strictly imposed but with exceptions, except in villages and small towns.
• It was easy to grow and raise food. Farmers still sold to people from the cities.
• Production quotas were more or less met. Farmers found ways to hide part of their production.
• 1943 – most farmers were also supplying the local maquis.

(b) **Occupied zone**
• Curfew and blackout more strictly enforced.
• Farmers struggled to meet quotas and keep back enough for themselves and customers from the cities.
• Germans were also frequent customers.
• Most farmers fed résistance members.

C. Food and Wine Stores
• There were no food supermarkets. Each type of food had its own store.
• It must be remembered there was no refrigeration in households. A few affluent families may have had an ice-box.
• Cafés, restaurants and food stores would have an ice-box.
• A large block of ice would be delivered and placed directly into the ice-box by the delivery man every second day.
• An ice-box was a kind of cabinet in three parts: top compartment for the block of ice, the middle compartment for the food and beverages and the bottom for the container that collected the water from the melting ice.

• Ice was collected in winter from mountain glaciers or frozen lakes, brought onto a train car, with some insulation, to towns where it would be transported by truck or horse wagon to a distribution point.

• The majority of families were Catholic. They were likely to give a blessing before eating and the more devout would give thanks as well after the meal.

• Affluent classes were also affected by restrictions but were more likely to resort to the black market on a regular basis.

NOTE: The word salad – *salade* – was always made up of lettuce. Mixed salad, as known in North America and England, a mixture of lettuce, tomatoes and other vegetables, would be called a *salade composée,* which was rarely served. Besides the lettuce salad, a tomato salad (nothing but tomatoes) or a bean salad (similarly, just beans) were likely to be served in season, especially if eating outdoors.

• Lettuce was never chopped with a knife but torn with the fingers in the kitchen.

• The less affluent classes drank more than the affluent classes. Alcoholism was prevalent among the poorer class, though public drunkenness was rare. Frenchmen did not drink to get drunk. With restrictions, wine became less and less available and the quality deteriorated.

• Wine was available with ration tickets. A drop of wine might be added to the children's water glass.

• Mineral water such as Badoit, Evian, Perrier, Vichy and Vittel was available without ration tickets for people who could afford it.

NOTE – in the description of meals, no mention was made of *family parcels* received from country relatives or from the foraging trips, as the supply of food thus obtained was not consistent.

i. After curfew

• One minute after curfew ended, women, old men and children hurried to the food stores and waited in line for the store to open.

• The day before, people had scoured the newspapers and listened to Radio-Paris (official German controlled station) to find out where food would be available, where food items, such as sardines or potatoes, had arrived and occasionally did not require ration tickets.

• When possible, families divided the tasks with children queueing before school. This was a source of conflict when a childless woman protested that children should not hold a place in line for their mother.

• The queues became places where social rules were relaxed. Women exchanged news, especially the BBC news, with trusted people.

• Women exchanged recipes.

• Various police agents (no uniform), spies, queued alongside regular customers in the hope to overhear talk of résistance or black market.

ii. Bread

• Bread was eaten with every course, except soup and dessert.

• It was never buttered except at breakfast. If jam was served, the bread was not buttered. It was either one or the other.

• In normal times, bread was broken from the loaf, not cut with a knife. If the type of bread did not lend itself to being broken, it might be sliced with a bread knife.

• During the Occupation there was less choice of bread and the Pétain's government had decreed that the only bread that could be sold had to be one day old and the housewife had to cut very thin slices.

iii. Breakfast

• French people did not eat bacon.

173

• In normal times, breakfast consisted of bread and butter or bread and jam. Never both on the bread. During the Occupation, if there was butter or jam, a thin layer would go onto the bread.

• In normal times, coffee, and *café au lait* (milk coffee), and now ersatz, was served in a small bowl (about 15cm or 6in in diameter) held in one hand. Children used both hands or had a bowl with a couple of small flat handles.

• No other food was served at an urban breakfast.

• Men of poorer classes frequently stopped at a café for a shot of brandy or Calvados.

• Men of middle class frequently stopped at a café for *un noir* – black coffee.

• Once the household's preserves were exhausted, jam was no longer on the menu for most families.

iv. Midday meal

• Office workers had a one-hour-and-a-half to two-hour break. They either went home or ate at a local café-restaurant, or they bought sandwiches and ate them on a park bench.

• Executives had a two-hour break which could be a business lunch at a restaurant.

• Factory workers took a lunchbox to work containing sandwiches and a flask of red wine. They had a one-hour break, sometimes less depending on the factory.

• The *déjeuner* was eaten at home by the housewife and schoolchildren. When the mother also worked, children ate in the school canteen (not cafeteria-style but a served meal) where they had a hot home-cooked meal served in the "réfectoire" (dining hall). High school students who lived too far to walk home at noon also attended the canteen. School lunch break was one and a half hour.

(a) Affluent classes

• In normal times there would be an entrée, or a hors-d'œuvre, followed by a fish course, followed by a meat or poultry course, followed by a vegetable course, followed by

174

cheese, or a salad and/or a dessert. The appropriate wine was served. A bowl of fruit in season was on the table. If a dessert was served, it would be homemade, though on special occasions, and often on Sundays, a cake was bought from the patisserie. An apéritif (such as Martini, Cinzano) was served while waiting for the meal.

• During the week, a business executive would eat lunch in a restaurant.

• During the Occupation – only one course of fish, meat or poultry on the appropriate day. Vegetables and fruit in season. Rutabaga was usually avoided. There would not be a dessert every day. Depending on the reserves, only one wine would be served. Either an apéritif or liqueur once or twice a week. Both on Sundays or special occasions if the cellar was well-stocked.

(b) Less affluent classes

• In normal times, the déjeuner consisted of a hors-d'oeuvre, a meat or poultry dish, vegetable dish and fruit in season. Fish would always be served on Fridays. Desserts only served on Sundays and special occasions. Wine was served.

• Middle-management office workers frequently ate lunch in a restaurant.

• During the Occupation there would be vegetables, salade, bread and cheese on ordinary days. The meat ration was saved for Sundays, fish on Fridays. Wine was measured out to make it last. Ersatz coffee was served and sometimes on special occasions real coffee if it could be obtained on the black market.

• An apéritif, (such as Martini, Cinzano) was served while waiting for the meal to be served if the cellar was well-stocked.

(c) Poorer classes

• In normal times, the déjeuner consisted of bread, leftovers and cheese. Ordinary red wine and coffee. If the husband came home for lunch, he would get the meat, or poultry, or fish. A dessert was served on special occasions.

• During the Occupation there would be bread, cheese and the meat ration, which went in the worker's lunch box. Ordinary red wine and ersatz coffee.

v. Evening meal
(a) Affluent classes
• In normal times the *dîner*, served at 7:00 pm, or later in affluent families or storekeepers – who often closed at 8:00 pm, consisted of a simple hors-d'oeuvre (cold meats), a vegetable dish or a potage or consommé (light soup), and a dessert, usually a fruit in season, were served. Select wines and coffee.

• During the Occupation, hors-d'œuvres were now reserved for special occasions. A light soup, a vegetable dish, followed by bread and cheese. One wine and ersatz coffee, unless real coffee had been obtained on the black market.

• Once the household's preserves were exhausted, jam was no longer on the menu for most families unless obtained on the black market.

• The scarcity of food was a serious problem. Most people lost weight. By 1943-44, most people had to make do with rations, but often supplemented with black market. Even though privileged, most children did not reach the appropriate size and weight for their age.

• Wine was available with ration tickets. By 1943, the ration decreased to one liter per person per week.

• People became conscious about waste.

(b) Less affluent classes
• In normal times, *dîner* consisted of an entrée or a hors-d'œuvre, a potage or consommé, cheese or salad. Wine and coffee.

• During the Occupation, hors d'œuvre were served only on special occasions and Sundays. A thick soup. A vegetable dish. Wine and ersatz coffee. Dessert on Sundays.

• The scarcity of nutritious food was felt. People lost weight. Children's growth was impaired. By 1943-44, there were serious signs of malnutrition as people were less and less able to afford the occasional black market.

• Wine was available with ration tickets. By 1943, the ration decreased to one liter per person per week.

• People of this socio-economic class relied heavily on rutabaga, potatoes and bread, and the occasional black market item. Whenever possible, families would make food gathering trips to the countryside. When they had a rural family, food parcels, which included vegetables, fruits, homemade cheese, dried meats, were a welcome supplement. It must be noted that the parcels were spaced out and irregular.

• Already somewhat conscious about waste, they became stricter and more creative.

• Used the black market for special occasions.

• Some families had a member classed as *worker doing heavy work* – category T, and benefited from extra rations.

(c) Poorer classes

• In normal times, *dîner* consisted of a substantial soup, often using any unused leftovers from lunch with bread. Occasionally cheese. Wine and coffee.

• During the Occupation – not much different, just less quantity. Most of the food went to the worker. Malnutrition was rampant as early as the winter 1941-42. Children's growth was impaired and they were highly susceptible to tuberculosis and later in the war, skin diseases.

• Wine was available with ration tickets. By 1943, the ration decreased to one liter per person per week.

• Most men in the family worked in factories. It was not considered *hard labor* and very few were classed as *workers doing heavy work*, category T, to benefit from extra rations, which went to the workers not the children as it did in more educated families.

• They relied heavily on rutabaga, potatoes and bread. Already conscious about waste, they became stricter and more creative.

• Rutabaga and Jerusalem artichoke – *topinambours* – were staples. Nothing was wasted.

• On Sundays, men who owned a bicycle rode out to a farm to buy fresh produce. Others took the train.

• Every traveler, whether on foot, bicycle or train, was subjected to control by the gendarmes and frequently a German controller as well.

• Those with rural family connections occasionally received food parcels.

vi. Rural areas

• In normal times. On a farm, the farmers and workers would work a couple of hours before breakfast and come in to have an egg or some saucisson with bread before returning to the fields. Coffee was served.

• Breakfast was served by the farmwife.

• Midday meals consisted of generous portions of meat, followed by a large serving of potatoes, sometimes followed by other vegetables from the garden, followed by cheese. Desserts were only on Sundays and special occasions.

• Evening meals consisted of soup made with vegetables in a meat broth. Bread and homemade sausage or ham or meat – *saucisson, garlic sausage, homemade smoked ham, cured raw ham.*

• Homemade preserves and jams were used in cakes or pudding-type desserts on Sundays.

• Farmers gathered in the village café after the evening meal for a glass of wine.

• During the Occupation, little changed except ersatz coffee replaced real coffee. Farmers were classed as *workers doing heavy work* (Category T) or *agricultural workers* and benefited from extra rations.

• Farms generally could provide enough food for themselves and were able to sell some.

• After January 1943, they also supplied food to the local maquis.

vii. Collaborators
• No change of lifestyle for collaborators. In fact, they lived better.

D. Rationing
• To begin with, people were only invited to consume less food and butchers had to close three days a week.

Note that rationing remained in place until 1949, the difference being the last person in the queue got her ration.

• Until November 1942, people in the non-occupied zone were able to obtain sufficient foods according to their rations. City dwellers also went on trips to the countryside. After the Germans occupied the south zone, the differences with the occupied zone disappeared.

• For city dwellers, food became a race against starvation by 1942. It must be remembered that there was no refrigeration in people's homes.

• Businesses, like butcher, charcuterie, café and restaurants, would have an icebox.

• A few well-to-do households may also have had an icebox. The housewife or maid still shopped every day.

• People read the official newspaper and listened to Radio-Paris, the official station, to learn of the arrival of foodstuffs, such as potatoes.

• The newspapers indicated any changes in the restrictions and when to renew the ration booklet.

• The obsession with food dominated people's lives.

• Cooks became creative. Ingredients normally reserved to feed cattle, such as rutabaga, appeared on the table. It did not require ration tickets.

• A lot of cooking was done in a frying pan. There were no non-stick frying pans. The preferred frying pan was of cast iron as it heated evenly and kept hot for a long time after the stove had gone out or the cooking gas switched off.

• Due to the lack of oil and butter, cooks would keep a small square of pork fat on a fork to apply a thin layer of grease to the pan.

• When a household obtained a ration of oil, after use it was filtered for reuse until it turned black

• Cookbooks adapted to the new conditions as early as 1940.

- *340 Recipes* by H.P. Pellaprat (published by Flammarion).

- *Cuisine et restrictions* by Dr. Édouard de Pomiane (from the Pasteur Institute).

• Both the Germans and the gendarmes were concerned about people buying food in the countryside to resell at inflated prices in the city on the black market. Those who had just enough for an average family were usually let go. Though later in the war, they sometimes saw their meagre booty confiscated.

• People foraged for wild foods, such as berries, dandelions, mushrooms, anything edible, in parks and woods.

• Most important, servings which were normally small became even smaller. Manual laborers were the only ones to be served bigger portions.

i. Ration booklets

• The first booklets of ration tickets for staples, such as bread and meat, were only issued in October 1940. The government had been hesitant to impose rationing after the declaration of war.

• Ration tickets for other food items were issued in February 1941.

• People registered with their local merchants. Registration did not guarantee that they would receive their food allocation, but they might get better service. A storekeeper might save enough for his favorite customers' rations.

• A person might patronize another store than the one they registered with if the lineup was shorter.

• Ration booklets were stamped with the town's official stamp.

• Tickets could only be redeemed on a specified day.

• Tickets for some item such as bread, meat, milk, butter, were renewed every month.
• Tickets not used in the correct month could not be redeemed.

ii. Forgery
• Ration booklets of tickets were relatively easy to forge. Penalties if caught were severe.

iii. Tickets and storekeepers
• Every month, the storekeepers would glue the collected tickets onto an official form to enable them to receive their quota of products.

iv. Rationing controls
• Three organizations were created – Price Controls, Mobile Control Units, Economic Police, separate from the national police or gendarmerie, and were universally detested by storekeepers.

v. Not rationed
• Rutabaga and Jerusalemn artichoke were the only food items that were not rationed.
• Cities, particularly Paris, ran out of those in early 1944. Before the war, those roots were only fed to cattle.
• Mineral water – Eau de Vichy, Badoit mineral water, Évian mineral water, Perrier mineral water (plain, no flavour), Vittel mineral water were available to those who could afford them.

vi. Population categories
• The population was categorized by age or occupation:
  - Category E – children aged under 3 years.
  - Category J1 – children aged between 3 and 6 years.
  - Category J2 – children aged between 6 and 12 years.

- Category J3 – Children from 13 to 21 years, as well as pregnant women.
- Category A – Persons aged 12 to 70 years employed but not in heavy work.
- Category T – Persons aged 14 to 70 years employed in heavy work.
- Category C – Persons 12 and older (no age limit) employed in agriculture.
- Category V – Persons 70 and older not employed in agriculture.

vii. Calories
• In normal times, the average daily calorie intake for a working man was 2,400 calories (more for extra heavy work) and 2,000 calories for a working woman. The war changed that to 1,200 calories daily, determined by the government. This amount diminished with each year of war to end at 850 calories per day. Irreversible starvation occurs at 600 calories.
• By 1944, many people, especially in poorer districts, older adults and children, barely reached 600 cal/day. Deaths from starvation were recorded.

viii. Bakery. Bread and pastries
• As early as the fall of 1940, bakers were obliged to sell day-old bread to customers as per an edict from the Pétain's government. The idea was that people would eat less of the stale bread than fresh bread.
• Pastries, croissants, brioches or any product containing butter, as well as ice-cream, were banned everywhere, except in the designated stores for the occupiers' consumption.
• Housewives did not make their own bread. An isolated farm might make their own bread if they were able to obtain flour, which was also rationed.
• There were three types of bakeries: 1. *boulangerie* – bread products. 2. *boulangerie patisserie* – bread and pastries. 3. *pâtisserie* – only pastries.

NOTE: As in cooking, there are terms that do not describe the product accurately. Do not trust the internet translations. Bread making has evolved since the war and has become fancier with new techniques and products varieties have been added that did not exist in the war era.

• By 1942, bakeries had difficulties obtaining the traditional baker's yeast and reverted to making levain and sourdough bread.

(a) There were several varieties of bread, made with traditional baker's yeast:

• *Pain de deux livres* (the traditional two-pound or 1 kg loaf, 80cm long). Your character could ask for "*Un pain*" or "a loaf" and would receive a two-pound loaf. The length was important as it could not be to be tied on a bicycle carrier if too long. Made exclusively with white flour, which during the war was of poor quality and mixed with other flours and even chaff and sawdust.

• *Bâtard* – was half the size of a pain de deux livres – 500g and 40cm long. Only made with white flour but during the war, a mix of flour, chaff and sawdust.

• *Baguette* – a long loaf, much thinner than the *pain*, weighing just over 250g and 70cm in length. Only made with white flour but in wartime used a mix of ingredients.

• *Boule* – as the name indicates, it was a round loaf, also called *pain de campagne,* meaning country loaf. It was made with different flours, according to the region, with barley, rye, spelt or whole wheat. The round loaves were made with sourdough *levain*. It was the traditional bread of rural areas. It, too, suffered from a lack of flour and was made with a mix of ingredients.

• *Pain de mie* – a soft bread made with milk. Delicate, it was more expensive and bought for a special treat. Only bakers serving German customers obtained the necessary milk to make *pain de mie*. Ordinary citizens could not buy it, except on the black market.

183

• *Pain de Vienne* – Vienna loaf was made with sugar, milk and butter. Only bakers serving German customers obtained the necessary ingredients. Again, moneyed people could buy it on the black market.

(b) Boulanger Pâtissier – a pastry chef who made both bread and basic pastries, such as bread pudding, croissants, *galette des rois* (an almond flat cake with layered pastry similar to flaky pastry), *Kouign Aman* – a bread-pastry from Brittany. This bread was a specialty that could be found in Paris and in Brittany, but unlikely in other towns. *Kuglof* – Kugelhoff, a bread pudding made with leftover breads, quatre-quarts, fruit tarts, éclairs and madeleines.

(c) Pâtissier did not make or sell any bread

• Individual pastries of which very few of them were available to the French public were *Baba au rhum, clafoutis(often made with leftover pastries), choux à la crème, éclair au chocolat, financier, l'Opéra, macaron, madeleine, meringue, mille-feuille, profiterolle* (usually with chocolate) and *religieuse.*

• Cakes – *Alcazar, canelés, Charlotte, envoi de Nice, fraisier, flan, fruit tarts, Génoise, Marquise, Napolitain, Pithiviers, Progrès* (also called a *Russe*), *quatre-quarts, Saint-Honoré, savarin, Tatin* tart.

• *Petits fours*, also called *mignardises*, and sometimes in English *small oven*, meaning baked at a lower temperature. When bread had finished baking in a traditional brick or stone oven, there was enough heat left to bake pastries. *Petits fours* could be glazed, salted, or made as miniature cakes.

ix. Coffee

• There was no such thing in France as *national coffee*. It might occasionally be erroneously mentioned by older people in a memoir many years after the war. The expression does not occur in the government's *Journal Officiel* or in books written during the first decade after the Liberation. People used the

German word *ersatz* or the French *succédané* to denote coffee substitutes.

• *National Coffee.* The expression came into use under British influence only after the war by writers, journalists and filmmakers, partly due to a lack of research. During the war, people used the German term *ersatz* for coffee substitutes. The French equivalent is *succédané*. There is one mention of *café national* in a Pétain government document in the archives of the État Français alluding to the proportions of one third coffee, one third chicory and one third barley. Had Pétain intended this blend to become the model for a *Café national,* the term never caught on, not in Pétain's non-occupied zone nor in the occupied zone. In the latter there was no coffee available at all – except on the black market – and people drank various concoctions of acorns, chickpeas, roots or grains, roasted and ground. They certainly had no notion of a *national* coffee.

• French people drank coffee, not tea. For an intimate gathering or significant dinner with mostly women in attendance, some affluent people might offer tea as well as coffee. It was considered snobbish or pretentious by the rest of the population. Neither was available during the war, except on the black market, and it eventually ran out as it was imported.

• In normal times, women of the affluent classes meeting with friends would serve tea. They may also go to a *salon de thé*, such as Ruc in Paris.

• In normal times, meals would end with a cup of coffee. Milk or cream was not offered by the hostess. If requested, it was poured in after the coffee, not before. There was no milk substitute during the Occupation.

• Cube sugar would be on the table in normal times. Guests brought their own saccharine ration.

• Coffee disappeared in the occupied zone, except on the black market and German supplies. Ersatz coffee was made of chicory, roots, grains or acorns, anything that could be dried and ground.

185

• In normal times, people bought coffee as roasted beans. There are no records of ground coffee being sold in stores. Every household had a hand operated coffee mill. Coffee beans disappeared from the market in 1940 and people used their coffee mill to grind replacement products, such rye, chicory, seeds, dandelion root or grains they may find.

x. Cooking oil
• Prewar, two-thirds of necessary oil for the food industry, mostly fish canneries, was imported.

• The Pétain's government encouraged the local production of oilseeds, such as sunflower, and a plant new to France – soyabean.

• Manufacturers experimented with different plants, seeds, fruits, without great success.

• Oil was preciously stored, used and re-used until it became so black and thick it could no longer be used. It was not thrown out, but went to grease bicycle chains, with mixed success.

xi. Fish and fishing
• Fish fell under the same restrictions as meat.

• Educational institutions, hospitals and restaurants were legally able to obtain more than housewives. The Secours National also helped provide the hospitals and schools.

• Fishmongers only sold fresh, dried and canned fish and shellfish.

• Fresh fish and shellfish were not rationed.

• Fishermen were allowed to resume fishing as early as July 1940, with some restrictions about distance and areas.

(a) **Fishing** was not allowed between 6:00 pm and 9:00 am.

(b) **Captains** had to indicate their departure.

(c) **Captains** had to provide a list of their crew members.

(d) **They could only fish** within three nautical miles from shore.

• Due to the lack of fuel, sailboats reappeared.

• The lack of vegetable oil, especially olive oil, led to innovations using water, lemon and tomato juice as well as white wine to preserve canned fish.

• The Wehrmacht and the Kriesgmarine bought two-thirds of the canned fish and facilitated its production.

• Unlike for other industries, the canneries were not requisitioned.

• The occupiers had freezing technology, which was still unknown in France, and brought it to one cannery near Douarnez in Brittany.

• Canneries were in fact collaborating but saw no alternative as 100,000 people were employed in the industry.

• Only the fish canning factory Noël Larzul closed for the time of the Occupation.

• Some of the fish and shellfish, fresh and canned, found its way to fishmongers in cities mostly to supply the occupiers.

• Fishmongers in rural towns and villages relied on fish from local streams and lakes to help feed the population.

xii. Meat. Charcuterie (Delicatessen). Poultry
(a) Fresh meat

• Slaughter facilities that exceeded their quota were shut down until their next quota period.

• In Paris, a decree dated December 23, 1939 forbade the sale of meat on Mondays, Tuesdays and Fridays at butchers, markets or other stores.

• February 29, 1940 – came a new decree forbidding the sale of meat for three consecutive days a week. The choice of days was the responsibility of the prefects in their jurisdiction.

• The restrictions also applied to hotels and restaurants. Only one meat dish, of 100g, without bone, could be served per meal, and only on permitted days.

• Because of the lack of refrigeration, the butcher's store had an open front, which was closed at night and in freezing weather.

• The butcher cut the meat as per customer's requirements and wrapped it in paper (reddish and thick). During the Occupation, cuts were no longer *according to requirements* but whatever was available.

(b) Charcuterie – delicatessen

• A charcuterie did not sell fresh meat, nor fish products.

• Charcutiers prepared the products themselves, salting, curing and cooking. They made preserves in glass jars.

• A charcuterie sold whole and sliced dried, salted or cured meat products.

- *Saucisson* – a dry large sausage made with raw beef, pork and fat, then cured by hanging several months in a cool place.

- *Jambon* – cooked by boiling leg of pork.

- *Jambon cru* – raw ham cured by hanging several months in a cool place.

- *Pâté* – made with ingredients such as goose liver, pork, rabbit (especially during the Occupation), turkey, partridge and other wild game. During the Occupation, other products found their way into pâté.

- *Boudin* – blood sausage, in Britain called black pudding.

-*Tripes* – tripe, stomach lining

- *Charcuteries pâtissières* – meat product contained in a pastry shell. For example, vol-au-vent. This was made fresh every day in prewar days but soon disappeared during the war, except for luxury and requisitioned restaurants.

(c) Poultry

• There were stores that sold only poultry – *un magasin de volaille*.

xiii. **Dairy** – *crèmerie* sold milk, butter, eggs and cheese (*beurre œufs fromage*)

(a) Milk

• Milk – *lait* – was reserved for Categories E, J and V.

• There was no milk substitute.

• The *crèmerie* sold cow's milk in bulk from a large basin. The merchant had different sized ladles – quarter liter, half liter, liter.

   • The merchant poured the milk into the customer's milk can – common size one liter – fitted with a lid and a handle.

   • Goat's milk was not available during the Occupation.

   (b) Butter – *beurre* – was cut with a wire from a large block and placed on a piece of wax paper.

   • During the Occupation, butter was replaced by *saindoux* –melted pork fat with salt added.

   (c) Cheese – *fromage* – prewar, more than 350 varieties of cheese were available.

   • Soft cheese like camembert was sold in a box of thin wood.

   • Hard cheeses were sliced with a wire onto a piece of wax paper.

   (d) Cheese was a staple of the family parcels.

   • Cheese varieties commonly available at the *crèmerie* were Camembert and Emmenthal.

   • Varieties in family parcels might include:

   - *Fourme d'Auvergne*, *Petit chèvre* – goat cheese, *Pont l'Évèque, Reblochon, Roquefort, Saint-Marcellin, Saint-Vincent, Saint-Paulin, Saint-Maure, Saint-Gilda, Saint-Albray and Tome de Savoie*.

xiv. Produce – Grocery

   • The grocery store only sold fruit and vegetables, fresh, dried and in cans, plus fresh herbs. By 1943, the storekeeper had to rely on growing produce in his own garden. Official supplies were insufficient. People in private houses cultivated a garden, but those in apartments had to rely on the grocer.

   • Spices ceased to be available during the Occupation in the occupied zone, except on the black market while stocks lasted.

   • After the invasion of the non-occupied zone, no more spices could be imported from North Africa.

189

• *Anis* – aniseed was grown in Provence and therefore available locally until the invasion of the free zone.

• Pétain had banned making *pastis*, a drink based on *anis*, (See résistant industrialists, Paul Ricard, in 13.   Collaboration).

xv. Sugar. Candy store – Confiserie

• Saccharine replaced sugar, which became unavailable by the end of 1943.

• When visiting, people brought their own saccharine.

• Candies were banned by the Pétain's government.

• When they did not close, storekeepers became ingenious at disguising candies and sold them under the term medicinal pastilles.

TRIVIA: The popular *cachou* La Jaunie, a tiny liquorice candy in an iconic small yellow round tin box, was sold as a remedy for children's constipation, upset stomachs or colds. Children just liked it as a candy.

• Due to the sugar restrictions, artisanal candy makers and storekeepers experimented with vegetables and herbs with varying results.

xvi. Wine. Liqueur and Liquor. Mineral water

• By 1943, wine became less available and was reserved for people in Category T.

(a) Apéritif : Cinzano, Dubonnet, Suze, Quinquina, Vermouth, Byrrh.

• Pastis: Ricard, Pernod – banned by Pétain, (See résistant industrialists, Paul Ricard, in 13.Collaboration).

(b) Liqueur (sweet) and Liquor (spirits). There is only one word in French – *liqueur*.

• Liqueurs included Bénédictine, Chartreuse – green or yellow, Cointreau, Grand-Marnier. These would be served at the end of a meal.

• Liquor included Armagnac, Calvados, Cognac, Marc, Marie-Brizard. These too were served at the end of a meal – to help digestion! A favorite of some workmen would be to buy a coffee with a shot of cognac in it in the morning on their way to work.

(c) **Wine** – red wine was the customary wine served with every meal.

(d) **Mineral water** in glass bottles was available without ration tickets to those who could afford it:
    • Eau de Vichy, Badoit mineral water, Évian mineral water, Perrier mineral water (it was plain, no flavor), Vittel mineral water.

xvii. Clothing
    • Textile ration tickets were prioritized for children up to seventeen years and special issue for weddings, pregnancy, mourning and liberated prisoners.
    • It took several tickets to buy enough material for an outfit or buy a ready-made garment.
    • 1942. Jews had to buy the yellow star with their textile tickets.

xviii. Coal
    • Coal was prioritized for households with children under six years of age or the elderly over seventy years and to households that had no gas or electrical stoves.
    • By 1943, the supply was insufficient and those households had to choose between cooking or heating.

xix. Soap
    • Soap became scarce, with fragrant and delicate soaps being the first to disappear.
    • 1941 – by the end of the year, stocks of laundry soap were exhausted.
    • Homemade soap was made with any oil or grease unsuitable for consumption and sodium hydroxide (lye).
    • Old recipes reappeared. Laundry was done with wood ash.

• Women grew saponine plants in balcony boxes or in gardens, which foams in contact with water, for personal washing.

xx. 1943-1944
• The lack of goods available meant that most ration tickets were useless.

xxi. Allotments
• August 1940 – the government encouraged municipalities to create allotments (community gardens) in public spaces and gardens.
• Public parks, like part of the Luxembourg Gardens and of the Jardins du Louvre in Paris, were turned into allotments. Other cities followed suit with their parks.

xxii. Soup kitchens
• After January 1943, food shortages were so dire that the government and the prefectures established official soup kitchens. Up to that point, a number of soup kitchens had been run by private and religious charities. They continued until after the war.
• The Secours National had already been supplementing schools and hospitals and running soup kitchens for the elderly and disadvantaged in poorer districts.

E. Typical wartime dishes
i. Ordinary dishes
• *Pot-au-feu* – a national dish of cabbage, carrots, celery, leek, onion, potatoes, beef and herbs. Due to rationing, the meat was a small portion of the cheaper cuts. And eventually no meat at all.
• *Cassoulet* – normally made with beans, mutton and sausages, was now made with mutton alone, or sausages when available, and eventually just beans.
• Potatoes

- Baked potatoes were baked in their skin to avoid waste.
- Stuffed potatoes, normally stuffed with meat, now stuffed with any available mashed vegetables.
• The above dishes were only occasionally served in affluent classes, but as the Occupation continued, they were added more frequently to the menu.
- Potato purée – normally made with butter and milk, was made with water and a saved ration of butter, if available, or a fat like oil, if available. The cook would add some milk to the children's portion.
• A typical rutabaga recipe – after washing thoroughly, the skin was grated off or peeled and kept to make soup. The rutabags were sliced as thin as possible and baked with fat, if available. If not, it was cooked in water and mashed thoroughly.
• *Topinambour* (Jerusalem artichoke) could be eaten raw or cooked into a purée. Washed with a brush, it was cooked and the skin eaten.

ii. Recipes for when everything is lacking

• People cooked on gas stoves (pressure became less and less until there was no gas in 1944) or propane or butane burners, as long as the cylinder could be refilled. Electric burners were subject to numerous electricity cuts from the end of 1942 to the end of the war. People used wood or coal stoves for as long as there was fuel, which was carefully managed.
• By 1941, gas and electricity were only on for a limited time at a given hour. Housewives scrambled to cook all they could during that short period.
- Soup was made with nettle, chickweed or clover, collected in parks or gardens, or fields in rural areas.
- *Pâté* – a cube of Viandox (a bouillon cube, available up to 1943) was mixed with water and flour or cornstarch and an egg to make a meatless loaf.
- Rhubarb grew easily and with saccharine made jam with must from grapes or wort from beer. It did not make many

pots, but at least it preserved the rhubarb or any fruit that could be obtained in quantity.

- Throw nothing away – stale bread made *pain-perdu*, literally lost bread, a moist cake-like pudding. The bread was soaked in water or milk in rural areas where it could be obtained. Any dried or fresh fruit in danger of spoiling was added, and the mixture mashed together and baked. Vegetables in danger of spoiling could be used instead of fruit.

- A scraping of flour, which could contain chaff, bran or something else, was mixed with a little water and spooned into a pan of hot oil – often re-used. When cooked, the fritter was drained of oil for later re-use. The nutritional value was virtually nil, but it kept the hunger at bay for another day.

- Beans and lentils were screened for weevils and bits of gravel and soaked overnight. They were then brought to the boil in water and simmered for as long as electricity or fuel supplies allowed. Lentils took less time to cook, beans a little longer.

F. Open-air markets and Les Halles de Paris
i. Prewar

• Before the invasion, open-air markets were held in many locations for the sale of farm and other produce.

• Open-air markets ceased with the invasion and rationing, when people had to register with their local stores for items such as bread.

• In Paris, there were street carts selling flowers in the early days of the Occupation.

• The flower and bird market on the Île de la Cité, remained open. The occupiers were the main clientele.

TRIVIA: – there was an underground tunnel from the métro station Cité to the Palais de Justice. Well hidden from view, this tunnel was much used by resistants.

ii. Paris. Les Halles

• Les Halles, located between rue de Pontoise and rue de Poissy in the 12th Arrondissement, was the fresh food

194

distribution center for Paris and its suburbs. It was also where flowers arrived from the south.

• Les Halles consisted of a series of cast iron and glass pavillons designed by Victor Baltard. Each pavilion offered a specialty product – meat, fish, flowers, etc.

• Employees and suppliers possessed a special Ausweis to be out at night.

• Producers arrived at the Halles between 9:00 pm and midnight.

• Only the *Forts des Halles* – men employed by the administration for their strength and endurance, were allowed to unload the goods.

• Outside the pavillons, at the street junctions, was *Le Carreau*, where small producers could bring their goods and sell them themselves. Everything went directly onto the ground – no tables allowed, other than boxes and crates.

• Housewives could come as soon as the curfew was over at 5:00 am

• The selling in the Baltard Pavillion opened at 10:00 pm until 8:00 am the next morning.

• Although producers from the countryside brought food for sale at the Halles, they also bought what was not available in their areas, especially exotic foods, which disappeared during the Occupation, but also fish and shellfish.

• Destitute people waited until the bell indicated the end of trading and would come to scavenge whatever was left before the arrival of the cleaners. By the end of the nineteenth century, such people were called *clochards*, from *cloche* – bell.

• Soon after the Occupation, not only destitute people but people rendered poor by the war and Occupation came to pick up what they could before being chased away by the authorities.

• There were food distribution centers in all major towns, none as grandiose as *Les Halles de Paris*.

G. Slow famine
i. 1940-1941

• The winter 1940-41 was extremely harsh. Urban areas particularly suffered from insufficient food and heat. With the introduction of the rationing categories, it made little difference whether a family lived in an expensive area or in a poor district. The ration tickets were the same.

• Affluent families were able to resort to the black market.

• Rationed supplies available in urban areas were superior to those in rural towns. The inequality created discontent.

• People blamed Pétain's government for starving the French to feed the occupiers.

• The French population was not accustomed to food shortages. The empire used to provide oil, coffee, cacao, fruit. The British Atlantic and Mediterranean blockade, plus the occupiers' requisitions, affected everyone. Insufficient food supplies made it to the non-occupied zone and even less to the occupied zone.

• While urbanites had to scramble for food, agricultural areas encountered fewer difficulties.

• Bread had always been considered as the staple of the French diet. The restrictions and requisitions affected the supply of flour. The government authorized the addition of chestnut flour, potato flour and buckwheat flour to wheat flour. By 1943, flour was in short supply and bakers added sawdust to make bread (gray, heavy, barely risen).

• While the distribution system was functioning, the promised produce often failed to arrive. It had serious consequences for people, whether in urban or rural areas.

• In both zones, prices simply doubled. People in the lower socio-economic range could not buy even the minimum food.

ii. 1942-1944

• The winters of 1942-43 and 1943-44 were again extremely cold, with heavy snowfalls. Agricultural output diminished.

• The even greater shortages in urban areas caused death by starvation.

• By the spring of 1944, cities, Paris in particular, had exhausted all food reserves, leading to a food crisis. Allotments, window boxes and other ways of growing proved insufficient. Vulnerable people died. By the beginning of August 1944, food reserves in Paris were totally exhausted and no foodstuffs arrived at Les Halles. Famine began to spread despite the resourcefulness of Parisians.

H. Medical Opinion

• The Medical Academy examined the rations available and declared they did not constitute a balanced diet and were insufficient to sustain life.

• Women who did not obtain additional food experienced erratic periods or none at all. Puberty in girls, normally starting age twelve or thirteen, was delayed .

• The most at risk were young children, pregnant women and the elderly. The Academy demanded more food for those categories. Demands were, more often than not, ignored by the supply authorities.

• Doctors were alarmed at the death rate of newborns and the elderly. Things were so bad they advised against breast-feeding, since mothers were too undernourished to provide adequate nutrients to the baby.

• Doctors reported that the height and weight of poorer and middle-class children and adolescents was below average.

• Hospitals, mental asylums and prisons strictly applied the rationing portions. This sector's death toll increased threefold.

• By 1942, doctors were reporting an increase in cases of tuberculosis.

• Rations were 20 to 30 percent below what was needed for minimum nourishment.

I. Household furnishing
i. Furniture stores. Forced labor camps. The M-Aktion

• M-Aktion – abbreviation for Möbel-Aktion – looted some 70,000 homes of French, Belgian, and Dutch Jews or other Jews who had either fled or been deported.

• The largest funiture store in Paris was Lévitan, rue du Faubourg Saint-Martin. It was immediately taken over by the occupiers. The furniture was sent to Germany, and the building became a clearing house for all items requisitioned by the occupiers.

• The store became one of three forced labor camps in Paris (the Lager-Ost). Some 800 inmates from the Drancy camps were selected and housed in three camps in the city: 1. The top floor of the Lévitan building. 2. Austerlitz camp, established in the warehouse of the *Magasins généraux*, 3 Quai de la Gare, near Gare d'Austerlitz. 3. Bassano camp, avenue d'Iéna, in the mansion – a *hôtel particulier* – of the Cahen d'Anvers family.

• A few Jewish properties in other cities were also looted and directed to those camps.

• The prisoners, sorted, cleaned, repaired, packed everything, from the largest cabinet to teaspoons, jewels, clothes and linen.

ii. Other Jewish stores
• **Les Galeries Barbès**, boulevard Magenta, a department store where Parisians could buy just about everything, were Aryanized.

J. Hardware stores
• A hardware store was a fascinating place. Items in powder form, granules or paste were sold in bulk out of large bins. For liquids such as bleach, customers brought their own bottles to be refilled.

• The merchant served the customers. Self-serve did not exist.

• Examples of what the hardware store sold included:

- Cocking supplies such as pots and pans, utensils, soaps, including fine soaps and laundry soap, which was a black sticky paste with a strong odor.

- Everything for the repairman – tools and supplies for plumbing, electricity and cooking gas.

- Oil lamps, carbide lamps, flashlights and the oil, carbide and batteries for them.

- Laundry items, such as boilers, basins and scrub boards.

- Scales, weights, and so on...

K. Laundry. Cleanliness

• There were no laundry facilities in apartment buildings. There were, however, local laundries which were mechanized and offered complete services to wash, press, starch garments and linen, as well as dry-cleaning.

• In high-income areas, a laundry worker would collect and deliver the client's laundry. Elsewhere, people took their dirty items to the laundry themselves.

• The hand steam iron was not available at this time in France. If needed, people used flat irons with a wet cotton cloth or sad irons.

• There were no electric irons. Flat irons were heated on the stove.

i. Commercial laundries

• Large setup employing a number of workers. Commercial laundries had large tubs to boil items and electrical washing machines. They had steam-presses to iron house linen and garments.

• Delicate items were ironed by hand.

• Items were ironed while damp. Woolen garments were ironed with a wet cloth on top.

• There were no electric dryers. Laundries had a stove to heat a special room equipped with fans.

ii. Small laundries

199

• Artisanal setup, run by a family. There were many local small laundries. They had a mechanical washing machine – but the operator had to turn a handle.

• Household linen was first boiled in a big tub and washed by hand.

• There were no electric dryers. Laundries had a drying room to hang linens and garments and a stove to maintain a high temperature. Laundry took a few hours to dry.

• Starching and ironing were done by hand.

iii. Dry-cleaning

• By 1942, it was difficult to obtain perchlorethylene (perc) – also known by the names trichloroethylene and tetrachloroethene – the solvent used in dry cleaning.

iv. Rural areas

• Rural people hand washed using a large tub boiler at home.

• Public washing place (*lavoir*) – a covered space often by a river or in a village square.

• In fine weather, laundry was hung on a line to dry. In inclement weather, only small items were washed and hung to dry in a laundry room or close to the stove.

v. Urban areas

• Small items were hand washed at home to save money.

• Everything that could not be done at home was sent to a commercial laundry.

L. Librairie-Papeterie – bookstore, stationer
i. Art supplies and paper-based items.

• The farther away from the heart of Paris, the bigger their inventory.

• They sold artist's materials, books, newspapers, notepads. Office supplies, writing paper, typewriter paper, files, blotting paper, pens and pencils. School supplies, including school textbooks.

Note that a *librairie* is a bookstore, plural *librairies*. English library is *bibliothèque*.

ii. Banned books

• August 27 to 31 – The Geheime Feldpolizei and Schutzpolizei, helped by French gendarmes, seized over 700,000 books on the Bernhardt List and destroyed them.

• The Bernhardt List, sent by Berlin in August 1940, was replaced by the Otto List in September of the same year. The Otto List was established by Otto Abetz, with the help of Parisian publishers. It was amended twice, in June and July 1941.

• The État Français adopted the Otto List by the end of 1940.

• When the Otto list was handed to the bookstores, many owners hid their banned books.

iii. Black market for books

• Booksellers, librarians and publishers hid banned books, which they sold under the counter.

• Some publishers succeeded in obtaining paper and clandestinely published banned authors.

iv American library-bookstore – Shakespeare & Company

• America being a non-combatant country, Sylvia Beach was allowed to keep operating her bookstore. She displayed a red label that certified it belonged to neutral America.

• It both sold and lent out books.

• In December 1941, the store closed for a couple of months. Under the patronage of the Countess of Chambrun whose connections with Pierre Laval and Philippe Pétain gave it a special status and it reopened. Proscribed books were not available, at least not overtly.

• Its clientele was varied and included educated Germans.

v. German Bookstore
• Located in boulevard Saint-Michel, on the Rive Gauche, anybody could go in and buy a book. German titles but also some French and translations.
• A homemade bomb was thrown at it, November 21, 1941.
• Novembre 26, 1941– a bomb attack against the German military library located at the corner of rue de Rivoli and rue Cambon.

vi. Newspapers
• Bookstores sold a selection of authorized French and German newspapers, as well as some magazines.
• Newstands, run by war widows and veterans, in Paris and major towns sold all the permitted newspapers and magazines.
• People bought official newspapers to learn where foodstuffs were available, any changes in the restrictions and when to renew ration tickets.

M. Libraries
• Elementary and secondary schools had no libraries. Students and teachers brought books to the class to be shared.
• Literature (See 8. Art, Entertainment, Literature).

i. Public libraries
• A municipal library could usually be found in each *Arrondissement*.
• Public libraries were run by municipal councils.
• Most municipalities had a library.
• Libraries in both zones were subject to the Bernhardt and Otto Lists.
• Libraries were caught short in August when gendarmes and the SD came to seize banned books. They were better

prepared in September and October. Books were hidden. Some loyal users took books home to hide.

ii. Promoted books
• The Matthias List contained books to promote pro-Nazi ideology and collaboration.

N. Lumber stores
i. Urban areas
• Lumber stores sold construction and carpentry timber. Nails, paint and other needed items were sold by the hardware store.
• Wood for fuel.

ii. Rural areas
• People went to the local sawmill for their needs.

O. Parks and recreation
• On June 11, 1936, all classes of workers were granted paid holidays. During July and August, city- and town-dwellers vacationed at the seaside or the mountains.
• During the Occupation, in the non-occupied zone, people were still free to go to the seaside and be on the beach, except in the forbidden Atlantic zone. Although when soldiers used the beach, local people could join them.

i. Affluent classes.
• On Sundays throughout the year, families went to parks, swimming pools or skating rinks.
• Children were not allowed to play in the street.
• They played *marelle* – similar to hopscotch – a game played by chalking an airplane shape on the cement yard.
• They played skipping ropes.
• They had a variety of balls, small and big.
• They went to a fashionable square where they played with a *cerceau* – a hoop.

• Boys took a toy sailboat to the pond in the Tuileries gardens. Girls walked their dolls in a doll carriage.

• Boys played marbles. Marbles came in different sizes and colors and had names such as *Sibérie* (the rarest), *Condor, Cyclone, Galaxie and Agate* (named after the gem stone but not made from the gemstone agate).

(a) Most marbles were made of colored glass .

(b) More fortunate boys had one or two marbles made of the precious gem, agate.

(c) Cheaper marbles were made of glazed terra-cotta. They detoriated over time.

• Children had no shortage of toys – but always gender defined.

• Children went to swimming pools and learned to swim.

• Many families from Paris and major towns owned a country house which was often the family's ancestral home .

• If it had not been requisitioned, those families who could obtain an Ausweis spent the summer vacation there.

• Children were free to explore their rural surroundings.

• 1943-44 – due to bombing and sabotage, traveling became unsafe and few went on holiday.

ii. Less affluent classes

• Sundays throughout the year, families went to parks or took the train to a place of recreation close by, such as the Marne river bank.

• Picnics – no tables were provided. People spread a cloth on the grass and laid out the food. Most food was eaten with fingers.

• Children played unrestrained either in the street, at a park or at home.

• They played *marelle* – similar to hopscotch – a game played by chalking an airplane shape on the cement yard or the sidewalk.

• They played skipping ropes.

- The more fortunate had a couple of balls they threw against the wall and caught while doing acrobatics.
- Although toys were gender defined, girls played ball with the boys and boys played *marelle*.
- Boys played marbles, but girls did not and were not invited. In less affluent classes, it was extremely rare that a boy would have agate marbles, but some glass marbles imitated agate.

(a) Marbles were made of colored glass.

(b) The most fortunate had one or two marbles of imitation agate.

(c) Cheaper marbles were made of glazed terra-cotta. They detoriated in time.

- Children went to swimming pools. The fee was minimal. They did not have swimming lessons and learned by themselves.
- Some had country relatives, where they went to spend the summer, that is if they were able to obtain the necessary Ausweis.

iii. Poorer classes
- Workers traditionally spent Sundays picnicking on the bank of a river, swimming, fishing, boating and games.
- During the Occupation, the Sunday pleasure trip was replaced by foraging excursions in the countryside.
- When a man owned a bicycle, he would use it rather than take the train.

P. Utilities
i. Electricity
- 1940-41 – supplies were more or less sufficient, until September 1, 1941, when restrictions were imposed. Electricity was only provided during certain hours.
- 1942-43 – additional restrictions in winter. Cuts due to bombing. Stores were not allowed to illuminate a window display.

• In areas where there was street lighting, it was dimmed and switched off after curfew.   •
1943-1944 – usage was strictly regulated to as little as one hour a day. Factories serving the occupiers were not subject to restrictions, nor were garrisons and places taken over by the occupiers.

(a) Electric heaters were no longer allowed. Industries were also limited in usage.

(b) Street lighting was terminated. Intense bombing and infrastructure and power station sabotage meant that electricity was more often cut for longer periods of time.

(c) In the city's poorer districts, tenants often only had a two-ring burner and suffered most.

ii. Gas
• There was no natural gas. Gas was manufactured from coal.
• There was a network of underground cooking gas pipes in Paris and large cities.
• Propane or butane was also available and was used in rural areas where there was no piped cooking gas.

iii. Water
• In nineteenth century Paris, Baron Haussman installed a large network of drinking water pipes and sewers. Most other cities and towns adopted his system.
• In Paris and some towns, artesian wells provided a constant supply of water.
• A gravity-fed system was often used in hilly and mountainous regions to distribute water to buildings and dwellings.
• Where a gravity system was not feasible, electric pumps were used.
• Rural areas, farms, had wells. In some villages, a fountain in the middle of the square was the only source of water.

• Filtration through layers of sand was commonly used for drinking water in the cities. No filtration in rural areas.

iv. Waste water
• Cities had an extensive network of sewers to handle wastewater, which was usually emptied directly into rivers, though solid matter was partially held back by grates, cleaned from time to time
• Rural buildings and dwellings had septic tanks. The clean liquid effluent drained directly into fields as fertilizer.

iv. Public baths
• Most apartments lacked bathrooms. Public baths were available in every town.

v. Public washrooms
• In Paris and major towns, urinals were found in cafés, hotels, restaurants, which men were free to use.
• Women were hesitant to use those facilities and limited themselves to department store toilets.
• Town halls also permitted people to use the toilets, though they might be questioned.
• *Vespasiennes* – a typical Parisian public urinal in the street, for men only. Resistants often met in a Vespasienne to exchange brief verbal messages.

Q. Système D
• System D stands for *système débrouillardise*, which means possessing ingenuity and resourcefulness and the ability to negotiate official red tape – namely knowing survival tricks.
• The French, particularly Parisians and those in big cities, became masters of the art of the System D.

O. Transportation (See 45. Transport)
• People needed to travel for work, pleasure or in the constant search of food.

207

• The bicycle replaced the automobile.
• The vélo-taxi – a sort of bicycle rickshaw – replaced regular taxis.
• People made an intensive use of trains and the Métro where they existed, plus bus, trolleybus and streetcars.
• Commercial trucks and people allowed a car, such as doctors, converted the gasoline engine to gazogène.

P. Zazous
• A fashion restricted to young people as a form of rebellion, dressing differently, hair styles going against the norm, which was short hair for girls and dancing to jazz music.

18. Demarcation line. Escape lines

• In all wars, prisoners have attempted to escape and return home.

• In all wars, soldiers have tried to avoid being taken prisoner.

A. Demarcation line until November 11, 1942

i. A border

• As a result of the June 1940 armistice – signed June 22 with the Germans, June 24 with the Italians and in force on June 25 – France was divided into two zones. The north was occupied by the Wehrmacht and the south became a free, non-occupied zone – the *État Français* – under the government of Marshal Pétain in the town of Vichy.

• The demarcation line was 1,300 km long (746 miles) but did not follow the cease-fire line. This meant that in many cases, Wehrmacht soldiers had to leave their positions and move north of the administrative line during July 1940. Most of the Wehrmacht behaved correctly during this withdrawal, but there were plenty of incidents.

• It was a controlled border, but it was not impenetrable.

• It was marked with signs and posts painted the Nazi colors, and included barriers and sentry boxes. There were empty spaces between control points which were less heavily patrolled.

• Wehrmacht soldiers controlled the checkpoints until February 1941, when they were replaced by German border guards and Feldgendarmerie.

• Opposite each post was a French post manned by French border guards.

• An Ausweis was required to cross the line.

• In the north-east, there was one other line – the *Nordostlinie* – that closed off Alsace and Lorraine. The line continued on to integrate the departments of Nord and Pas-de-Calais under the Brussels' administration. Crossing this line was more complicated than the one from occupied to non-occupied zones. An Ausweis was required.

• Although not designated as a demarcation line, the whole coastal area from Belgium to the Spanish border was classified as a forbidden zone. Many inhabitants had left or later had been obliged to leave when they were within the construction area of the Atlantic wall, which saw construction begin in March 1942.

• Fishermen and cannery employees remained.

ii. Life on the line

• There were many disruptions in the life of the inhabitants along the border as the line was moved back and forth in places to accommodate the Germans.

• Inhabitants within 50 km (30 miles) were issued a special Ausweis and permits

• A farmer or an employee might need to work in one zone, while having his home in the other. It facilitated the smuggling of letters and documents. It led to some daring schemes to help downed airmen.

• Many inhabitants lived in fear that at any moment the Germans could invade the free zone, which they did on November 11, 1942.

iii. Ausweis

• No one was issued a permanent Auweis, except Pierre Laval.

• The application for an Ausweis was made at the local Kommandantur. The applicant had to state a valid reason to cross the line. An Ausweis was difficult to obtain.

iv. Forgeries

• Before people could escape, they needed official papers, which gave rise to artist-forgers.

• Forging documents was an art. If it wasn't done well, the recipients were caught at the first checkpoint. The best forgers had a background in art or calligraphy and were able to copy handwriting and imitate signatures with convincing accuracy.

• Later, as the authorities became aware of forged Ausweis, they changed the design frequently.

• Each set of papers was custom-made to fit the individual person who only had to produce a photo.

• Some photographers joined the résistance. There were also resistants who were amateur photographers and were skilled at developing and altering photos.

v. Official rubber stamps
• Each town and village had its own rubber stamps, kept at the town hall.

• Forgers became skilled at reproducing these stamps.

• Stamps were sometimes stolen, or borrowed with employee complicity, a plaster cast made and the stamp returned to the town hall. From the plaster cast, a mold was made, usually in lead as lead is relatively easy to melt.

vi. Registers
• In France lacked a central registry of people's birth.

• Each municipality kept a registry of births, marriage and deaths.

• Some registries dated back a hundred years. If a municipality's town hall was bombed and the registries destroyed, there was no other means to trace people. This was exploited by resistants and the forgers.

• Frequently, with the complicity of a mayor or civil servant, papers were issued in the name of a dead person.

vii. Printing paper
• Special paper was used for identity cards, ration tickets and the Ausweis. Such paper was frequently stolen from a town hall.

• A young man would also have to have his military book showing where and when he was demobilized.

• Paper rationed for printers was unavailable to ordinary people.

C. Demarcation line after November 11, 1942

• The inhabitants close to the line had to have a special Ausweis to move across the line. Situations arose where a house was on one side of the line and a school on the other.

• Even after the Germans invaded the non-occupied zone, and the line removed in March 1943, it remained a source of stress, with the authorities threatening to re-instate it.

• Some 109,000 Jews fled the occupied zone for the non-occupied zone, crossing the demarcation line clandestinely.

• Some village inhabitants near the line had never met a Jewish person.

• After November 1942, many Jews attempted to flee into the zone occupied by the Italians.

B. Escape lines until November 11, 1942
i. The beginnings

• June 1940, English soldiers and downed airmen who were unable to be rescued under Operation Dynamo, were hidden by inhabitants of the Pas-de-Calais. Immediately after the June armistice, people saw the need to get them to safety in the non-occupied zone. The first escape line was created.

• Norbert Fillerin, from the Pas-de-Calais, was probably the first one to lead two British airmen to Marseille after the armistice. Soon, others join him. This developing escape line became known as the Pat O'Leary Line.

• Initially, escape lines were spontaneous offers of help but soon became highly organized and provided clothing, extra foodstuffs and false papers.

• In 1940, the word *résistance* was not in use, though that is what the people were doing.

• Besides Allied soldiers and airmen, there were people who had reasons to fear for their lives and needed to relocate to the non-occupied zone.

• Long chains of helpers were organized, made up of people who understood the risks. If caught by the occupying forces, it was death for men and deportation for women, when it was not death on the spot.

• The 1,300 km (746 mile) demarcation line was a major obstacle, aggravated by the fact the occupiers occasionally altered the line to suit their purposes.

• The escape lines were an initiative of French citizens. Soon it became apparent that more was needed, especially after the first SOE agents were infiltrated into France. The SOE organized and financed new escape lines.

• The contribution by women to the success of the escape lines has been largely unrecognized. Besides providing for the escapees, they also guided them, sometimes traveling as pretend couples. The risks they took carried the same penalties as the men if discovered.

ii. Guides and safe houses

• Guides were people who knew the local area and could guide an evader from one safe house to another.

• Ways to lead an evader included commercial vehicles, often equipped with a gazogène (45. See Transports), as they were the only ones that could circulate legally with an Ausweis. Other means were bicycles or simply following or pretending to follow the guide on foot. At times, escapees used available public transport. Very often, a measure of subterfuge was needed to avoid detection.

• Near the demarcation line, those guides who specialized in crossing the line became known as *passeurs*.

• Safe houses were not necessarily a house. They could be an empty apartment in a town, a barn, an abandoned farm, a brothel or a barge. Many were ordinary people's homes.

• Security was strictly enforced, with passwords and codes used when knocking on doors.

• Besides downed airmen needing repatriation, others, such as French and foreign Jews, résistants on the run, Alsatian deserters, needed to cross from the occupied to the free zone.

213

iii. *Passeurs*

• With the occupation of the northern zone came the flight of foreign refugees, resistants, escaped prisoners and persecuted people, along with downed airmen.

• Those who made their own way to the demarcation line needed help to evade the border posts.

• Passeurs were men and women who did not accept the Occupation.

• Passeurs from the occupied zone into the non-occupied zone were in the majority, but there were also some passeurs who operated in the other direction. Those mostly helped agents who had landed in the non-occupied zone and needed to work in the occupied zone and resistant leaders who needed to coordinate and meet with leaders of réseaux in the occupied zone.

• SOE, resistance movements and resistance réseaux secured the services of passeurs.

(a) Altruism

• Passeurs came into existence as early as July 1940, with the flux of people wanting to leave the occupied zone.

• Local people with intimate knowledge of the area led people to the safety in the non-occupied zone. They did not accept money. It was simply the right thing to do. They shared food and lodgings.

(b) Collaborator passeurs

• Local collaborators posed as passeurs and aimed at groups, the larger the better, usually Jews, collected money and led them straight into a pre-arranged ambush.

(c) For profit

• Other locals viewed helping people as a business with a high level of risks and charged a fee. They also had to feed – buying on the black market – and shelter the escaping people, sometimes for more than a day, and felt justified in getting paid.

(d) Swindlers

• Another category of local was attracted by money and did not care about helping people. After pocketing the money, every scenario was possible, from denouncement to the Feldgendarmerie to abandoning the people, even killing them.

19. Deportations
A. Jews
• Pétain had negotiated that no French Jews would be deported. Laval and René Bousquet did not comply.

• 75,721 Jews, of whom 11,400 were children – one quarter of France's Jewish population and only one third being French citizens – were deported. An estimated 3,000 to 4,000 returned.

• Some 3,000 were executed as hostages or died in internment camps. (Serge Klarsfeld sources).

• August 15, 1944 – *Le convoi de Pantin* or The Last Transport. All Paris prisons were emptied. 2,600 men and 400 women in total. Railroad workers, Red Cross, and even the Pétain government fleeing to Germany interceded to have the transport stopped and prisoners liberated. The SS commander refused to listen. The rail workers tried without much success to prevent the train from leaving.

• August 17, 1944 – *Transport N. 79* departed from Royallieu, near Compiègne with 482. prisoners. Despite all efforts, diplomatic and resistant, the transport arrived in Buchenwald on August 22. A number of personalities of the Résistance, were on board. 130 of them did not return.

• March 27, 1942 – first train to Auschwitz.

• May 30, 1944 – the seventy-fifth and final train to Auschwitz left Drancy.

• August 9, 1944 – laws relative to the status of Jews were declared null and void by the Provisional Government in Algiers.

• Some small villages near the line had never before met a Jewish person but willingly helped.

• After November 1942, Jews attempted to flee to the Italian-occupied zone.

i. Census of the Jewish population
• October 20, 1940 – deadline for the census in the occupied zone. 149, 734 Jews registered.

• July 1. 1941 – deadline for the census in the non-occupied zone. 140,000 Jews registered.

ii. Detention camps (See 45. Transports)
(a) Under French administration.
• Fifty detention camps in both the occupied and non-occupied zones for Jews and other persons deemed undesirable. A short list – Beaune-la-Rolande. Drancy. Gurs. Camp des Milles. Montreuil-Bellay (Roma). Les Tourelles. Pithiviers. Rivesaltes. Fort de Romainville. Saliers (Roma). Le Vernet. Schirmeck in Alsace in the restricted zone but not annexed and therefore not under MBF control.
(b) Under direct German administration.
• Natzweiler-Struthof, in annexed Alsace.
(c) Under Wehrmacht's control.
• *Ilag* (*Internierunslager*) camps established to hold Allied civilians – Besançon, in Doubs department, Frontstalag 142, in the Vauban barracks, Saint-Denis, near Paris, Vittel Frontstalag 121, in Vosges department.
(d) Labor camps for Jews were created by the Pétain's government in Algeria and Morocco.

iii. Protests against deportations
• The first public protests came from the clergy – Monseigneur Saliège, in Toulouse. Protests were taken to the Vatican with no response or condemnation from the Vatican.
• Protests remained silent, but thousands of anonymous people helped save most of the 225,000 Jews who escaped deportation.

iv. Raids – *Rafles*
• May 14, 1941 – first raid, known as *rafle du billet vert* – Green notice raid – on foreign Jews.
• July 16-17, 1942 – *rafle du Vel d'Hiv*.
• August 20 to 23, 1942 – a massive raid in Paris rounded up 4,232 Jews, 1,602 of whom were French.

• January 22 to 29, 1943 – 4,000 Jews arrested in Marseille in Operation Tiger.
• February 22, 1943 – the Italian occupiers refused to deport Jews from their zone.
• April 6, 1944 – raid on children's home in Izieu.

v. **Restrictive measures**
• September 27, 1940 – MBF forbade the return of Jews into the occupied zone.
• June 7, 1942 – wearing the yellow star was made compulsory in the occupied zone.
• Pétain government objected. Jews in the non-occupied zone were not made to wear the yellow star, even after it was occupied November 11, 1942.
• In the Paris métro, Jews were relegated to the last car of a train.

B. Roma, Sinti
• 1935 in Germany, Roma – Zigeuner – were rounded up and interned in camps.
i. Status of Roma in France
• According to the law of 1889 , Roma in France had French citizenship.
• A ruling in 1912 categorized the Roma into three groups, each with identity papers. 1. Traveling merchants. 2. Operators of fairground attractions. 3. Jobless nomads.
• There were many myths about the Roma and rural people in particular wanted to see them settled in one place. Dislike and indifference were widespread.
• In their travels, they had to register with the town hall or the gendarmerie on arrival in a community and sign out when leaving.
• At the same time, they received a medical exam.
• By the law of 1912, the vehicles carried a registration plate with specific identifying numbers. Descriptions of the

vehicles were kept at the prefecture of the department in which they spent the most time, usually the winter.

ii. April 6, 1940 – travel restrictions
• The French administration forbade all the Roma and Sinti – some 3,000 to 6,000 (figures vary) residing in France at the start of the war from traveling in order not to interfere with troop movements.
• Police kept them under surveillance in their encampments. There were fears they could become spies.

iii. June 1940 – MBF internment demands
• After the occupation, the occupying authorities demanded that the Roma be interned in camps.
• Roma remained under the French administration.
• Camps were set up in the occupied zone as well as the non-occupied zone.
• Internment camps in the non-occupied zone included Salters, Lannemezan.
• There were twenty-four internment camps in the occupied zone, the main ones being Moisdon-la-Rivière (Loire Inférieure) and Montreuil-Bellay (Maine et Loire).

iv. Lack of resources
• Because Roma did not mix with the population and were self-sufficient, the French population was generally mistrusting and indifferent to them. Interning them was viewed as merely preventing them from traveling and people did not offer help like they did with camps holding Jews.
• People living near Roma internment camps were upset by the Roma's presence and wanted them gone, not for altruistic reasons, but because of the long-held belief that the Roma were thieves and kidnapped children.
• Used to freedom, the Roma did not take well to internment and men constantly escaped. Except on rare occasions, they received no help.

• In Montreuil-Bellay, a priest named Abbé Jollec offered them help and support. Many priests and nuns tried to alleviate the conditions of the camps, which helped Roma to remain in the camps and thus avoid arrest.

v. Systematic deportation in other occupied countries
• Roma in France being interned and under French jurisdiction, were not deported, except those in the Nord and Pas-de-Calais departments which were under the jurisdiction of Brussels.
• The Nazi authorities systematically arrested and deported people without fixed address throughout the occupied countries.
• According to records of the Roma that were deported to Auschwitz-Birkenau from Belgium, 145 were French. Other than this, no other Roma were deported from France.
• Total of Roma murdered in Nazi concentration camps amounted to 600,000.

C. 1945 and the return of the deported
i. Statistics
• Approximately 166,000 persons were deported from France.
• About 1,800,000 POWs were repatriated.
• 48,000 civilians were repatriated.
• 90,000 French citizens died in concentration camps.
• From March 1942, 76,000 Jews, among them 11,000 children, were deported. Only 3,000 survived.
• Local newspapers published the names of the returning deported, who were able to give the names of their compatriots who would not be returning.
• People read every line of these bulletins searching for family and friends.

ii. Reaction of the population

• Reactions varied from being horrified at the state of the returnees to mistrust that those emaciated people in striped pajamas were French citizens. After four years of occupation, some people did not want to hear more horror stories. Others bent backward to welcome the deported.

• Many people, especially in rural areas, did not understand what the deported were telling them.

TRIVIA: A twenty-year-old resistance woman returned to her village from Ravensbrück concentration camp. A neighbor complained, how they had suffered during the Occupation, being so hungry despite having a garden. "The lack of meat and cheese was terrible." The Ravensbrück survivor, reduced to a mere 35 kg (77 lbs) just smiled.

• *The Comité des œuvres sociales de la Résistance* (SOCOR) – an underground organization helping the families of resistants, went public and provided help, and funding, to returning deportees, including children of foreigners who had fought for France.

D. Trains

• The MBF authorities warned the rail employees – the *cheminots* – of the Société Nationale des Chemins de fer Français(SNCF) that they would incur the death penalty if they refused to obey orders.

i. Trains

• *Les trains de la honte* – The trains of shame.

CAUTION: This widely known expression was coined only *after* the war to designate those artists, performers and writers who eagerly accepted the Reich's offer to visit Germany.

• During the Occupation, people looked the other way. People who did not live close to a station or a major rail line were not necessarily aware of the trains. For many, it was only rumor, even within the supporters of the résistance.

• Of the 410,000 SNCF employees, 40,000 became registered resistants.

• Engineers of trains deporting Jews only drove the locomotives as far as the German border.

• A car, or sometimes two with a machine gun on the roof, of German Order Police men was attached to each train carrying deportees.

• As in every other walk of French life, there were collaborators and those who sat on the fence, those who did not want to take part in the résistance but did nothing to stop it, and then there were the resistants.

ii. Railroad résistance (See 46. Transports, 43. Résistance)

(a) Avoid your having French characters talk about the deportation trains, unless they are directly involved as rail employees. Even these knew only that the trains were going to Germany. When the trains were about to depart, the station was cleared of French rail employees, thereby increasing the mystery surrounding the deportation trains.

• The majority of people knew nothing about those strange trains unless they lived near a transit station or were somehow involved as when delivering food to the SS train car before the deported were brought in. If they talked to family or closed friend, they all agreed to keep quiet. Toward the end of the war, when the deported were allowed out, a rare occurrence, in the middle of the countryside, some nearby villagers brought water and food, only to be chased away by the guards, though a few let the villagers put the food on the ground and the deported grab it.

• When résistance groups near those transports learned about such trains, they informed London, but were otherwise powerless. Sabotaging such a train would only have resulted in more victims, as the lives of those inside could not be guaranteed. As well, if a train was successfully stopped, it would have been impossible to hide the hundreds of people inside. On occasion, *cheminots* succeeded in unlocking some cars. Imprisoned résistants escaped, but few Jews dared to.

Often, a man had family on board and refused to abandon them. All this under the threat of the machine guns on the roof of the guards' car.

• When the deported threw notes through the holes of the cattle car, cheminots went to pick them up and forwarded them to the address.

(b) The railroad resistants passed information about train timetables, troop movements and what trains transported.

• They switched labels, and switching points, sending trains elsewhere.

• The resistant cells had to choose between derailing or blowing up a train.

• In preparation for D-Day, resistant cells and rail workers sabotaged every line.

• Locomotive engineers blew the whistle when they approached certain pre-arranged locations to signal to escapees on board to jump off. Sometimes a door had been unlocked, other times the windows had been loosened.

(c) The hidden face of the rail workers.

• Despite the Allied landings in Normandy on June 6, 1944, and the increased résistance pressure on German troops, the Nazis still issued deportation orders and the État Français complied.

• Germany needed still more forced labor from the camps to continue its war effort and did not want that labor to be liberated and take up arms against them.

• Violent reproaches have been made against the *cheminots* for having driven the deportation trains. Such criticism is unjustified. The history of the period reveals that thousands of rail workers, through often small acts of resistance, disrupted the functioning of the railroad and saved lives. It must be remembered that there were two guards in the locomotive cabin with a gun trained on the locomotive engineers. As many as 2,500 rail workers were shot or killed by the occupiers.

(d) Deportation trains in the summer of 1944, some tragically known as *trains fantômes* – ghost trains – or *trains de la mort* – death trains.

• July 3, 1944 – *Le train fantôme*. A train departed Toulouse with a total of 800 men, women and youths on board, whom the Germans had taken from prisons and camps. They were resistants, two-thirds of them Spanish who had fled Spain at the end of the civil war. The *cheminots* did everything they could to halt the train – shunting it onto dead-end tracks and sidings, inventing mechanical problems, deliberately stopping to take on water at a tower that was damaged, so the locomotive had to be filled by hand using buckets. Anything and everything to delay the train, all this with guns trained on them. On the way, they facilitated the escape of 200 prisoners. The RAF, unaware that this train was a deportation train, because every fourth car carried anti-aircraft guns, bombed the train. The SS commander refused to listen to pleas to stop the transport. Fifty-four days later, it arrived at the border and three days later at Dachau.

• July 31, 1944 – Transport No. 77. 1,309 prisoners from Drancy camp, 324 children among them, left Bobigny station for Auschwitz. It was the last transport of Jews from Drancy. Only 251 survived. The train was driven by German engineers.

• August 11, 1944 – *Le convoi de Lyon-Perrache*. A transport train left Lyon. Despite all the *cheminots*' efforts, the train arrived on the border with Germany on August 22.

• August 15, 1944 – *Le convoi de Pantin* or the Last Transport. Paris' prisons were completely emptied of 2,600 men and 400 women. Rail workers, Red Cross, and even members of Pétain's government fleeing to Germany interceded to stop the transport and free the prisoners. The SS commander refused to listen. The *cheminots* tried without success to prevent the train from departing.

• August 17, 1944 – Transport N. 79 departed from Royallieu, near Compiègne, with 482 prisoners on board. Despite diplomatic and resistants' efforts, the transport arrived at Buchenwald on August 22. A number of notables of the Résistance were on board and 130 of them did not come back.

• August 22, 1944 – *Le convoi de Clermont-Ferrand*. The cheminots were unable to prevent a transport train from leaving Clermont-Ferrand. It reached Germany on August 30. The bishop of Clermont-Ferrand and the Prince Bourbon de Parme were among the prisoners, but the Germans, always respectful of titles and rank, put them in a Third-Class compartment rather than the cattle car.

• September 1, 1944 – *Le convoi de Loos*. Just before the arrival of Allied troops, 870 prisoners were boarded onto the train, all of them were to be freed the next day. Despite cheminots' efforts, the transport arrived at Sachsenhausen. 570 prisoners did not come back.

20. Diplomatic relations

NOTE: The United Nations Organization only came into being on October 24, 1945. Prior to that date, there was the largely ineffective body known as the League of Nations, founded January 10, 1920 in the hope of preserving world peace. It formed the basis of the United Nations.

• Switzerland maintained an embassy in Paris until June 25, 1940, when it was moved to Vichy. A consulate replaced it in Paris. The legation had to deal with the MBF. For matters requiring Berlin's approval, diplomats negotiated with the German embassy in Bern, Switzerland.

• The United States maintained an embassy in Vichy until December 1941.

• From December 1941 to March 1943, a U.S. consulate remained in Vichy.

• May 23, 1943 – the MBF orders all consulates to leave occupied France.

• Switzerland alone obtained permission to keep a consulate with reduced staff in Vichy.

21. Economy. Industries. Factories. Banks
A. Aeronautics industry
• Under the terms of the June 1940 armistice, France could not build any aircraft. A joint Franco-German aerospace program of aircraft construction was permitted. It avoided the removal of entire factories to Germany, along with advanced technical plans, which were immediately hidden.

• With the law of August 16, 1940, Pétain's government created *Comités d'organisation* – organizational committees – to satisfy MBF production and delivery quotas.

• The French aeronautics industry had been nationalized before the war. After the armistice, this meant that factories in the non-occupied zone worked for the German-controlled factories in the occupied zone.

• After November 1942, the MBF took direct control of all the factories.

• The best-known figure is factory owner Marcel Bloch, who refused to work for the Germans. He was deported to Buchenwald, survived, returned and took the name of Marcel Dassault in 1946.

• Engineers secretly designed prototypes.

NOTE: The Communist Party, taking their orders from Moscow, carried out sabotage in the aviation factories that manufactured planes and parts for Finland, a country at war with the USSR, following its invasion of Finland – the Winter War. The MBF did not pursue the communists, because of the Non-Aggression Pact, but the État Français did. When Nazi Germany invaded the Soviet Union on June 21-22, 1941, the communists turned against the Germans. Hunted by the État Français and the occupiers, the communists paid a heavy price for their guerrilla actions.

• The MBF ordered that all airfields in France be plowed up, except for those they were using.

B. Agriculture
i. Changes

• 400,000 agricultural workers had been made prisoners of war, plus the deaths on the battlefield.

• The Ministry of Agriculture and Supply was a complex organization supervised by the MBF.

• Before regulations could be put in place, the Wehrmacht requisitioned crops and other foodstuffs.

• All aspects of agriculture and the distribution and supply of its output were identified and regulated down to the number of eggs a farmer produced.

• To some degree, these measures helped protect the agricultural sector, while enabling producers to fudge figures. The lack of fertilizer, lack of manpower and the inability to run machines because of a shortage of fuel were cited as reasons for lower numbers than anticipated by the government.

• Farmers were an independent group who hated regulations and quotas. Without being organized, they entered en masse an era of passive résistance and cheating the authorities. That dislike of authorities, particularly "foreign authorities," made them receptive to hiding people on the run, selling food they hid from the authorities, providing food and assistance to their local maquis and at times actively participating in sabotage.

• Agriculture still operated along traditional lines and relied on horses and oxen. Since most of these were requisitioned by the Germans, production by hand could not achieve the required output.

• There was a small increase in meat production, hampered by the fact not enough hay could be stored for the winter.

• Pétain's government created an agricultural *police*, to counter agricultural fraud brought about by hunger and or political resistance.

• Prices were fixed, thus limiting competition and favoring the black market.

• Farmers, who had always been regarded as lower on the socio-economic status, became important. With the rise of the black market and the influx of urbanites desperate for food, they were the ones who dictated prices and conditions.

ii. Quotas
• The occupiers' demands had to be met. Each municipality was responsible for enforcing quotas determined by the MBF in consultation with the prefecture.
• Trade between the non-occupied zone and the occupied zone was restricted and required special permits.

iii. Political resistance (See 42. Résistance)
• Farmers resisted the occupiers by hiding produce and livestock numbers. When discovered, it meant death or the burning down of the farm.
• Farmers who chose resistance provided resistants with food and concealment. By the end of 1942, this aid was extended to *les réfractaires* – young men avoiding forced labor and the nascent maquis.

C. Automobile industry
• Upon the declaration of war, the automobile industry was transformed into military vehicle production, with only a few cars still manufactured for the use of administration officials.
• After June 25, 1940, German technicians were immediately put in place in every automobile factory.
• Some companies worked outright for the MBF, while others navigated the dangerous path of sabotage.
NOTE: The origin of the word *sabotage* comes from *sabot* – a wooden clog – a derisive name given to sloppy, inefficient and clumsy workers who caused problems in the manufacture of goods in the eighteenth century. Following social unrest, rather than strike – an action with grievous consequences – workers undertook to spoil the production in a way that it could not be traced. The practice soon became known as *sabotage*.
i. Interior resistance
(a)**The Citroën** factories located in the Paris suburbs of Suresnes and Boulogne-Billancourt sabotaged the trucks they were forced to produce by moving the *Full* line lower on the

engine dipstick. As a result, the motor ran on insufficient lubricating oil and soon seized up.

(b) The Michelin tire factory in Clermont-Ferrand (they also produced maps and guides).

• Sabotage of tires for the eastern front that disintegrated in the cold, stocks that caught fire, etc.

• The local resistant cell did not have the means to disable the factory. The Allies wanted a total stop on the production of tires for enemy use and planned a bombing raid for March 16, 1944.

• The local resistants made sure there were no workers in the factory on that date.

• Michelin secretly agreed with the Allied Staff to have the latest – 1939 – version of the comprehensive *Guide Michelin de France* printed in Washington and distribute a copy to every officer taking part in the D-Day invasion.

• Every Michelin family member was involved in the resistance, hiding resistants, organizing the local maquis, stealing confidential documents from BMW or joining the Free French Forces in London.

(c) Peugeot automobile factory in Sochaux, in north-east France.

• Involved in the résistance and helped sabotage their production.

• Family members, managerial staff and workers were all involved in the resistance.

• The Germans wanted Peugeot to manufacture the V1 Rocket fuselage. Engineer Cortelessi was summoned to Germany to arrange for the cooperation of the French company. He succeeded in copying the plans which were then sent to London. The RAF was thus able to bomb the factory where the first V1s were being made.

(d) Marcel Bloch aircraft company, in the Paris suburb of Suresnes.

• *La Société anonyme des avions Marcel Bloch* refused to collaborate. Pétain's government arrested him and the Germans deported him to Buchenwald in 1944. He survived and on his return took the name Marcel Dassault in 1946. The Germans were particularly interested in the company's technology. The staff accepted German congratulations while knowing that the parts and planes they provided would malfunction in good time.

ii. Role of the résistance

• Résistance groups communicated many of the targets to Allied forces. They were concerned about the impact of the air raids on civilians and offered to sabotage important factories to avoid bombing raids.

• The Berliet truck factory in Lyon refused to allow sabotage. As a result, the factory was bombed.

• The Dunlop tire factory in Montluçon in Allier, central France, refused to allow sabotage and as a result, it was bombed.

• The Gnôme et Rhône factory in the Gennevilliers suburb in the north-west of Paris manufactured airplane engines, as well as motorcycles and bicycles, refused to sabotage and was bombed.

• The Michelin Tire factory in Clermont-Ferrand in central France). Although supporting the résistance they did not allow sabotage of the factory itself, as the résistance cell did not have sufficient means to carry out significant damage. This would have brought severe repercussions on the population. They did carry out limited sabotage of the tires produced. The factory was bombed repeatedly by the RAF and the USAF.

• Renault factories in the Boulogne-Billancourt suburb of Paris. Louis Renault, a pro-Nazi who visited Hitler, refused to sabotage. Consequently, the factory was bombed repeatedly by the RAF and the USAF.

• March 1, 1942 – the RAF dropped leaflets warning of the raids on the Renault factories on March 3. April 4, 1943 – USAF daylight bombing raid. September 1943 RAF night bombing raid.

• Villacoublay aviation factories in north-central France were taken over by the Luftwaffe and were heavily bombed from 1943 onward.

D. Banks
• Unlike at the start of WWI, when people withdrew their assets all at once, the banks in 1939 were better prepared. They had transferred assets well away from the country's northern borders.
• On arrival in Paris, the MBF requisitioned the British-owned Lloyds Bank.

i. Status of banks
• Banks were either national, private or cooperative banks.

ii. Major banks
• Banque de France, Crédit Lyonnais – a cooperative, Comptoir National d'Escompte, Société Générale, Paribas, Rothschild, La Banque d'Indochine, Banque de l'Union Parisienne – BUP.
• In addition, there were regional banks, commercial banks and savings banks.
• Rural areas were mostly served by cooperatives – Mutuelle Agricole, Caisse nationale de Crédit Agricole.
• The PTT – postal service – also served as a savings bank.
• Some banks were nationalized after the liberation.
• Banks in the French colonies were not subject to German demands and were either Pétainist or Gaullist.

iii. Collaborationist banks
• The private Worms & Cie bank was pro-Nazi.
• Crédit Commercial de France, Banque Nationale pour le Commerce et l'Industrie, La Société Générale collaborated in order to stay in business.
• Paribas appeared to collaborate but its director Émile Moreau was ousted for refusing to comply with the MBF

demands. André Debray, a senior executive, succeeded in financing the Résistance. He took part in the liberation of Paris.

iv. Currency
• For control purposes, the MBF needed to impose a monetary system on its occupied countries. Due to France's different status, it did not work that way.

(a) As soon as the armistice was signed, the Banque de France and all other banks returned to Paris, and other towns, to prevent the Germans from using the obsidional currency, namely emergency money used in time of war or invasion, that they had prepared. Hence, the French currency prevailed for the rest of the war alongside Reichmarks used by the occupying troops. The exchange rate was twenty francs to one mark. Storekeepers could refuse to take Reichsmarks in payment, but few did, since the Germans would simply have walked out with the goods. They then exchanged the Reichmarks at the bank at face value.

(b) The Reichsmark was imposed on the annexed territory of Alsace-Lorraine.

(c) Occupying troops could obtain Reichmarks from the *Reichskreditkassen* – the financial institution responsible for supplying currency in occupied territories.

(d) Some enterprises working for the Germans had access to the Reichskreditkassen.

(e) The État Français being sovereign, at least in theory, maintained the French franc. Since the administration of the occupied zone was, again theoretically, under Pétain's control, the franc was used along with the Reichsmark, albeit with a different value – twenty francs to one Reichsmark.

(f) June 27, 1940. The Reichskreditkassen issued a 50 Reichspfnig coin and paper 1, 2, 5, 20 and 50 Reichsmarks. After July 1940, zinc coins of 1, 2, 5 and 10 Reichspfenig were also in circulation.

(g) Marshal Pétain had replaced the French Republic's motto *Liberté Égalité Fraternité* on currency with *Travail Famille Patrie*. He issued one-cent coins of nickel with a hole in the middle as well as 2, 5, 10, 50 cents and 1 and 2 franc coins. Paper money consisted of 100 and 200 franc bills.

• The 5-cent coin was nicknamed a *sou*. 50 cents was nicknamed (10) *dix-sous*. 1 franc was nicknamed (20) *vingt-sous* and 5 francs was nicknamed (100) *cent-sous* – a play on pronunciation *sans-sou*, meaning without money. Older people often referred to the 5-franc coin as a *thune* – ancient money.

(h) **After the 1944 liberation**, the new French government immediately changed the motto on all the currency back to *Liberté Egalité Fraternité.*

v. Gold reserves

• A country's economic viability was measured by the weight of gold bullion held by its banks. In a normal economy, investments are linked to the gold reserve. Germany had little gold. To finance its re-armament and obtain foreign currency to import needed raw materials, it devised a system of selling, lending and borrowing on paper investment.

• The national *Banque de France* had large gold reserves and also stored some of Belgium's gold. As the Wehrmacht advanced, the gold reserves were evacuated to different places, namely Canada, U.S.A. and to French overseas territories.

vi. Transporting gold reserves

• France did not have enough ships to carry the gold bullion and asked the United States to help. Because the U.S. was neutral and, according to international laws, was not allowed to transport a belligerent country's gold. France therefore 'sold' the gold to the U.S. who then transported it. On its arrival at the U.S. Federal Reserve Bank, France bought it back.

vii. Résistance and the banks

• Banks did not actively take part in the Résistance.

• Only some individuals within a bank skillfully filtered funds to the Résistance and hid some Jewish assets, such as at the Crédit Lyonnais and Banque d'Indochine.

• Banks did take part in the process of Aryanization of businesses. If they had not, the German banks would have taken them over and records might have been destroyed.

• They did business with German banks. They were tightly controlled, both by the État français and German inspectors.

• The Banque de l'Union Parisienne, Crédit Lyonnais, Comptoir National d'Escompte, constantly tried to keep their dealings with the occupiers to the minimum.

(a) Their executives did not engage socially with the occupiers. Seven of them were arrested by the occupiers for not complying with the demands.

• For the banks to have refused cooperation would have meant a total collapse of the economy and the nazification of the country. Banks navigated a narrow path. Even some of the top officials who were extreme right wing, as with the Worms & Cie bank, wanted the country to remain independent and French. The war was not over and they looked to the future, while being complicit with the Nazis.

(b) The Banque d'Indochine avoided participation in the worst aspects of collaboration thanks to its chief executive, Jean Laurent, who was an active resistant.

(c) The Rothschild Bank was Aryanized. Guy de Rothschild, whose parents were dispossessed, was left as a manager, as the German authorities had little desire to enter the banking business. He governed the bank from the non-occupied zone until 1942, when he and his wife left for the United States.

viii. American obsidional currency

NOTE: Obsidional currency was otherwise known as *siege money* or *emergency money,* as throughout history it was currency issued by a town or region under enemy attack to enable the local economy to continue functioning. Obsidional coins were usually of base metal and poorly struck.

235

• Prior to the 1944 Allied landings, the U.S. administration had planned to establish a government of occupation in liberated France, as well as in other previously occupied countries or a defeated country. To that end, they printed currency which they gave to American troops to use after they landed in Normandy. By that time, France was claiming a provisional government, headed by General de Gaulle in Algiers, and on August 26, 1944, the provisional government transferred itself to Paris and became the official French government. The Americans were thwarted in their attempt to install a government of occupation under their control and their obsidional currency never came into use.

• The French considered that an American government of occupation would simply mean exchanging one occupier for another. This is one of the reasons why de Gaulle received massive support from the French population, much to the dismay of President Roosevelt, who, unlike his generals, had not understood the French résistance and de Gaulle's prestige.

• French people in the liberated towns of Normandy refused to accept the strange money the American troops tried to use before being officially told they could not use it.

E. Bicycle industry

• *Bicyclette* is the official French term. *Vélo* is the familiar form.

• There were eleven millions of bicycles in France during the Occupation.

• The bicycle with two equal wheels and pedals dates from the mid-nineteenth century.

• The bicycle had a chain but no gear mechanism – not until the 1950s.

• When it became impossible to repair the tires and the inner tube, various materials were used to fill the rubber tire or patch it. Finally, wooden wheels made their appearance.

• People who needed to go places during the Occupation often used Fidèle Outterick's ingenious invention, the vélo-taxi –

a bicycle-taxi similar to a bicycle rickshaw found in many Asian countries.

i. Brands
• Peugeot commercialized its first bicycles in 1886.
• Michelin invented the inner tube in 1891.
• The major brands were Peugeot, Manufrance and Mercier.

ii. Customers
(a) **The Wehrmacht** equipped soldiers with bicycles when invading Norway and Poland.
(b) **Other armies** had bicycle-mounted troops – such as Japan to invade Malaya.
• The United States for easy transport within a base.
• Britain produced the BSA folding bicycle for the use of paratroops.

iii. Bicycles coveted items
• Thefts of bicycles were common. In some instances, the theft was catastrophic.
• Chaining the bicycle to a lamp standard did not prevent thieves from dismantling parts.
• Owners of bicycles went to great lengths to keep them secure.

iv. General usage
• Housewives who had a bicycle used it to get to a store that had an arrival of foodstuffs not requiring ration tickets.
• Working men to go to work.
• Men to go to the country to buy food or to forage.

v. Résistance and the bicycle
• Being silent, safe and easy to maneuver, the bicycle was favored by resistance fighters.
• Bicycle usage was highly regulated. A bicycle carried a

yellow identification plate and in Paris an additional license plate. In addition, there were tax duties to pay and a mandatory safety certification.

• Résistants were always on the lookout for a German female postal official, who might leave the bicycle unattended while making a delivery. An agile resistant would jump on the bicycle and ride away to a workshop where it would be quickly repainted and fitted with the necessary plates.

• A bicycle with its hollow frame was an ideal hiding place for messages.

• A resistant courier would often ride as much as one hundred kilometers a day.

• A bicycle is also useful to transport anything – clandestine papers, tracts to be thrown to a people lining up, arms and food.

TRIVIA: A true story. A pursued resistant saw an unguarded bicycle, jumped on it and escaped. Sometime later, he wrote to the bicycle's owner, apologized and included some money as compensation.

vi. Repairs

• Tires wore out and soon after the Occupation began, it was impossible to buy new tires. Even the occupiers had difficulties obtaining rubber tires.

• Inner tubes were unavailable and after being repaired with various ingenious materials, there came a point when they were unusable. Tires were filled with any number of possible and ingenuous materials, including in wine country, corks threaded on a string inside the tire.

F. Chain of supply

• Until November 1942, the État Français received reduced quantities of products from North Africa and imported a limited quantity from Spain.

i. Food distribution

• Merchandise was directed to the distribution centers in cities and towns. A small quantity of products, such as cooking oil, was allowed into the occupied zone – until November 1942. It arrived at Les Halles (See 17. Daily Life).

• Although the demarcation line was abolished in March 1943, there were still checkpoints. The goods still did not circulate easily and were often seized by the German guards.

• Résistance cells and local maquis also helped themselves to food products, but made a point of paying for them or giving IOUs, which were honored after the Liberation.

ii. Import/Export

• Due to the British naval blockade, almost no foodstuffs arrived from the French colonies. A limited quantity of products made its way across the Mediterranean from North Africa.

• Exports of wine and cheese were directed to Germany.

G. Cinema

• In the name of cooperation, the Propaganda Abteilung organized cultural trips to Germany for producers and actors.

i. MBF and Pétain's control

• Cinema production fell under MBF-Pétain control. The main studios were in Paris and Nice. The French-made films made no reference to the war or the daily difficulties of the occupation. German films carried underlying propaganda and anti-Semitic themes.

• Nazi Germany financed a new French cinematographic company called the Continental.

• Besides forbidding the screening of Anglo-American films, the occupiers confiscated the blank film and all the materials necessary to produce a film in order to facilitate the production of an allowed French film.

• Many of the workers were either prisoners or taken by the STO.

• Some producers and actors, such as Julien Duvivier, Jean Renoir, Jean Gabin and Louis Jouvet left the occupied zone.

ii. Producers
• Producers were mandated to make entertaining films to make the population forget about the difficulties of the Occupation.
• Censors ensured that the films upheld moral standards and respected traditional values.
• 1942 is the year when French films began to disseminate subliminal messages of dissidence, hope and liberty right under the noses of the occupiers and the État Français' censors. Pétain's censors, who had not experienced occupation, failed to understand the subtleties. Only after the war were the messages pointed out.
• 1942 – *Félicie Nanteuil, Le voile bleu, Les visiteurs du soir, Le corbeau*
• 1943 – *Donne-moi tes yeux, Adieu Léonard*
• 1944 – *La fiancée des ténèbres*

iii. Wartime production
(a) **1940**, French-made films.
• *Paradis Perdu* (Abel Gance), *L'Empreinte de Dieu* (Léonide Moguy) – shown in 1941 without the producer's name, as he'd fled to the United States. *La fille du puisatier* (Marcel Pagnol) – the first film made in the free Zone after the Armistice.
(b) **1940**, German-made films.
• *Le Juif Süss* (Veit Harlan).
(c) **1941** French-made films.
• *Premier rendez-vous* (Henri Decoin), *Le dernier des six* (George Lacombe), *Romance de Paris* (Georges Lacombe).
(d) **1941** German-made films.
• *J'accuse* (Wolfang Liebeneiner).
(e) **1942** French-made films.

• *Nous, les gosses* (Louis Daquin) – children's film encouraged by Pétain, *Le Mariage de Chiffon* (Claude Autant-Lara), *Les visiteurs du soir* (Marcel Carné), *Le corbeau* (Henri-George Clouzot).

(f) 1942 German-made films.

• *Sang Viennois* (Will Forst), *La Ville Dorée* (Veit Harlan).

(g) 1943 French-made films.

• *Goupi Mains rouges* (Jacques Becker), *Marie Martine* (Albert Valenin).

(h) 1943 German-made films.

• *Titanic* (Herbert Selpin & Werner Klinger), *Lumière dans la nuit* (Helmut Käutner).

(i) 1944 French-made films (shown after Liberation).

• *Premier de cordée* (Louis Daquin), *La fiancée des ténèbres* (S. de Poligny).

H. Electricity
i. Hydro-electricity

• After WWI, France realized the importance of producing as much electricity as possible by means other than coal. Coal was mined in northern France in the regions that were occupied by the Germans.

• In 1940, the majority of electricity came from hydro energy. Some of the hydro-electricity was connected to coal-fueled electrical stations in order to economize the coal immediately after the declaration of war.

ii. Destruction

• The destruction of electricity power stations during the invasion was repaired by the winter of 1940.

• Railroad destruction prevented the supply of coal to thermal power stations. The preventive measures adopted in 1939 ensured an adequate supply of electricity throughout the winter 1940-1941.

iii. MBF demands
• March-April 1941 – the MBF ordered the reduction of coal deliveries to the French thermal power stations. Supplies were diverted to Germany.

• Pétain's government issued a decree on August 12, 1941, which remained in force until 1944, under which electricity was rationed according to needs. First, the needs of the occupiers, second industries and workshops that served the occupiers, third retail stores, lastly households.

iv. Shortages
• By the end of 1943, due to sabotage and bombing destruction, electricity became severely rationed. It was prioritized for the occupiers, though they too had to face cuts.

I. Gasoline, domestic gas and oil industry
i. Gasoline was produced from coal and from oil.

• During the Occupation, only the occupiers could buy gasoline. Special permit holders of cars were allowed a few coupons of gasoline.

• Gazogène power, invented in the nineteenth century and used during WWI and the interwar years, re-emerged. A vehicle equipped with such a device burned coal or charcoal to produce a gas that powered the engine. The gazogène engine was not highly efficient.

ii. Domestic gas
• Natural gas was not available. Gas was manufactured locally in gasworks, where it was extracted from coal in ovens and stored in large gasometers before being delivered to consumers via a network of pipes. The spent coal, now called coke, could still be burned in stoves.

• There was a network of domestic gas pipes in Paris and large cities, with gasworks on the outskirts. These were targets for the RAF and USAF, with intensified bombing in 1944.

• Propane was also available. It was used in rural areas where there was no piped gas. It was manufactured in gasworks.

(a) By the end of 1941, domestic gas rationing was imposed due to insufficient coal supply.

(b) 1942 – domestic gas was limited to a couple of hours a day.

(c) 1943 – limited to one hour a day.

(d) 1944 – there were days with no supply. By the end of 1944, with most of the occupiers gone, engineers were able to ensure a limited but regular supply of gas.

iii. Oil and refineries

• There was no oil extracted in France. All was imported. The *Compagnie française des pétroles* (CFP) had holdings in the Middle-East.

• The enemy succeeded in capturing some of the oil reserves that the French had not been able to set fire to.

• There were seven refineries close to ports which were requisitioned by the MBF. The most important were in Normandy, near Bordeaux and near Marseille. They were bombed and some of the reserves were set on fire to prevent their use by the Germans.

• The oil industry was in the hands of the *Compagnie française des pétroles*.

• The managerial staff practiced passive resistance and slowed down the production to almost nothing. Crude oil imports were not getting through. Some refineries completely shut down.

• Résistance groups also carried out sabotage.

• Some of the directors were deported.

• Britain listed the CFP as *Trading with the Enemy*.

• The MBF demanded that the refinery in Normandy be retooled to manufacture aviation fuel. Since crude oil was unavailable, the refinery staff used the bottom sludge in the reservoirs to manufacture industrial grease, and the occupiers transferred various components to Germany.

• Before the war, an underwater pipeline had been built between France and Britain. It supplied the Allied armies during the Normandy campaign, but it was not sufficient and the USAF brought additional fuel by air.

J. Mining
• Miners were not mobilized upon the declaration of war.
• Although falling under German control, miners were not subjected to forced labor. They were a vocal group. Although the repression was severe, they went on strike several times.

i. Location of coal reserves
• The major coal production was centered in the Nord, Pas de Calais and Lorraine. Secondary mines, though still important, were located in the Auvergne, Provence and Dauphiné provinces.
• In the occupied zone, the occupiers had priority on output. To meet the needs of the population, some small, uneconomical mines that had previously closed reopened in the non-occupied zone.
• Wehrmacht soldiers and SD police supervised mine crews above ground.

ii. Resistance and strikes
• The occupiers had hoped to increase the coal production by 35%. It fell by 30%.
• The workday was already eight hours long. The occupiers wanted to lengthen it by one-half hour. They wanted to abolish the daily two fifteen-minute breaks.
• More than 1000,000 miners, including some 40,000 Polish miners, went on strike from May 27 to June 10, 1941. It began with 1,500 women – wives and daughters of miners – marching to the main offices of the Pas-de-Calais mine.
(a) **Grievances** included the lengthening of the workday, the need for better rations – mining was classed as *hard work* – the removal of restrictions on soap, and pay increases.

(b) Women defied the occupiers' ban on street gatherings by marching and forming picket lines to discourage miners from entering the mines which were protected by the soldiers and French gendarmes. When the SD police tried to arrest a woman, the others surged around to protect her, thwarting the authorities.

(c) The strike spread to the factory manufacturing tools for the mines and to the textile mills.

(d) The occupiers accused the mayors of the regional communities of negligence and they were ordered to call an end to the strike. The mayors delayed orders or outright refused. Some were imprisoned.

• General Hermann Niehoff ordered mass arrests, special courts, seizure of T.S.F. radios to create a psychological effect on the population. The move failed.

• The occupiers arrested 500 men and deported 270 to Sachsenhausen – half did not come back – and executed 220 men.

• The mine management collaborated with the occupiers by supplying lists of personnel.

(e) Work resumed on June 10, 1941, with the evening shift. The miners had obtained all their grievance demands.

• Miners continued their slowed work, thus sabotaging production.

• In the summer of 1942, the occupiers brought in Ukrainian and Soviet prisoners to work in the French mines. They quickly adopted the French miners' tactics.

(f) At the liberation, the managers were dealt with as collaborators, but most escaped real punishment as it was imperative to restart coal production for the sake of the economy.

K. Publishing and printing
• The declaration of war led to the censorship of any publication viewed as detrimental to the nation. First to be banned was the communist newspaper, *L'Humanité*, due to the

Germano-Soviet non-aggression pact. The USSR was considered a hostile country.

• Publishers avoided printing any material with a pacifist or fascist slant.

• Everything changed with the Occupation, when the occupier imposed censorship and propaganda, helped by collaborating publishers.

• The German embassy and the German Institute, with their extensive knowledge of French life, established good relationships with publishers and authors and organized cultural trips to Germany.

i. Aryanized publisher
• Ferenczi and Calman-Lévy.

ii. Banned books
• August 27 to 31, 1940 – the Geheime Feldpolizei, helped by French gendarmes, seized over 700,000 books on the Bernhardt List and had them destroyed, among them works deemed to be anti-Nazi and also anti-Stalin, due to the Germano-Soviet non-aggression pact, as well as books by Jewish writers.

• The Bernhardt List, issued by Berlin in August 1940, was replaced by the Otto List in September of the same year. The Otto List was established by Otto Abetz and aided by Parisian publishers. It was revised twice, in June and July 1941.

• When the Otto list was handed out, many booksellers hid their banned books. In July 1941, the Otto list prohibited the re-printing of books by British authors published after 1870, both in English and in translation. Later, in May 1943, the same list banned all Russian books, both in Russian and in translation.

• Pétain's government adopted the Otto List by the end of 1940.

• The eclectic nature of the Otto list, coupled with its numerous errors, hindered its full implementation.

• Pétain wanted publishing to reflect the esthetic and moral ideals of his Révolution Nationale.

iii. Black market in books
- Booksellers and librarians hid banned books which they sold under the counter.
- Publishers who had hidden banned books also sold them under the counter.
- Some publishers succeeded in obtaining paper to publish banned authors clandestinely.

iv. Collaborating publishers
- René Julliard, Robert Denoël, Bernard Grasset.
- Hachette obtained the monopoly of paper distribution.

v. Résistance in publishing
- Éditions de Minuit published *Le Silence de la mer* (1942) by Jean Bruller, under the pseudonym Vercors.
(a) Ambiguity
- Éditions Gallimard – chief editor Jean Paulhan was replaced by Drieu de la Rochelle, a virulent pro-Nazi. Paulhan and Gaston Gallimard were resistants linked to the Musée de l'Homme network.

vi. School books
- 1941 and 1943 – two lists of approved school textbooks imposed revisions to show a better relationship with Germany and eliminate any Jewish authors.

vii. Supplies of paper and ink
- Paper was requisitioned by the occupiers. Publishers and printers had to submit a monthly account of their paper use.

L. Réquisition of non-ferrous metals
- The État Français asked citizens to bring non-ferrous items voluntarily, especially copper, to their town halls. They would receive money or wine or fuel in exchange. They were also

promised that the copper would be used to make copper sulfate and cupreous salts for the use in vineyards.

• The majority of people were sceptical and the drive met with very little success.

• October 11, 1941 – the État Français passed a law ordering that public statues and other art objects in non-ferrous metal must be delivered to smelting works either in France or Germany. Municipalities had to decide which objects ought to be saved as part of the cultural heritage.

• February 9, 1943 – imposition of a tax on non-ferrous metal. Each household was obliged to hand over a certain quantity of non-ferrous metal objects or pay an equivalent sum of money.

M. Textile industry
i. Locations

• The textile industry – spinning and weaving – was centered in northern France around Lille, Roubaix, Tourcoing. During the war, some factories were destroyed in bombing raids.

• Some small factories, especially in Alsace, were relocated farther south.

(a) **In the non-occupied zone**, the Occupation gave a boost to smaller enterprises that had closed or stagnated under competition from larger factories in the north.

(b) **Calais** was a center for lace making but was heavily bombed first by the Luftwaffe and then by the Allies.

(c) **Lyon** and area was the center for silk making, though during the Great Depression the demand for silk declined and the demand for synthetic rayon increased. Lyon became a hub for résistance.

• Lyon had been declared an open city and only the Bron airfield was bombed. Its factories were spared. Unable to import raw silk and not having sufficient silk-worm production, the industry had to experiment with making synthetic materials.

ii. Production

• The MBF authorities managed the textile factories for the needs of the Reich.

• Despite the incentives from Nazi Textistell and the improvements made to factories, production fell. Machines were unsuited to synthetic material production and had to be adapted. The French management made no real effort under the direction of the Texilstelle.

• Only the factories using wool were able to continue, although below the prewar output.

• As the Liberation progressed, factories were damaged in the fighting.

• After the German forces left, the Americans seized all the stocks. This action created bitterness in the population "No better than the Boches!".

iii. Restrictions

• Imported raw materials such as hemp and flax became unavailable and synthetic substitutes were used.

• 1941-1942 – coal supplies diminished, creating endless delays.

• By March 1943, Nazi Germany was in need of labor and began to transfer workers to Germany or to the building of the Atlantic wall.

• April 1944 – The Daimler motor company demanded the use of the factories and swiftly moved the textile machines out. Many were damaged beyond repair.

22. Education. Children and adolescents

• Whenever you need to portray children or teachers in your novel, be aware that online information almost never applies to prewar, the Occupation or the decades immediately after the end of the war. In fact, the school system in France did not change until 1968.

A. Administration of the school system

i. The education system was centralized in Paris but during the Occupation was administered from Vichy by the État Français.

• The État Français ministry of education doubted the loyalty of teachers, viewing them as the bastion of the previous republic and its liberal ideas, and suspected them of being freemasons, Jews, communists or free-thinkers. This did not fit the doctrine of Pétain's État Français and many teachers were purged.

• In addition to the loss of teachers through dismissal, together with those who had been conscripted and made prisoners of war, women teachers reaching age fifty were also let go as an excuse to relieve unemployment. Yet there were not enough graduates, especially men, to fill the vacancies. In October 1941, the government was forced to hire teachers still in training, many of them young women.

• The majority of children went to public schols, i.e state schools for both elementary and secondary schooling.

• There were some Catholic church schools, especially at the elementary level. There were also some Jesuit schools at the secondary level.

• The Occupation caused widespread disruption of education, through the displacement of children, the requisition of school buildings for troops' housing and the relocation of students to other schools.

ii. Forms of address

• School pupils at all levels were addressed by teachers using the title *Mademoiselle* or *Monsieur*, followed by the student's last name.

• Students addressed their teachers as either *Mademoiselle*, *Madame* or *Monsieur* – never followed by a last name.

• The *Maître* or *Maîtresse* forms of address (as shown incorrectly in the French Village series) were only used by preschool children.

• A constant feature of French education was homework, from the lowest grade to the highest.

iii. The school year

• The elementary school year ran from October 1 to July 13, the day before the national Bastille Day holiday – the July 14 Bastille Day celebrations were suppressed by the occupiers.

• Elementary pupils had classes every day except Thursday, with classes all day on Saturday.

• The school year for secondary level lycées and colleges ran from October 15 to June 30. They had Thursday classes – usually morning only – and classes on Saturday morning.

• The two exams during the secondary cycle were the *Brevet*, which students sat in their fourth year of secondary schooling and the *Baccalauréat* three years plus another year for the second part, equivalent to a first year university in either the maths/sciences or philosophy/the humanities.

• Secondary level exams were held from the beginning to mid-June, after which those students were free.

• A secondary school teacher was referred to as *professeur* – both male and female – and addressed solely as *Madame*, *Mademoiselle* or *Monsieur*.

B. Elementary schooling.
i. School age

• Schooling was compulsory for children from seven to fourteen years of age.

• Those students who had not entered a lycée or a collège took a *Certificat d'études*, school-leaving examination.

ii. Teachers
• Elementary school teachers were referred to as *instituteur* if male or *institutrice* if female. Forms of address were the same as for the secondary level – *Madame, Mademoiselle* or *Monsieur*.
• While some schools, especially rural schools, used a bell to summon students, most schools employed supervisors or proctors who used a whistle.

iii. Boys and girls attended separate schools. There was no co-education in this period.
• Students of schools out of commission from bombing or requisitioning had to be accommodated in the nearest school. Otherwise, schools remained separated by gender throughout the war.
• If one school housed both boys and girls, the building was divided, with boys on one side and girls on the other, each with their own entrance and schoolyard. In larger urban areas, schools for boys and girls were in separate buildings.
• In normal times, boys were taught by male teachers and girls by female teachers.
• Due to many male teachers having being made POWs after being conscripted, having fled to England or dismissed by the Pétain's government, women teachers were frequently called upon to teach in boy's schools.
• Male teachers in cities were often brought out of retirement to fill vacancies.

iv. Rural schools.
• Villages with less than 500 inhabitants were allowed to have a one-room school with mixed classes of both boys and girls.

• In areas that were bombing targets, schools were often closed for days at a time.

• Sometimes, when the boy's school had been requisitioned by the occupying troops, boys were relocated to the girls' school.

v. Student Health.

• During the Occupation, elementary school children were supposed to receive a daily vitamin-fortified cookie. In reality, it was hit and miss whether its supplies reached the school.

• Although schools were allowed extra food to supply the *cantine*, there still was not enough to feed children adequately.

• There was an upsurge of tuberculosis among children.

vi. School children.

• A boy in elementary school was *un écolier*, a girl *une écolière*. At the secondary level, a male student was *un étudiant*, a female *une étudiante*.

• There were no school buses. Children walked or bicycled to school.

• Morning classes ran from 9 am to 12 noon.

• Children living close to the school went home for lunch, others went to the *cantine*, which was not a cafeteria. Students sat and were served a fixed meal – no choice of menu.

• In most jurisdictions, classes resumed at 1:30 pm and ran to 4:30 pm, with optional study time to do homework until 6:00 pm if there was no one at home. Workplaces ended work at 6:00 pm.

C. Secondary Education
• There were three different streams at the secondary level.
i. Lycée
• Admission was by a somewhat competitive examination. A lycée targeted academically inclined students, aged eleven to twelve and taught, in addition to mainstream subjects, Latin and Ancient Greek as well as two modern languages.

253

• The final exam was the *Baccalauréat*, which was administered in two parts over a two-year period. The first part would be equivalent to a North American twelfth grade. The second part was equivalent to first year university. In the second part, students specialized in either philosophy/humanities or mathematics/sciences.

• Teachers, both male and female, were referred to as *professeur*.

• Professeurs were addressed as Madame, Monsieur, Mademoiselle.

ii. Collèges
• A *college* was identical to a lycée in targeting academically inclined students but the curriculum did not include Latin or Ancient Greek, though two modern languages were offered. Admission was by competitive exam at age eleven or twelve.

• Colleges grew out of nineteenth century girls' establishments which concentrated on domestic arts and just a little schooling, in the belief that girls were not considered capable of learning complex subjects like literature and mathematics, this despite an ever-growing number of protests from high-achieving women. Attitudes changed after WWI.

iii. Technical and commercial colleges. Admission by non-competitive exam. The focus was on vocational trades, practical arts, commerce and hotel work.

• Teachers were referred to as *professors*, both males and females, and called Madame, Monsieur, Mademoiselle.

iv. Students of lycées, collèges and Technical collèges
• They were referred to as *étudiant*, *étudiante* and attended only the required classes in their chosen subject, each class being one to two hours long. Students were free the rest of the time.

• A study room was available for when there was only a short time between classes.

• Classes ran from Monday to Saturday.

• On Thursdays and Saturdays, classes were morning only.

• Classes started at 8 or 8:30 am. The last class ended at 5:30 pm. On some days, a student might have one class at 10:00 am and be finished for the day at 12:00 pm.

• Students ate in the *cantine* – a served meal, with no choice of menu – from 12:30 to 13:30 pm (France used the twenty-four-hour-clock).

D. Grandes Écoles
• Elite institutions of higher (than university) education.

• They instilled the ethos of public service.

i. Admission
• By selective competition.

• To prepare for the entrance examination – at the same time as preparing for the Baccalauréat – students studied for two years in a program called *khâgne*.

ii. Goals
• The formation of leaders, cadres for commerce and industry.

• Formation of leaders in government and public office.

iii. List of the principal Grandes Écoles, with areas of specialty
• La Sorbonne, Paris – literature, sciences, medicine.

• École normale supérieure, Paris – education, sciences, literature.

• Polytechnique, aka l'X, Paris – engineering.

• Sciences politiques, aka Sciences Po – political and social sciences, law.

• École des Mines et Ponts et Chaussées, Paris – engineering, physics, geology, metallurgy.

• École des Hautes études de commerce, Paris – business administration, hotel management.

• École militaire, Paris – military officers.

• École Saint-Cyr, Saint-Germain-en-Laye – military officers.
• École de Saumur, Saumur – military officers (formerly cavalry officers).
• École vétérinaire de Maison-Alfort – animal sciences and animal husbandry.

E. Teacher Training
i. For the elementary level
• Candidates for the teaching profession trained at the École normale – equivalent to university teacher training – after successfully passing the competitive entrance exam.
• There were Écoles normales in every prefecture.
• The Pétain government closed all the Écoles normales.
• Formation of *instituteurs* and *institutrices* – elementary school teachers – dropped below the demand. The État Français had not prepared alternative training for teachers.

ii. For the secondary level
• Candidates for the teaching profession at the secondary level trained at the École Normale Supérieure – part of the *Grandes Écoles*.
• They had to pass the *Aggrégation* –higher-level exam (they had to have obtained a Master before they could apply for the agregation) to become professors in a lycée or collège.
• Further studies were needed to obtain a doctorate to teach at the university level.

F. University
• Admission solely from colleges and lycées after successfully obtaining a *baccalauréat*.
TRIVIA: there is a bronze statue opposite the entrance of the Sorbonne of Michel de Montaigne, the sixteenth century Renaissance philosopher who greatly influenced education. Students would touch Montaigne's foot before exams for good luck.

G. Home influence
i. High-income households
• Opinions about the war and the occupation were usually shared with adolescent children.

ii. Medium-income households
• Among the middle class, adults tried to shield the children from the war and its consequences. If the children asked questions, they would be told to concentrate on their homework and leave politics to the adults. Nonetheless, young children and adolescents eavesdropped and not surprisingly, there were many resistants among them.

iii. Low-income households
• Adults in working-class districts discussed the war and the occupation in front of the children, but the children were not included and would be rebuked if they tried to express an opinion.

• Except in more enlightened families, the prevailing ethos was still very much that children should be seen and not heard.
• The FTP recruited among young people and it was not unusual to have a father in one cell and his sixteen-year-old son in another.

H. Making choices
i. Fascism
• Among the collaborating segment of the population, adolescents frequently espoused the family's beliefs, and since it meant material comfort, they did not look for another point of view and found the propaganda attractive.

ii. Resistance
• Adolescents, in general, were looking for a purpose in life. They were idealist and ready for adventure. During the

occupation, young people matured quickly and fitted easily into the résistance movements.

• Even children as young as ten were receptive to the notion of résistance. Parents who were themselves involved in résistance work felt the need to shield them and, when possible, sent the children to stay with family in the countryside. It did not stop astute children from getting involved. The occupiers failed to recognize the skill of youngsters to carry messages and perform other acts of résistance.

I. Understanding the Occupation
i. Adolescents

• For the most part, they had a realistic view of the war, despite not fully understanding their place in the world. Even those who started employment at age fourteen were dependent on their parents, lived at home, handed over their wages and submitted to paternal authority until age twenty-one – the age of majority.

• For students at a lycée, collège or university, and strongly influenced by their home environment, peer pressure played a large part in their decision-making.

• Until this period, students enjoyed little personal autonomy and had to ask permission even to go out with friends. The outbreak of war and the Occupation changed this. In many households, the absence of the father contributed to earlier youth emancipation, in some instances resulting in juvenile delinquency.

• For many adolescents, the total defeat of the French Army made them resentful towards any uniformed authority – gendarmes and police in particular.

• These young people matured quickly well beyond their chronological age.

ii. Younger children

• Children were influenced by the milieu to which they belonged and accepted what they were told.

• Children under seven years of age were shielded from the realities of the situation. If a child was scared during a bombing, adults would make up some story while cowering in an air-raid shelter.

• Young children were unble to view events in the larger context of the war. They were exposed to lies every day from schoolteachers following the Nazi-imposed curriculum. Parents would then counter these views, thus leading to more confusion.

• Sometimes, children were also sent to buy products with false ration tickets, in the belief that a storekeeper might be less suspicious of a child. If found out, the child would be thrown out of the store, whereas an adult might be arrested.

• When asked what they knew of the war, children's replies were personal, not reflecting the events themselves but their reactions to it. For instance, if asked about electricity outages, a child might reply, "I bumped my knee in the dark and it hurt." An older child might say, "I hate the dark. I have to share the candle with my brother, sister and mother."

• Allied bombings reinforced the notion of how powerless they were and how dangerous was the outside world.

J. Pétain's Chantiers de la Jeunesse
• After the June 22, 1940 Armistice, compulsory military service for young men was abolished and replaced by the Chantiers de Jeunesse, an organization that performed civilian work, such as forestry, but in a military-type setting.
• They were only in the non-occupied zone.
• The MBF forbade all youth organizations, though later relented for church organizations, in the occupied zone, such as the Scouts de France.
• Jews were forbidden to take part.
i. Reasons behind the creation of Chantiers de Jeunesse
• In June 1940, there were 100,000 young men that had just been drafted into the army. After the June armistice, they were left without a direction.

• The authorities realized they could not simply send them back home without anything to do and no work. Aged nineteen to twenty, they would normally have been performing two years of military service. Conscription gave young men from rural areas an opportunity to broaden their horizons. Normally, rural people could spend a lifetime without leaving their village.

• The mandate of the *Armée d'Armistice* did not include training new recruits.

• July 4, 1940 – Defense Minister General de La Porte du Theil was asked to deal with the problem of those youths in order to avoid delinquency.

ii. Formation

• The Chantiers duration of service was fixed at six months later extended to eight.

• General de La Porte du Theil organized 52 military style camps with a maximum of 2,000 young men per camp.

• Enrolment was compulsory.

iii. Goals

• The main goal of the general, himself a former scout leader, was to ensure the physical and moral well-being of the young men through outdoor living and other scouting-like pursuits. They undertook agricultural and forestry work or marine activities, principally fishing.

• The Jeunesse et Montagne is the name of the Chantiers in the mountainous regions of the Alps and Pyrenees, where the main activities included skiing, mountaineering and the rebuilding abandoned chalets.

• Helping alleviate unemployment was a secondary goal. At the end of their service in the Chantiers, the young men could find useful employment.

• The unspoken goal behind the Chantiers organization was to maintain and reinforce the veneration of and loyalty to Marshal Pétain and his ideals.

iv. Leadership
- The overall direction was entrusted to Général Joseph de La Porte du Theil.
- Each group was under the direction of a demobilized military officer assisted by officer cadets.
- Discipline was along military lines.
- A cadre school for training leaders was opened in the Château Bayard in Uriage, near Grenoble, Isère department.

v. Activities
- The ministry of Agriculture saw the benefit of this workforce and organized work for them.
- The ministry of Forestry followed suit.

v. Final Outcomes
- The Chantiers de Jeunesse was a de facto paramilitary organization.
- Although not trained in arms or combat, it was the nucleus of a paramilitary group.
- It formed a reservoir of young men who went on, either to join the résistance or the Milice.
- The MBF had always been cautious about the Chantiers de Jeunesse, but after invading the non-occupied zone in November 1942, they saw it as a source of labor.
- A fatal blow to the organization took place when Laval created the Service de Travail Obligatoire (STO). General de La Porte du Theil refused to call and send men to the STO. He was arrested and sent to a prison camp in Austria.
- A large number of young men took to the hills. The nascent maquis groups integrated them. The trained former members of the Chantiers de Jeunesse helped them adapt to life in encampments.
- Regional Commissaire Adolph van Hecke, took about 40,000 of the youths from the Chantiers in his jurisdiction and went to Algeria shortly before the Allied landing of November

1942. They went on to fight successfully with the Armée d'Afrique alongside the Allies.

23. État Français
• The *État Français* – the French State – was the government of the southern part of France after the country was invaded by German Forces and the 1940 Armistice imposed. It was headed by the collaborationist General Phillipe Pétain, a national hero from WWI. Theoretically, the État Français governed the whole of France, but its control of the occupied north was purely nominal.

A. Capital Vichy
• Located 50 km south of the demarcation line separating the two zones. Chosen by Marshal Pétain for the government of the *Zone Libre* – the non-occupied or free zone, nicknamed *Zone nono*. The government brought 35,000 government officials to Vichy, normally a town of 23,000 inhabitants.

• Neutral and non-belligerent countries maintained a diplomatic presence in Vichy.

• Neither the occupiers nor the French in either zone seriously considered Vichy to be the capital. In everyone's eyes, Paris remained the capital of France. The term *État Français* was relegated to administration.

B. Milice – Milizia (See 13. Collaboration)
• November 19, 1942 – the occupiers requested a police force be set up to control dissidents. Joseph Darnand created the Milice, recruiting from the SOL.

• The Milice was an army of 30,000 men – though that figure is still contested – 15,000 of them active in the hunt of résistants.

• Other units of the Milice controlled administration, police and prisons.

• The Milice was fascist, anti-communist, anti-Semitic, anti-Republic. Nominally under Pétain's prime minister, Pierre Laval, its de facto chief was Joseph Darnand.

• Joseph Darnand pledged allegiance to Hitler and was awarded the grade of Obersturmführer of the Waffen-SS.

• Pétain and Laval both fully supported the Milice.

• The Milice participated in all Wehrmacht and Waffen-SS operations against the maquis, hunted Jews, communists and Romas.

• To keep up their numbers, Darnand recruited anyone, whether young men escaping the STO or criminal prison inmates.

• The numerous extortions by the Milice coupled with racketeering, rapes, burglaries and assaults turned the fearful population against them.

• 1944 – the Milice fled to Singmarinen in Germany, where most were drafted into the *Division Charlemagne*. Darnand had to hand over control to a German officer.

C. Révolution Nationale

• Marshal Pétain blamed the French Third Republic for the military defeat and wanted to straighten out the country with his own program, the *Révolution Nationale*, based on Nazi ideology.

• To young men occupied and replaced military service, which had been abolished according to the terms of the armistice of June 1940, Pétain launched the Chantiers de la Jeunesse. Their leaders were recruited from among the *Armée d'Armistice*.

• To occupy the older war veterans, Pétain created the Légion Française des Combattants(LFC), a paramilitary wing, deployed exclusively in the non-occupied zone.

• January 1942 – Joseph Darnand created the Service d'Ordre Légionnaire(SOL), an adjunct to the LFC.

• January 20, 1943 – Joseph Darnand transformed the SOL into the Milice – *Le Franc-Garde* and pledged allegiance to Hitler.

D. Volunteer workers

• Pétain's government encouraged young workers to apply to work in Germany and commissioned propaganda posters with the promise that one POW would be liberated for every three volunteers. It was dubbed *La Relève* – the relief.

• Due to insufficient volunteers, the Reich pressured the État Français for labor. This led to the creation of the Service du travail obligatoire (STO) in January-February 1943.

24. Exodus – *l'Exode*

• An exodus is a spontaneous mass movement of a population fleeing a danger.

• Most people had not planned for it. The driving force was the escape from the danger posed by the advancing German forces by any means possible, taking only what possessions they could.

A. Departures
i. North to south

• As the Wehrmacht invaded neutral Denmark, April 9-10, 1940, people from Holland, Belgium and Luxembourg left their homes to make their way to France.

• Any semblance of order disappeared when the Luftwaffe started bombing and strafing the columns of refugees on the roads.

• At their appearance in the Nord department, people panicked and threw themselves on the road.

• People in northern France had memories of WWI and the brutal German occupation. They were fearful.

• Neither the military nor the local authorities were able to put order to the chaos.

• Early June, the French front was broken, Parisians were caught up in the panic and swelled the mass of fleeing refugees.

• There were approximately nine million refugees out of a population of some forty million on the roads of France.

ii. South to north

• After the Wehrmacht entered Paris, some refugees who were still on the road, turned round and attempted to go home, adding further confusion and chaos.

B. On the roads
i. Bombing, strafing

• The majority of people on the roads were women and children, along with elderly men.

• The Nazi authorities hoped that by attacking civilians, the government would quickly capitulate and stop fighting.

• The renewed German offensive of June 5-6 pushed even more people on the roads. One million Parisians had joined the mass of refugees heading south.

ii. Chaos
• Panic was contagious. Houses, stores and farms were abandoned. Prisoners were transported toward the south with their guards, who would have preferred to go back and make sure their families were safe.

• Some towns had no police force, mayors or administrative personnel left in place.

• The International Red Cross offered limited help, with roadside first-aid stations in major towns and took charge of lost children. They directed the refugees to lodgings, places to get water and food.

• People had in mind that if they could cross the Loire River, they would be safe. The army would hold the line.

• In Chartres, Prefect Jean Moulin tried to maintain in place the administrative and police personnel. Most left. He, personally, went out and helped refugees.

• Soldiers whose regiment had gotten dispersed were trying to rejoin any unit. Others wandered about aimlessly. Some were going south where there were defense posts.

• A few people had cars, others bicycles or a horse drawn-cart, but many had just a handcart, a baby carriage or a wheelbarrow. Others were on foot, dragging a suitcase.

• In the middle of the chaos, good samaritans organized help with food, water and sleeping accommodation in farms and villages along the way.

• Officials who remained in post attended to urgent matters, such as lost children, orphans or the wounded.

iii. People
• At the start of the war, evacuation of border areas had been ordered. During the Phoney War, many of these people had returned home. They were now evacuating again.

- Affluent families left after May 10 for their country houses.
- As the news of the Wehrmacht's advance was broadcasted, people living north of the Seine River left, especially if they had family in more southern regions.
- During the first days of June 1940, especially between June 8 and 13, 1.2 million Parisians out of a total 2.9 million inhabitants rushed to the rail stations, where the overwhelmed SNCF cobbled together trains to carry them south.
- The weather at the height of the exodus included a short heatwave, followed by thunderstorms and rain, then a second heatwave and more thunderstorms.
- On Saturday, June 8, 1940 – the temperature was 25°C (77°F) with thunderstorms
- On Sunday, June 9 – the temperature rose to 30°C (86°F) also with Thunderstorms
- On Monday, June 11 – hotter still at 31°C (88°F) thunderstorms continuing
- On Tuesday, June 12 – temperature at 26°C (78°F) more thunderstorms
- On Wednesday, June 13 – the temperature eases to 20°C (68°F)
- On Thursday, June 14 – 22°C (71°F)
- On Friday, June 15 – 29°C (84°F) with renewed thunderstorms
- At rail stations, people slept in front of the gates in order to be first through as soon as the station opened. Fistfights and other rowdyism occurred.
- The government gave no orders. They, too, were on their way south.
- June 13 – stations closed for lack of rolling stock and personnel.
- When the Wehrmacht entered Paris (declared an open city – no fighting) two-thirds (1,200,000) of the population had left.

iv. Mental state

• Fear dominated the exodus. Most people had either endured occupation in northern departments or heard horrific stories from older members of the family.

• Fleeing created an 'everyone-for-themselves' state of mind.

• Some proved to be good Samaritans, others uncaring and selfish.

v. Vehicles
• People with cars piled high with belongings and mattresses on the roof did not advance much faster than the pedestrians. They ran out of gas at some point and abandoned their vehicles on the side of the road.

• After a bombing and strafing by the Stukas, many cars were disabled.

• To add to the confusion on the main roads, some military vehicles were moving north to the front and others trying to join the defense line on the Loire River.

v. Timeline for the Blitzkrieg
• April 9, 1940 – invasion of neutral Norway and Denmark.

• May 10, 1940 – invasion of neutral Holland, Belgium and Luxembourg. France, a belligerent in the conflict, was invaded.

• May 15, 1940 – Holland surrenders.

• May 28, 1940 – Belgium also surrenders.

• June 10, 1940 – Norway surrenders.

• Evening of June 10, 1940 – German forces occupy Luxembourg.

• June 14, 1940 – German forces occupy Paris.

• June 17, 1940 – Marshal Pétain requests an armistice.

   - 12:30 pm, Marshal Pétain orders the army to lay down arms.

   - The message is immediately relayed to the Wehrmacht.

• June 18, 1940 – General de Gaulle's appeal from London.

• June 22, 1940 – France and Germany sign an armistice.

   - The fighting continues.

• June 24, 1940 – France and Italy sign an armistice.

• The armistice comes into effect June 25, 1940 at 0:35 am.

• The Wehrmacht had fought its way to the south, reaching Bordeaux, Saint-Étienne, Grenoble and Lyon – a curved line which was known as the cease-fire line, not to be confused with the demarcation line established later under the armistice conditions.

• Although the French mountain troops in the Alps –*les Chasseurs Alpins* – had won the battle against the Italians and the Italians were not on French soil – except for a small area near Menton – the disgruntled Chasseurs had to withdraw and cede territory to their adversary.

• Italians occupy a relatively small area in the Alps and Menton on the coast.

• A demilitarized zone 50 km (30 mi) wide was created from the Swiss border to the Mediterranean. It included the cities of Grenoble and Nice.

C. Return home
i. Despite the Occupation
• Despite the Occupation, most people wanted to return home once the fighting ended.

• After the armistice, the French government, in agreement with the MBF, proceeded with the repatriation of several million people into the occupied zone.

ii. German organized returns
• The Wehrmacht was tasked with helping the repatriation, which they authorized as of July 25, 1940.

• They were mandated to behave correctly and display a friendly attitude.

• The MBF assigned additional trains and controlled passengers at the demarcation line between the free and the occupied zones.

• A small fraction of the refugees had already made their own way back as soon as the armistice took effect, likely concerned about their property, coupled with a good dose of fatalism.

iii. Restricted returns
• The decree of July 23, 1940 – any person having left France to go abroad between May 10 and June 30, 1940 without a valid reason would lose French nationality and their assets confiscated.

• The MBF limited the return of certain categories of people deemed undesirable, namely communists, freemasons and Jews, plus colonial troops, mostly black.

• In the annexed territories of Alsace and Moselle, all persons with a French name or known to French sympathizers, rather than pro-Nazi, were forbidden to return.

• Roma & Sinti were nomadic and thus considered to be homeless. For them, travel to the occupied zone was forbidden.

25. Health, medications, medicine

• In the period covered by this book, antibiotics did not exist. There were sulfonamide drugs, but they are not antibiotics. Penicillin was still under development in the United States.

• Medicine was not very advanced in 1940 and medical diagnostic errors were common.

• Germany had done advanced research into the harmful effects of smoking and Hitler wanted to ban the habit. German researchers had linked smoking to lung cancer (See 39. Propaganda). Nonetheless, cigarette smoking was widespread among all combatants.

• Tuberculosis was believed to be incurable and a stay in a sanatorium was considered but a respite. The Koch bacillus had been identified, but the medical corps believed it was indestructible and death unavoidable.

• Women had babies at home, aided by a midwife or an experienced older woman neighbor if a midwife was not available. Only when the midwife diagnosed an especially difficult birthing would the patient be sent to a hospital for a cesarean section. Maternal and infant mortality was high by modern standards.

• Men were not allowed near the birthing room and generally had nothing to do with the newborn.

• After the birth, women stayed in bed for many days, weeks even.

• A woman who had several miscarriages was automatically treated for syphilis.

• Any spots on the body raised the fear of smallpox and the patient was isolated.

• Although the stethoscope had been invented, doctors still relied on placing their ear directly on the patient's chest covered by a sheet.

• The use of leeches was still current in cases of hypertension, as was blood-letting.

• In the absence of systematic vaccination, childhood diseases were often fatal.

• In France abortion was illegal. A woman who had a clandestine abortion which went wrong ended up in hospital and often died of sepsis.

A. Dentists, doctors, nurses, veterinarians

• German chemists, Alfred Einhorn and Emil Uhlfelder, in 1915, put together a local anesthetic they named Novocain.

• X-rays – invented in 1895 by the German physicist Wilhem Rötgen. In many languages, they are still called Rötgen rays.

i. Dentistry

• Dentists set up a practice in the largest front room of their house.

• Very few dentists owned an X-ray machine. By the end of the 1930s, it had been recognized that repeated use of X-Ray caused cancer in the hands of the operators.

• During the Occupation, it was almost impossible to obtain the necessary film for the X-ray machines that had not been seized by the occupiers.

• Toothpaste in tubes had been invented in the last decade of the nineteenth century.

• Toothbrushes of various sorts had been around since antiquity, the modern-style of toothbrush – natural bristles on a wooden handle – had been invented at the end of the nineteenth century. Although teeth brushing had become common, it was not universally practiced until after WWII.

B. Drugs/medicines

i. Penicillin

• There was no penicillin until 1945 when three hospitals – Claude-Bernard, Enfants Malades and the Pasteur hospital, together with the American Hospital in Paris, received a small quantity of the antibiotic from the American forces. It would not become available to family doctors until after the war, in late 1946.

ii. Iodine

• Iodine was widely available, but not necessarily present in every household, to treat wounds and to disinfect. Dark yellow in color, it stained the skin and caused stinging on open wounds.

iii. Mercurochrome
• Mercurochrome was widely used to treat minor injuries like scraped knees, cuts and similar. Bright red in color, it stained skin. Present in every household.

iv. Methylene blue
• Methylene blue was readily available to treat sore throats. Present in every household. A soft metal rod with a wad of cotton at the end was dipped into the bottle and the throat coated with the methylene substance. Unpleasant taste.

v. Morphine
• Morphine was available to pharmacists and doctors.

vi. Sulfonamides
• Sulfa powder and tablets were available on prescription.
• It was used to treat infections and deep wounds.

vii.Other medications
• Other medications, such as aspirin and laxative tablets, were readily available and present in every household, at least early in the war. By 1943, common remedies had disappeared from the pharmacies, obliging people to rely on the black market.

C. Home remedies
i. Medicine cabinet
• In many household medicine cabinets, there would be an assortment of medicinal herbs, such as a licorice twig – given to children to relieve constipation – camomile, lime-blossom, mint

tisanes, and other local plants, all with various levels of effectiveness.

• Aspirin and laxative tablets – laxative chocolate had not been invented.

• Mercurochrome, iodine, methylene blue.

• Hydrogen peroxide, rubbing alcohol.

ii. Cupping glass

• Cupping glasses and scarification were applied to the chest to relieve chest congestions, cough, even bronchitis.

iii. Common illnesses

• During the war, common illnesses, especially among children, were tuberculosis, whooping cough, scarlet fever, measles, *rubella* – German measles. There were no vaccines available for these diseases.

iv. Malnutrition (See 17. Daily life)

• The calculated rations were below the essential minimum. If on paper they were deemed adequate, in reality they could not sustain life.

• By mid-1941 – signs of malnutrition appeared, especially among the poorer classes.

• By the spring of 1944 – there were deaths from extreme malnutrition.

• Some of the deaths were attributed to either the lack of food or the lack of heat or both.

D. Doctors

• Medical studies took six years plus one preparatory year.

• Medical doctors had to compete with folk healers and bone setters, as generally people were reluctant to pay for a consultation and treatment and were mistrustful of the highly educated physician. Folk medicine had been passed down for generations and was widely trusted. Patients made a donation.

• Doctors and medical personnel, including nurses and orderlies, were under the authority of the French administration – the *Assistance Publique.*

• Instructed by the BMF to fire doctors born of foreign parents, the Assistance Publique reluctantly followed the order by transferring such doctors to other hospitals of less interest to the MBF.

• As late as January 1944, the MBF ordered the director of the Assistance Publique to transfer the Jewish patients and the Jewish doctors to Rothschild hospital where they could more easily be seized for deportation.

• Hospitals, particularly in Paris, were hotbeds of résistance.

i. Doctors

• Family doctors had an office in a front room of their house. Others practiced in a private clinic or a hospital.

• For family doctors, making house calls was the norm.

• They dealt with minor interventions such as stitches for a low level injury. In rural areas, they would also apply casts. They were also able to remove an appendix in an emergency.

• They had the assistance of a nurse.

• There were very few women doctors prewar. Less than five percent of female candidates were admitted to medical school. Those who were admitted were banned from surgery and general medicine. They could only practice in pediatric and gynecology.

• The women who persisted were often daughters of doctors or scientists. The fathers supported their daughter's application.

• These women doctors were defying what was expected of a woman at the time.

ii. Dispensaire – dispensary

• The *dispensaire* was basically a health care center in cities and towns managed and paid for by the state for low-income patients. Doctors were usually volunteers, though some were employed. They provided basic care and would refer the serious cases to the hospital. *Dispensaires* were located in poorer districts.

iii. Orthopedics
• Orthopedics were only provided in hospitals and private clinics.

iv. Pediatric
• Pediatricians worked out of a front room of their house, or practiced in a private clinic or a hospital.
• In the absence of systematic vaccination, childhood diseases were often fatal.

v. Surgery
• Surgeons practiced in hospital settings or private clinics often owned by the surgeon himself.

E. Nurses
• Whereas women were not welcome as doctors, they were welcome as nurses. Traditionally, the nursing profession had been the preserve of nuns who also ran hospitals.
• Generally, nurses in WWI had not received formal training, That changed in the interwar years Nursing became an accepted profession for women, though they were expected to abandon it upon marriage and maternity (!).
• A wave of patients during and after WWI obliged the nuns to train girls of good families.
• By the end of the 1930s, there were enough qualified nurses and the nuns were able to devote their time to the administration of hospitals and training.
• After WWI, tuberculosis brought home by returning soldiers increased to alarming proportions among low-income families. Nurses were entrusted with home visiting to teach hygiene to families. They were the forerunners of the social worker. This was not well-regarded by some people, men in particular, in the upper class.

• Except in Paris where visiting nurses received an official certificate, nurses elsewhere were considered volunteers and although trained, received no official recognition and little money.

• The French Red Cross opened its own nursing school in the mid-1930s, focusing on the medical aspect more than the social aspect of nursing.

• May 10, 1940 – the government ordered the evacuation of hospitals in northern France coming under attack from the advancing German forces. Nurses were tasked with organizing and taking care of the move, with the help of a few dedicated doctors.

• June 10-15, 1940 – those five days saw the exodus from Paris. The remaining few nurses, and even fewer doctors, staffed the hospitals.

• In 1940, the Pétain's government declared that all nurses had to possess a diploma from the *État Français*, as Pétain had abolished the Third Republic, along with qualifications it previously recognized. Nurses were obliged to re-sit their examinations. Doctors did not.

F. Pharmacies

• A pharmacist would have a storefront with an apartment above.

• Pharmacists provided first aid for free.

• They gave advice and prescribed certain medications for mild ailments or chronic cases.

G. Veterinary medicine

• Veterinarians in the country had a separate building for big and small animal surgery, with or without a dwelling above.

• They made farm and house calls.

• There were few veterinarians in the cities and towns.

• In rural areas, they practiced out of a small building that could accommodate a horse or two.

• There may have been an apartment or two above the veterinary building.

• They sometimes had an assistant who might be a trainee veterinarian.

26. Hospitals
A. Paris American Hospital
i. Timeline
• September 26, 1939 – admitted its first injured soldiers.

• December 31, 1939 – New Year's Eve, Josephine Baker sang and danced for patients and staff.

• June 14, 1940 – Dr. Thierry de Martel, the hospital's Chief Surgeon, took his own life.

• Summer 1940 – the hospital and the American Red Cross created a service to provide assistance to POW camps near Paris.

• October 11, 1940 – the hospital was awarded the French *Croix de Guerre* war medal by the État Français War Minister.

• August 1941 – the board of governors put the American Hospital of Paris at the disposal of the French Red Cross.

• May 25, 1944 – Dr. Sumner Jackson was captured by the SD, transferred to the Gestapo and deported with his wife and son.

• August 24, 1944 – the Kommandantur of Western Paris laid down its arms at the American Hospital of Paris.

• September 1944 – the hospital was requisitioned and transformed into an American military hospital named the 365th Station Hospital.

• In February 1946 – the hospital returned to its status as a civilian establishment.

B. Other hospitals in Paris
• The MBF oversaw all hospitals, in addition to those that received tortured prisoners, the sick from the camps and regular patients.

• Fifty thousand patients in psychiatric hospitals died of malnutrition and starvation during the Occupation.

i. Paris
• American Hospital – private.

• Hôpital Rothschild – private. After the family foundation was dissolved and all their assets seized except the hospital, both the MBF and the Assistance Publique ran the hospital. The

ophthalmology section was reserved for German officers –
Ortslazaret Hals-Nasen-Ohren-Augen – staffed by German
personnel. Another part, staffed by French personnel, was
allocated for the Jews from Drancy camp and prisoners from the
Tourelles prison, as well as résistants tortured by the Gestapo,
before their deportation. At the end of 1941, the hospital was
encircled with barbed wire and guarded by gendarmes as escapes
were numerous. Jewish women gave birth there. The newborns
were whisked away to safety and were registered as still-births.
  • Hôpital de la Croix-Rouge – private.
  • Hospice des Enfants-Assistés – for children.
  • Clinique Antoine-Chantin – private.
  • Hospice des Petits-Ménages – near Paris.
  • Hôpital des Enfants-Malades – children.
  • Armand-Trousseau – for children.
  • Notre-dame du Bon-Secours – maternity.
  • Hôpital Boucicaut – general.
  • Hôpital du Quinze-Vingts – ophthalmology.
  • Hôpital du Val-de-Grâce – general.
  • Hôpital Cochin – general.
NOTE the difference in meaning between French and English
use of the term *hospice*. In English, the term denotes palliative
care for the terminally ill. French *hospice* is a health facility
providing care to disadvantaged members of society – more of a
charity hospital.

ii. Requisitioned hospitals in Paris
  • Hôpital Beaujon – for Luftwaffe – and Hôpital
Lariboisière – for Wehrmacht – employed German staff only.
    • Hôpital de la Pitié, Hôpital de l'Hôtel-Dieu and Hôpital
de la Salpêtrière – employed French personnel under German
supervision.

C. Outside Paris

• Near Amiens in the Pas-de-Calais, which was in the Zone Interdite, Hôpital Allart de Fourment was located in the Château de Cercamp.

• Lyon – the Hôpital Desgenettes military hospital, Hôpital de la Croix-Rousse and Hôpital de l'Hôtel-Dieu.

• Marseille – Hôpital Ambroise-Paré.

• Toulouse – Hôpital Purpan.

• Vichy – Hôpital les Quatre-Chemins.

27. Identity
A. Ausweis – a pass
i. Crossing demarcation lines
• Issued by the local Kommandantur. It was needed to cross demarcation lines.

• An Ausweis was moderately difficult to obtain to cross the north-south zones, but extremely difficult to obtain to cross into the restricted territory in the north and the forbidden zone along the Atlantic coast.

ii. Circulation permit
• A travel permit was a type of Ausweis that a person entitled to drive a car or a commercial vehicle had to display on the inside the windshield in addition to their personal Ausweis.

iii. Vehicle permit
• Vehicles also had to carry a permit showing they were authorized to obtain gas, coal or charcoal for their gazogène.

B. Identity cards prior to July 1940
i. Identity
• In 1921 the government of the Third Republic imposed identity cards but only in the Seine department, which included Paris. In 1935, Pierre Laval's government extended the requirement to all of France.

• The aim of the identity card was to distinguish foreigners from native-born French citizens and control the movement of the population.

ii. Residency
• Proving one's identity could be as simple as having one's concierge certify that you were who you claimed to be and resided in the building. She would sign the form.

• A neighbor or a café owner could certify someone's identity. He would sign the form.

iii. Centralization in Paris

• Each regional prefecture issued ID cards on the same paper and in the same style as the Préfecture de Paris.

• The authorities believed such cards could not be counterfeited.

• Especially in rural prefectures, officials experienced technical difficulties in producing the same type of cards required by the Préfecture de Paris.

iv. Identity cards under the Pétain regime

• The government of Marshal Pétain imposed a single standardized identity card as part of the so-called renewal of the country – *La Carte d'identité de l'État Français.*

• At the same time, the government collected an enormous amount of information on each individual when they applied for the new card.

• Foreign refugees, anti-fascists – mostly found in the resistance groups – foreign Jews and stateless persons were easily identified by the new card.

• The July 22, 1940 law revoked the citizenship of foreign-born persons who acquired French nationality after 1927. The law was mostly directed at Jews. It was a source of conflict within the Pétain government. Not all ministers and elected politicians agreed with the law.

• Technical difficulties persisted and some municipalities continued to issue the old card. In addition, résistance groups succeeded in forging and falsifying identity cards, thus adding to the confusion.

• The *Carte d'identité de l'État Français* was abolished at the Liberation. It was replaced by a standard national identity card.

v. Naturalization of foreign-born persons

• The August 1927 law determined that a child born to a French mother and a foreign father was French.

• A foreigner, registered with a municipality, could apply for French citizenship after three years residency.

• He or she lost their native nationality and became wholly French – no dual nationality.

• Prewar France did not subscribe to the racist theories of other countries, such as the U.S.A., Germany, Italy and others.

• In the thirties, in the midst of the depression, employment preferences were given to native Frenchmen.

vi. France *terre d'accueil* – the universal refuge

• Traditionally, France had been a haven for those fleeing persecution or danger, as occurred, for example, after the Russian Revolution.

• In 1938, France welcomed 83,000 exiles fleeing religious and political persecution.

• In April 1939, exiles were encouraged to join the army. They received French citizenship in return.

vii. Ration identity cards and a fistful of ration tickets

(a) **An individual was issued** a ration identity card, listing the person's category, order number, address and status, an ink stamp from the town hall that issued it, the mayor's signature and the length of time it was valid for.

(b) **Included with the identity card** was a sheet of daily ration tickets enabling the person to buy a specific quantity of rationed foodstuffs. Different colors indicated a person's category. Food tickets were valid for one month.

(c) **Along with the food tickets** came tickets for various household items, such as textiles, china and cutlery, enabling the person to buy one item per category with the requisite number of tickets. These were valid for six months.

(d) **For larger items** such as a coat, shoes, bed linen or furnishings, a person had to apply to the town hall, which then issued or not a ticket authorizing the purchase.

viii. Résistance laissez-passer – pass

• In 1944, with the FFI holding many areas, they issued a *laissez-passer* proving the identity of the bearer, a French flag with FFI, and a stamp.

C. Certificates
i. Military discharge
• For men of military age, a discharge certificate would be issued by the local gendarmerie or, if there was no gendarmerie in a small village, by the prefecture, proving the bearer had been officially discharged from the disbanded French Army in 1940. Men had to carry that certificate and their military booklet with their other identity papers.

ii. Work exemptions and STO (See 22. Education)
• Men and women working in agriculture, or other occupations considered vital to the economy, were exempted from the STO.

D. Forgery
i. The forgers
• The forgers. Forging documents developed into a high art form. Poorly made fake documents endangered their users. The best forgers had a background in art or calligraphy. They were well-versed in forging handwriting and signatures.
• Each set of papers was custom-made to suit the individual person, who only had to produce a photograph.
• Since cameras were forbidden, it was an added risk for the person who was asked to take the photo.
• A resistant photographer ran great risk in using his dark room to alter photos when needed.
• The recipient of the forged papers also ran a risk if attending the photographer's studio.
• Some resistance members were amateur photographers and skilled at developing clandestine photos.
• Only those photographers who also served the Germans could officially obtain the chemicals necessary to process film.

• Forgers also forged postage stamps, as buying large quantities to post letters and clandestine newssheets would have drawn attention to résistants.

ii. Official town hall stamps

• Each town had its own rubber or brass stamps, kept at the town hall.

• Forgers were skilled at reproducing duplicates of these stamps.

• There had been instances when rubber stamps were stolen, or borrowed with an employee's complicity and a plaster cast made and the stamp returned to the town hall. From the plaster cast, a mold was made, usually in lead as it was relatively easy to melt lead, and rubber was not available. Other materials, such as linoleum, clay, even potatoes, were also used. They were not as durable.

iii. Centralized registers

• There was no general directory of people's names. Each municipality kept its own register of births, marriage and deaths. When full, another register was started. Some registers dated back hundred of years.

• If a municipality's town hall was bombed, and the documents destroyed, local people were called upon the use their memories to re-create the records.

• The local résistants made use of these circumstances to garner names and details. Thus, information of deceased persons was often used to create more secure false identity papers for résistance members.

iv. Paper

• Special paper was used for the identity card, ration tickets, and Ausweis. It was only available to the prefectures and town halls. Precise quantities were then handed to printers.

• Paper was rationed for printers and unavailable to ordinary people.

E. Yellow star
• The six-pointed star known as the Star of David was made of cloth, with the word *Jew* printed in the center in imitation Hebrew writing.
• Jews were obliged to buy their star and surrender one textile ration ticket.

i. Exemptions
• Special exemptions to individuals might be granted in the interest of the Reich, usually for prominent figures.
• Foreigners from belligerent countries, from neutral countries, and from Germany's allied countries would be exempt to avoid retaliation on German nationals or intervention from neutral countries.
• Certain mixed marriages whose children were born French were exempt at the request of Pétain's government.

ii. Non-occupied zone
• Pétain refused to impose the wearing of the yellow star in the non-occupied zone.
• Wearing the yellow star was not compulsory even after November 1942, as the MBF authorities feared an uprising of the population if they tried to enforce it in the formerly non-occupied zone.
• Identity cards had to carry the word *Jew*.

iii. Occupied zone
• May 28, 1942 – MBF's decree that all Jews aged six years and older must wear the yellow star in the occupied zone.
• It was a punishable offence not to wear it.
• A number of Jewish professionals refused to comply. Some were denounced and arrested.

iv. Religious and other protests

• Catholic bishops and archbishops tried to intervene with the MBF but to no avail. One bishop was obliged to wear the yellow star as his grandparents were of the Jewish faith, even though he had renounced Judaism and had embraced Catholicism at age sixteen.

• Small acts of defiance sprung up everywhere, such as Abbé Jean Flory, Montbeliard parish priest. At the midnight mass of Christmas 1942, with many Wehrmacht soldiers in attendance, the abbé had the infant Jesus, Joseph and Marie wear the yellow star as well as all the choir children and altar boys. There was no repercussion.

• Most Parisians were angry. Young and not so young people came out wearing a yellow star with mocking inscriptions, such as *Swing*, *Breton*, *Paris*, *zazou*.

28. Internment Camps. Prisoner of War camps

NOTE: Whereas the French population was aware of the existence of internment camps, Nazi concentration camps were known only through rumors of *labor camps*. No one talked about *concentration camps* or knew what they were. Only after the first Nazi camps were liberated in January 1945 did the truth began to filter into the news, despite the censorship imposed by the Allies.

When the former camp inmates began arriving in Paris, many people were bewildered and asked what was going on. Research has since shown that British and, to a lesser extent, American authorities had received intelligence from Polish resistance fighters about the existence of concentration camps as early as 1942, followed by highly detailed reports in the summer of 1943. This information was kept secret, as the main goal was to defeat the Third Reich militarily.

Because of this lack of knowledge on the part of ordinary French people, it is advisable to avoid having your fictional French or English or American characters talk about concentration camps, their horror or the camps in the east. Those who heard of labor camps assumed they were in Germany, and maybe prisoner of war camps which did not elicit the same horror. There were not many escapees or refugees who made it to France, and when they did, their knowledge did not go beyond the few people who hid them. It was too dangerous to talk.

A. Internment camps
i. Creation of internment camps

• Internment camps were created after WWI as centers for administrative detention and processing of displaced persons or prisoners of war.

• By September 1, 1939, the camps had been more or less abandoned. A new decree was issued that in case of war, all enemy nationals between the age of 17 and 65 would be interned.

• November 1939 – persons considered as dangerous to national and public security would also be interned.

ii. Phoney war
• The term refers to an eight-month period at the start of World War II during which there was only limited military activity on the Western Front. In French, it is known as the *Drôle de guerre.*   **NOTE:** the British form of the term *phoney* is used both in British Standard and American Standard English to denote this period.
• During the phoney war, the camps were filled with:
   (a) Germans, **Austrians**, anti-Nazis, and Jews who had fled their country.
   (b) Nomadic people such as Roma, Sintis, all falling into the category of Tziganes – gypsies.

iii. After June 1940
   (a) Camps varied according to their locations, either in the occupied zone or in the non-occupied zone.
      • Pétain's government had six categories of camp – refugee camps, internment camps, residency camps with minimal surveillance, camps with heightened surveillance, POW camps (for French and Allies) and transit camps for those to be transported to Germany.
   (b) Natzweiler-Struthof, located in annexed Alsace, and therefore under Nazi control, was the only concentration camp on French territory.
      • Another camp in Alsace created by the occupiers was the Vorbrück-Schirmek rehabilitation camp for Alsatians and Mosellans opposed to the occupiers. Some men were forced into the Wehrmacht and sent to the eastern front.
   (c) Camps were guarded by French gendarmes in the occupied and non-occupied zones. Many were mostly lenient toward their charges, some even taking them shopping, until November 1942, when Schutzpolizei police were added to the French gendarmes.

(d) There were camps in French territories, such as Algeria and Senegal, that had sided with Pétain.

iv. At the Liberation and afterwards

• Camp inmates were freed as the liberation of the territory progressed.

• Collaborators, traitors and German POWs were interned in the camps, guarded by gendarmes and FFI members, neither being lenient toward their charges.

v. Humanitarian organizations

• Internees wanted to be freed and return home but felt powerless. Some, however, organized escape committees in the camps with varying degrees of success.

• Protestant organizations were the first to mobilize and provide help. Despite the camps' physical and material conditions, they created centers with libraries and cultural activities.

• Humanitarian organizations repeatedly met with obstacles from the Pétain's government.

(a) *La Fédération universelle des associations chrétiennes d'étudiants* – the Universal Federation of Christian Student Associations – mobilized their teams upon the declaration of war to help with refugee resettlement, particularly those from Alsace and Lorraine, and later from Holland and Belgium.

(b) *Le Comité inter-mouvements auprès des évacués* **(CIMADE)** – a committee for integrating the movement of displaced persons – was an umbrella organization for five youth organizations, which still exists today as a NGO (non-government organization).

(c) Pétain's government finally gave CIMADE authorization to operate and, even in some cases, live in the internment camps.

(d) Quakers, otherwise known as the Society of Friends, also worked in the camps and faced the same difficulties as other organizations.

(e) Some important figures who strove to improve the situation of internees included Suzanne de Dietrich, Jane Pannier, Violette Mouchon, Madeleine Barot (an activist), Georgette Siegriest, Jeanne Merle d'Aubigné, Jeanne Tendil, Jeanne Sénat, Pastor André Morel, Pastor Marc Bognel, Pastor André Dumas and Pator Trocmé.

(f) *L'œuvre de secours à l'enfance* (OSE) headed by Dr. Eugene Minkowski employed legal and illegal means to rescue children. (See 32. Jewish organizations)

(g) Funds were obtained from individual donors and, via Switzerland or Sweden, from personalities such as Eleanor Roosevelt and Princess Bernadotte of Sweden who fundraised in their respective countries.

vi. Red Cross in the camps

• The authorities were more inclined to allow the French Red Cross into the camps. The Red Cross did not do as much social work nor provide as much material help as the Protestant organizations and, because of this, were heavily criticized after the war.

• The Red Cross occasionally facilitated the Protestant organizations' presence in the camps.

vii. Total Occupation and changes

• In 1942, as the deportation of Jews intensified, CIMADE attempted to intervene to have exemptions respected. Unsuccessful legally, they resorted to illegal means, including arranging escapes, particularly the rescue of children.

B. Prisoners of War camps
i. Escapes

• There were many escapes from the POW camps on French territory. Many French gendarmes simply looked the other way.

• The most famous escape was from Voves camp, near Chartres, in the occupied zone. Requisitioned by the Wehrmacht, it initially housed POWs, but soon other categories of prisoners joined them. In May 1944, forty-two prisoners successfully escaped after digging a 42 meter-long tunnel. Later, this inspired a Hollywood movie.

ii. Metropolitan French armies

• Most French POWs were taken to Germany into Stalags and Oflags – the latter being prison camps for officers.

iii. Colonial soldiers

• POW soldiers from the French colonies were kept in various camps in France (and in Poland) called Frontstalags and guarded by German ex-servicemen from the 1914-18 war. Later, these were replaced at the request of the Germans by French former officers from metropolitan France, giving rise to the bizarre situation of the POWs being held prisoner by their former commanders. There was no escape, Black men being too visible, and life in the camps under French command was acceptable.

29. German invasion 1940
A. End of the Phoney War
i. May 10, 1940

• Hitler's armies invaded neutral Holland*, Belgium, Luxembourg. They also invaded France, which had declared war on September 3, 1939.

NOTE: Be aware that the *Netherlands* is today the accepted name for the country, but in the period up to and during WWII, *Holland* was the name used.

ii. Controversies

• It is easy to fall into generalities when reading the frequently biased journalism, with scathing headlines about the Belgian and French armies fleeing in the face of the enemy. Later, equally biased historians took up the refrain, focusing on the defeat and not on the fighting, due to Marshal Pétain requesting an armistice. Marshal Pétain was not in the army. He no longer commanded the soldiers. He was a politician who quickly blamed the rank-and-file soldiers instead of the incompetent high command.

• Fact check – Holland, Belgium and Luxembourg, being neutral, had small armies that fought to the maximum of their abilities.

NOTE: The German General Alfred Wägner granted the honors of war to the French army under the command of General Jean-Baptiste Molinié after the siege of Lille, June 1, 1940.

• The French Army fought to the last man in many parts of the front and in particular at Dunkirk, where General Fagalde's 35,000 men, outnumbered 1:10 in one place and 1:30 in another, held back the Wehrmacht long enough to permit almost 200,000 men of the British contingent and some 120,000 French, Belgian and Canadian soldiers to be evacuated.

• 100,000 French soldiers alone died in the Battle of France.

iii. War crimes

• As the Wehrmacht advanced into France in 1940, they were followed by a small contingent of SD and SIPO of the Schutzstaffel – not the combat units but the political and police arm. The Wehrmacht committed war crimes against POWs, such as when one hundred British POWs were locked in a barn into which the Germans threw grenades. There were also war crimes committed against the population, such as when fleeing civilians were fired upon, or in Pont-du-Guy, when Wehrmacht troops locked twenty-two civilians in a barn and set it on fire.

   • On May 28, 1940, at Oignies, after a hard-fought three-day battle, eighty local civilians were massacred. A British officer was burned alive by Wehrmacht soldiers.

   • Any civilians attempting to resist their homes being pillaged were shot summarily.

   • It is sometimes said that the résistance started with Jean Moulin, the Prefect of Chartres, who refused to sign a German document blaming Senegalese soldiers, shot and tortured, for a massacre of civilians tortured and raped.

   NOTE: There is a tendency in subsequent writing to absolve the Wehrmacht of wrongdoing, that the ordinary troops were innocent and the crimes were committed by the Waffen-SS and other fanatics. This does not reflect historical facts. Wehrmacht units bear responsibility for a number of war crimes, both in 1940 and 1944 (See 43. Retreating armies).

B. Cities and countryside
   • Paris and Lyon were declared open cities and were not bombed. The term *open city* denotes a city or town that did not fight the besieging forces in order to save lives and property.

   • Surrounding areas, such as the industrial suburbs of Paris and the airfields in Lyon, were bombed.

   • The northern areas and port towns were heavily bombed, with no consideration whether they were military installations or civilian.

C. Armistice

• Monday June 17, 1940 – Marshal Pétain requested an armistice (See 7. Armistice).

• Two zones were created – the occupied zone comprising three-fifths of the territory, and a non-occupied zone.

• Italy occupied a fifty-kilometer band of territory from Léman Lake to the Mediterranean, as well as the French island of Corsica.

• The costs of the occupying powers were paid by the État Français to the tune of 400 million francs per day.

• The Germans were not to occupy the French colonies.

• An agreement made at the Wiesbaden Commission of Armistice was an undertaking to protect historical monuments, such as Mont Saint-Michel, even when under occupation.

D. Occupied zone

• July 1940 – the north-east line named the *Nordost Linie* and also referred to as the Führer Line extended from the Somme River to the Swiss border. It was more difficult to cross this line than the north-south demarcation line between the free and occupied zones.

i. Annexation (See 2. Administration of France)

• October 18, 1940 – by an unpublished decree, Hitler declared that Alsace and Moselle were a de facto part of Germany, in clear violation of the armistice conditions signed June 22, 1940.

• Alsace was the only part of the territory to have a Nazi concentration camp – the Natzweiler-Struthoff camp (See 28. Internment Camps).

• Annexation meant germanization of the region, as it was deemed to be part of Germany.

• Young Alsatian and Mosellan men, dubbed the *Malgré Nous* – Against our will, were forcibly conscripted into the Wehrmacht.

ii. Forbidden areas

• Alsace and parts of Lorraine provinces, having been annexed, were declared foreign countries to the rest of France. Travel was forbidden.

iii. Restricted areas

• The Nord and Pas-de-Calais departments were attached to the Bruxelles military command.

• Seventeen departments in the north and east of France, behind the Nord-East line, were declared restricted, with refugees forbidden to return − with the exception of miners and essential industrial workers. These territories were reserved for German settlers.

• A band of twenty to thirty kilometers wide of the littoral, from Dunkirk to Hendaye, became forbidden to all non-residents.

(a) Exceptions

• Fishermen were allowed to resume fishing as early as July 1940, with some restrictions about the distance and areas.

• Fishing was not allowed between 6:00 pm and 9:00 am.

• Captains had to indicate their departure.

• Captains had to provide the list of their crew. Everyone had to have a special identity card.

• Initially, they could only fish within three nautical miles from the shore. For economic reasons, the distance was abolished, but the Kriegsmarine determined the allowed area according to the season.

• Fishing boats had to fly a distinctive yellow guidon below the French flag.

(b) Pleasure boats had to register with the MBF to be issued with a special identity card to remain at their mooring place.

• A forbidden zone three kilometers wide along the Vosges and Swiss border was decreed in October 1942 to persons older than fifteen − the decree was issued as the result of numerous escapees taking advantage of the mountainous terrain.

iv. Nazi goals

(a) German archeologists began excavating in the megalithic site at Carnac, to try to find Germanic elements to prove that the ancient *Germains* had been present there to justify Nazi expansion and prove the superiority of the Aryan race. They deployed Luftwaffe aircraft to find sites elsewhere in France.

(b) At Margival, in the department of Aisne, north-east of Paris, in the middle of nowhere, eight hundred reinforced concrete structures spread over ninety square kilometers, were built. It was planned to be Hitler's HQ in France. Observation bunkers were built on surrounding hills.

(c) Protection of the Atlantic coast.

• The Nazi priority was to control the Atlantic coast and the ocean. The Germans expected some attacks from England, though they believed that to be improbable. In Hitler's mind, the most likely attacks would come from Britain's attempts to retake the Channel Islands that Germany had occupied.

• October 1941 – defenses were built on the Normandy coast to protect the islands.

• There was also the need to protect the submarine bases at Brest in the Finistère department, at Lorient on the Keroman peninsula of the Morbihan department, at Saint-Nazaire in the Loire Inférieure department, at La Rochelle in the Charente-Inférieure department and at Bordeaux in the Gironde department.

• The United States' entry into the war accelerated the need to protect the French coast.

• After the aborted Dieppe landing in August 1942, Hitler was convinced that the Allied landings would take place at or near a port.

• The Todt organization was to execute the protection work of what became known as the Atlantic Wall.

• December 1943 – Field Marshal Erwin Rommel inspected the Atlantic wall and saw that the beaches were unprotected – soldiers and some locals used the beaches for recreation. Within six months, he had all the beaches mined and anti-tanks defenses installed. Behind the coastline, he had low-lying areas flooded and ordered stakes to be planted in fields to prevent planes from landing. Those and **only those** were nicknamed Rommel's asparagus –*Rommelspargel.*

v. Population

(a) The Wehrmacht in Paris

• Friday, June 14, 1940 – the Wehrmacht entered Paris, an open city, at 5:00 am, not as one smartly attired unit marching up the Champs-Élysées, but dispersed units assigned to take possession of various areas and buildings. An informal parade for the benefit of the soldiers and the photographers took place in the late afternoon on Avenue Foch.

• Saturday, June 15, 1940 – the first of the formal daily military parades took place along the Champs-Élysées at 11:00 am.

• The photographs and the Nazi propaganda film of the victorious Wehrmacht parade on the Champs-Élysées was shot on Tuesday, June 18, 1940 after Marshal Pétain had requested an armistice.

(b) Public reaction.

• The Parisians were variously stunned, unbelieving, sad, furious with their government, or fearful.

• Reaction was varied – for some it was acceptance, others a wait-and-see attitude, still others opted for collaboration or opposition, which later led to outright resistance. Many WWI veterans felt a profound shame of defeat.

(c) The Wehrmacht continued to advance, bombing its way through France and randomly shooting civilians and committing war crimes against soldiers and civilians (see. iii. War crimes above), until the official end of hostilities on June 25, 1940.

30. Italian invasion, 1940

• The Italian government demanded a large part of the
territory, the French fleet, air force and cities in French Algeria
and Corsica. Hitler did refuse. The French also protested. They
had not been defeated by the Italians. On the contrary, the
French Chasseurs Alpins Corps had won the battle of the Alps
against the Italians.

• Italy was granted 800 square kilometers in the Alps, along the
border and part of four departments, including the town of
Menton in the department of the Basses-Alpes.

• The Italian occupiers attempted to Italianize the town of
Menton on the model of the germanization of Alsace.

• The Savoy region of Haute-Savoie and Corsica remained
entirely French.

• A demilitarized zone of fifty kilometers from the occupied
zone was established from Annemasse on the Swiss border to
near Antibes on the Mediterranean.

31. Invasion of the non-occupied zone
A. Operation Anton
• On the morning of Wednesday, November 11, 1942, the Wehrmacht invaded the non-occupied zone and reached the Mediterranean by evening.

• At the same time, the Italian army invaded the demilitarized zone and Corsica.

• German forces supported by Italian troops invaded Tunisia.

B. The French fleet at Toulon
• The Germans had intended to seize the French fleet at Toulon – Operation Lila.

• By November 1942, the French armed forces' allegiance to the État Français government was waning. Admiral Darlan had defected to the Allies.

• His replacement in Vichy, Admiral Gabriel Auphan, contrary to Admiral Darlan's order to rally to the side of the Allies, gave the order to scuttle the fleet. He did not want the French ships in the hands of either the Germans or the Italians, nor did he want to send them to England. There was still anti-British sentiment and a lingering allegiance to Marshal Pétain.

• Admiral Auphan instructed Admiral Jean de Laborde and the Toulon Prefect, André Marquis, to scuttle the fleet.

• The naval crews used deceit to delay the Germans until the preparations to scuttle were completed – November 27, 1942.

• Not all sailors shared the same allegiance to Marshal Pétain and five submarines escaped and rallied to the FFL.

C. Consequences of total occupation
• The Armée d'Armistice was disbanded.

• Jews from the former non-occupied zone fled to the Italian zone, as the Italians refused to round up Jews.

D. Italy joined the Allies

• When the Italian government signed an armistice in September 1943 with the Allies, the Wehrmacht invaded the French territory formerly occupied by the Italian army.

• The occupiers immediately began rounding up Jews for deportation.

32. Jewish Affairs (See 19. Deportations)
  A. At the start of the war
  • At the start of the war, Jews numbered just under 330,000 in France – 200,000 French Jews plus 130,000 foreign Jews. At the end of the war, there were a total of 220,000 Jews remaining. From Serge Klarsfeld's figures, seventy-five percent of the Jewish population in France survived the Occupation, the Sipo-SD and Pétain's government, despite denunciations and raids. The number does not include those who fled to neutral or allied countries via escape routes. Unlike some books and films, which deliberately portrayed rampant anti-Semitism everywhere in France, Klarsfeld, Semelin and other historians maintained an objective point of view. These writers were supported by documentation and statistics, as well as interviews with survivors, to throw light on why an impressive seventy-five percent of the Jewish population in France was able to avoid deportation.
  • A controversy persists still whether the Nazi regime ordered Pétain's government to enact anti-Semitic measures. One thing is clear is that the MBF made demands from the Pétain's government to provide a certain number of Jews for labor camps, and the government was willing to round them up. At the same time, the government occasionally opposed the Nazi's demands.
  • The other thing that is clear is that Pétain himself signed the decrees limiting Jews' freedom. Firstly, the July 22, 1940, denaturalization order, stripping Jews of their citizenship. Secondly, the October 3, 1940, initial status order for Jews, excluding them from public office, commercial and industrial work. Thirdly, the October 4, 1940 order for all foreign Jews to be immediately interned.
  • There was anti-Semitism among parts of the population (aristocracy and upper-class), but the majority took a neutral attitude, until 1942, when the *Rafle du Vel d'Hiv* changed

people's minds. From then on, people helped Jews to hide or escape.

• One factor that favored the survival of the French Jewish population was their geographical distribution. For the Nazis, forcing the Jews into a controlled location made it easier to deport them, but there were no ghettos in France. There were internment camps where the État Français had rounded up foreign Jews and *undesirables* to fill the quotas. It did not work very well and quotas were never met.

• In Poland, almost all Jews were eliminated. In Holland, 84% of them were murdered. In Belgium the figure was 50%, France 25% and Denmark 5%.

• Berlin depended on the collaborating governments of occupied countries to get their hands on Jews.

• The MBF authorities were attentive to public opinion, which could disrupt and hinder the flow of deportations, as in France after July 1942, when public opinion shifted in favor of the Jews.

• 75,721 Jews , which included 11,400 – representing one quarter of the Jewish population of France, only one third being French citizens, were deported. An estimated three to four thousand returned.

• Some 3,000 were executed as hostages or died in internment camps, according to Serge Klarsfeld sources.

• Some 109,000 Jews fled the occupied zone for the non-occupied zone, crossing the demarcation line clandestinely, the majority with a passeur's help, others on their own initiative.

• Some villagers near the demarcation line had hitherto never before met a Jewish person, but willingly helped.

NOTE: A reminder that all through the war and until May 14, 1948, there was no country called Israel. Earlier, Jews, especially those embracing Zionism, had made their way to the British Palestinian Mandated territory to lay claim to the land they said belonged to them in biblical times.

B. Chronology 1940-1942

i. 1940

• October 20 – deadline for the census in the occupied zone. 149,734 Jews registered.

• Jews were expelled from Alsace and Moselle as soon as the Wehrmacht entered the area.

• Jews were prohibited from returning to the occupied zone. Their assets were seized.

• July 22 – loss of citizenship for all foreign Jews by law of Pétain's government.

• September 27 – first German statute for Jews in occupied France by the MBF.

• Posters, with the word *Jew,* appeared in the window of Jewish businesses.

• October 3 – Pétain's first status of Jews order, excluding them from public office, commercial and industrial work.

• October 4 – all foreign Jews to be interned immediately.

ii. 1941

• March 1941 – Pétain's government created the Commissariat Général aux Questions Juives(CGQJ), under the direction of Xavier Vallat, and in March 1942 under the direction of Louis Darquier de Pellepoix.

• June 14 – second German statute for Jews which extended the first statute to the non-occupied zone and implemented by the État Français.

• July 1 – deadline for the census in the non-occupied zone. 140,000 Jews registered.

• November 29 – in order to control the Jewish population systematically, the MBF created the *Union Générale des Israélites de France*(UGIF) – the General Union of French Israelites.

iii. 1942

• February 7 – curfew from 8:00 pm to 6:00 am imposed on Jews.

• March 27 – First deportee train departs from the Nazi-controlled Compiègne camp to Auschwitz.

• May 29 – decree by the MBF that Jews over six years of age must wear the yellow Star of David, to take effect on June 7 in the occupied zone.

• Although Pétain approved of the wearing of the yellow star, his government did not make it mandatory.

• June 10 – Jews were obliged to travel in the last car of Paris métro trains.

• The Sipo and Schutzpolizei were ordered to search for and arrest every Jew in Paris.

• July – the MBF and SD announced their objective to deport 100,000 Jews aged 16 to 40. After negotiations with the secretary general of police, René Bousquet, only foreign Jews were to be arrested in both zones.

• July 3 – prohibition for Jews to use the telephone.

• July 8, 1942 – prohibition for Jews to attend a theater show or movie.

• July 16-17 – the Vel d'Hiv roundup of 13,152 persons – 4,115 of them being children.

• After November 11 – there were numerous attempts by Jews to flee to the Italian-occupied zone. The Jewish population, particularly in Nice, tripled.

iv. 1944

• May 30 – the seventy-fifth and last train to Auschwitz left Drancy camp.

• August 9 – laws relative to the status of Jews were declared null and void by the provisional French government established in Algiers.

v. Raids – *rafles*

• When the Nazi authorities requested a shipment of Jews, the French police filled a train and the SNCF *cheminots* – rail workers – took charge of the logistics under the scrutiny of the German inspectors.

• May 14, 1941 – the first raid on foreign Jews, known as *la rafle du billet vert* because of the green advance notices.

• July 2, 1942 – the Nazi regime demanded 20,000 Jews. Preparations were made for massive roundups in Paris as well as in other cities. In Paris, René Bousquet was directly involved with SS Karl Oberg in the organization of the raid to take place July 14, then changed to 16 because to make the raid on the day of France's national day would have precipitated riots.

• July 16-17, 1942 –la rafle du Vel d'Hiv.

• August 20 to 23, 1942 – massive raid in Paris, 4,232 Jews among them 1,602 were French.

• August 26, 1942 – to supplement the raids planned for August 26 in the non-occupied zone, Bousquet ordered the arrest of women and children no matter how young. Children under five were taken from homes and orphanages and put on trains, either by themselves or with a few of their caregivers. There were also non-Jewish caregivers who sacrificed themselves to accompany the young children.

• January 22 to 29, 1943 – 4,000 Jews were arrested in Marseille – Operation Tiger.

• February 22, 1943 – the Italian authorities refused to deport Jews from their occupied part of France.

• April 6, 1944 – raid on a children's home in Izieu in the Ain department.

C. Foreign Jews
i. Justification for deportation

• They were refugees from countries that the Nazis considered inferior.

• The Nazis viewed Jews as subhuman.

• Marshal Pétain and his government were not only anti-Semitic but also xenophobic.

• Pétain's goal was collaboration to ensure the political and ideological success of his Révolution Nationale.

• A hardening of the collaboration in the fight against communism.

• The eagerness of the État Français to take part in Nazi schemes and programs.

ii. Local attitudes
• Initially, there was little reaction from the non-Jewish population to the measures taken against the Jews, particularly foreign Jews.
• The year 1942 marked a turning point. The non-Jewish population became outraged that women and children were being rounded up with the help of French gendarmes, and in general, by the treatment of the Jews through restrictions and internment. The non-Jewish population began to provide assistance, sometimes actively by hiding them, providing them with false papers or passively by keeping quiet about their neighbors' activities. French people made no distinction between French or foreign Jews.
• At the same time, there were collaborators who denounced the hiding of Jews, and police informants were paid to do so.
• Pastors and some bishops protested overtly. Individual Catholic priests quietly engaged in helping Jews.

D. French Jews
• Legally, French Jews were not a people apart. They were French citizens of the Judaic religion, just as other citizens were Catholic or Protestant or no religion. French law made no distinction.
• The notion of a Jewish nation was alien to French culture and life.
• The occupation of the south zone marked the end of all appearances of normalcy.

E. Protests against deportations
• The first public protests came from the clergy: Archbishop Saliège of Toulouse, by a public letter of August 23, 1942,

followed by Bishop Théas, in Montauban, Cardinal Gerlier, in Lyon, and Bishop Delay in Marseille.

 • The protests were communicated to the Vatican. No follow up nor condemnation from the Vatican.

 • Silent outrage, coupled with the complicity of thousands of anonymous people, helped save most of the 225,000 Jews who escaped deportation.

F. Yellow star

 • Yellow star wearing was compulsory in the occupied zone.

 • The Jewish population in the non-occupied zone was not required to wear the yellow star, even after the total occupation. Identity cards were stamped with the word *Jew*.

 • For most Jews, it was not only a humiliation but a way to stigmatize them, to keep them under surveillance and control.

 • Up to 1944, 40,000 Jews in Paris did not wear the yellow star and were not troubled by the police unless caught in an incident or denounced.

 • Exemptions were made for foreign Jews from belligerent countries and neutral countries for fear of reprisals against German citizens in those countries and from Germany's allies.

 • Some Jews refused to wear the star. The medical profession and the law profession protested on behalf of their Jewish colleagues. They were threatened with arrest if they continued gathering petition signatures.

G. Jewish résistance

 • Jewish Réseau André helped Jews escape.

 • Youth groups initiated legal organizations that soon had to become clandestine.

 • Legal organization of *Œuvre de Secours aux Enfants* (OSE) conducted illegal activities to save children.

TRIVIA: Founded in Russia, moved to Germany, forced to leave in 1933 and re-established itself in Paris, the OSE was forced to integrate with the *Union Générale des Israélites de France* (GIF). From that point on, they operated illegally behind a legal façade. Not all the 426 OSE workers were of the Jewish faith. The OSE succeeded in removing children from internment camps, and with help from the Quakers, many were able to emigrate. The OSE took care of 3,000 hidden children placed in urban and rural families or farms. It supported 2,500 children who remained in hiding with their family.

• Formation of a Jewish secret army: *Armée juive* (AJ). They formed a maquis in the Montagne Noire region, a mountainous area south of the Massif Central.

• Some Jews belonged to non-Jewish résistance groups.

33. Language
i. Language according to class
• To preserve the *couleur locale* and the flavor of your fictional French settings when writing in English, it is advisable to use terminology, both English and where needed, French, that was current during the wartime era. Some English words came into common usage *only* after the war.

• For instance, the now widely used word *guy*, to denote a person, came from American English and its use was pretty much confined to U.S. troops stationed in Europe. Only *after* the war did it become adopted by the civilian population. It is unlikely that your novel's wartime British civilian character would be using the term, nor would the French.

• For the sake of authenticity, an author should develop an awareness of the cultural and chronological differences within a language. The same goes for customs by avoiding having your French characters sit down to a bacon and egg breakfast.

A. Class usage, slang and swearing
• Egalitarian France did not recognize classes, but society as a whole separated itself into various levels according to wealth and education. An author's fictional characters should reflect these distinctions in their speech patterns. Class awareness was more pronounced prior and during the war than today.

• More refined speech was used by members of the rump of the old aristocracy, with its inherited wealth and obsolete titles, which they used among themselves. These people tended not to mingle outside of their social milieu. Many aristocrats were favorably disposed to Nazism and cozyied up to officers, many of whom were also aristocrats.

• A polished form of the language was also spoken by *la haute bourgeoisie* – the wealthy, whose money came largely from commerce. Those in the professions and the arts were also in this group.

• More colloquial language patterns would be found among the ranks of the middle class – small business owners,

tradespeople, office staff and government workers –
fonctionnaires.

• Factory workers, agricultural laborers, domestic servants, store clerks and wage earners in general would be more likely to use regional speech patterns and non-standard language forms.

• The military constituted a class in itself – with career officers reflecting the upper-class and enlisted men the other levels of society – using military terms and slang.

ii. Slang

• Slang constitutes treacherous territory for a writer, as slang usage changes quickly from one time period to another and from one class and generation to another. If in doubt about using a certain slang word or expression, it is advisable to check with a slang dictionary to get the precise meaning of the term and an etymology dictionary to see if it was in use during the period.

• If you decide to include French slang in your dialogue passages, note that even a mild word can take on a stronger connotation depending on the tone. Some common slang expressions current in the 1930s and early 1940s:
- *cibiche* – a cigarette.
- *épatant* – great!
- *blaguer, c'est de la blague* – to joke, you're joking.
- *couper la chique* – interrupt someone or being astonished.
- *godillots* – work boots.

ii. Young people's slang

• Only used by teenagers:
- *chouette* – good.
- *ça me botte* – I like it.
- *flûte* or the milder *zut* – darn, damn.

iii. Familiar and ironic words

- *café Pétain* – ersatz coffee.
- *colis Pétain* – a parcel whose content were stolen.
- *gâteau Pétain* – food made without sugar.

313

- *haricots Pétain* – beans containing weevils.
- *une robe Pétain* – clothing made of various scrap
material.

iv. Swearing
• Less offensive swear words can be included in a novel.
Although there is a distinction in what the different classes used,
it was not quite as neat as set out below and there was some
crossover.

(a) **Middle or upper-class women** might exclaim, *juste
ciel!* – good heavens!

- *Mon Dieu* – Lord! good Lord! This expression is only
swearing if the person was deeply religious. It was common
among women to express dismay.

- *Crétin, feminine crétine* – cretin or idiot.

- *Fichez-le camp, foutez-le camp* – Get out of here, beat
it.

(b) **A lower-class woman** might say *Bon Dieu* – Good
Lord! with more of a swearing emphasis. She might also use
foutez-le camp and other male swear words.

(c) **Upper-class men**, particularly military veterans and
rural people, might use *Sacrebleu!* originally *Sacré Dieu* – my
goodness! Holy moly! – an old expression dating from the
Middle Ages.

- *Zut alors* – damn, darn.

- *Cré nom de Dieu, crénom, cré* is an abbreviation of
sacré – sacred. A familar swear to reinforce surprise,
impatience.

- *Bon sang* – dammit.

(d) *putain,* which literally denotes a whore, prostitute,
when used as an invective with another word had a milder
meaning, such as in *putain de guerre* – an awful war or this
goddamn war. As a swear on its own, it expressed surprise or
disbelief. *Putain!* possibly the equivalent of bloody hell or
goddammit, but often stronger and more vulgar, was used solely
by men of all classes, perhaps with the exception of those in high

314

positions, and not when women or children were present or on formal occasions.

(e) Lower-class men would use *con* – jerk, usually combined with a demonstrative adjective, *quel con!* – what a jerk!

- *connasse* – what a jerk, was more vulgar.

- *Nom de Dieu, cré nom de Dieu* – in God's name.

- *la ferme* – shut up.

- *la vache, quelle vache* – bastard, what a bastard.

- *ta gueule* – more vulgar than *la ferme*, used to tell someone to shut up.

(f) Universal swear words employed by all classes to express discontent, with the degree of vulgarity dependent on the context and the social milieu, include *merde, merde alors* – the equivalent of shit! Go to hell!

TRIVIA: according to legend, *merde* became famous when used by the French General de Cambronne during the 1815 Battle of Waterloo and addressed to the English commander who had asked him to surrender. Cambronne replied, "*Je vous dis merde*" which today would be translated by the vulgar "Go f*ck yourself."

B. Non-swear words commonly used in France before and during WWII
i. Endearments

• Adults. To a man, *mon chéri, ma chérie* to a woman – my dear. *Mon amour* – both masculine and feminine – my love.

To children:

• *mon chou* – my little cabbage.

• *mon trésor* – my treasure.

• *mon p'tit cœur* – my little heart, *p'tit* is an abbreviation of *petit*.

• *petit diable* – my little devil – playful and teasing.

• *mon petit*– addressing a small boy. Sometimes used in a patronizing manner to adolescents.

• *ma petite, ma puce* – addressing a small girl.

• *mon lapin* – literally, my little rabbit, often with the addition of *p'tit* – *mon p'tit lapin*.

• *mon grand* – at home to a boy over ten years, *ma grande* – to a girl over ten years. In public *chéri, chérie* would be used.

ii. Pejorative names for the occupying forces
(a) Common for soldiers and officers

• *Boche*, plural *Boche*s – to designate all German troops, they hated the term. Used particularly by older people of the WWI generation. Their grown-up children used the term. The younger generation also used it, but were quick to find new nicknames. Most of the time it was pronounced in anger at the occupier, as in the Boches take everything from us, which became a common refrain throughout the Occupation. It was always used in the plural in France – *les Boches*, unless to denote a specific soldier or entity – *Le Boche* – the enemy. There is no rule about using a capital or not.

• *Chleus* or *Schleus* – from a tribe in North-Africa, a pejorative term for soldiers. Likely to be used by older French people.

• *Doryphores* – literally the term refers to the Colorado beetle that devastates potato plants, a staple of German food. Hence the association, but also because, historically, Germany introduced the potato into France. The epithet was often used ironically by everyone to complain that the occupiers were taking everything, especially food.

• *Fridolins* – perhaps from its use as a common German first name – used mostly by young people.

• *Frisés* – spoken ironically, as the term had designated German Jews since 1836. Always in the plural. Likely to be used by the working class.

• *Fritz* – a term preferred by the Germans themselves and pronounced with neutral emotion. Used by all.

• *Haricots verts* – green beans. The occupiers never quite got the allusion to the uniform of the Schutzpolizei which was more green than gray.

• *Huns* – widely used during WWI in reference to the ruthless Attila the Hun, after German forces invaded Belgium with extreme brutality. In WWII, more likely to be used by older people and students showing off their knowledge.

• *Prussiens* – likely to be used by older people whose parents had experienced the 1870 Franco-Prussian War.

• *Souris grises* – literally, gray mice, widely used to designate female German military, from the color of their uniforms.

• *Teutons* – from the name of an ancient Germanic tribe. Likely to be used by academics and librarians.

• *Vert-de-gris* – verdigris – uniform of the Schutzpolizei being more green than gray.

(**b**) Names for the Feldgendarmerie – the military field police and alluding to the gorget they wore. A gorget, a crescent-shaped piece of metal worn about the neck on a chain, is a remnant of medieval armor adopted by Nazi formations with a police function.

• *Vache à bavoir* – a cow with a bib, also *vache* means malicious.

• *Barrière à vache* – a cow fence.

• *Vache primée* – prize cattle.

C. Words not used in France during WWII
i. Maquis

• Maquis designates a place, not a person and not an organization.

• The English language adopted the term *maquis* as a noun to mean an organization. It was not an organization. Until 1943, the term was not in use in France. People did not *join the maquis* like one might join an automobile club. Résistants and *réfractaires* (young men avoiding STO) made their way to a camp hidden in the forest, mountains; they took to the maquis.

317

• The term *maquis* originally described the rough scrubland in Corsica. This was the place where people on the run from a vendetta, or from the police, went to hide and set up a camp.

• The résistants living in a maquis camp and military trained were *maquisards*.

• Today, in novels, one can often find lines such as *the maquis blew up the railroad.* The correct form would be *the maquisards blew up the railroad* – a distinction which will help keep your novel sounding authentic – and this only from the summer of 1943.

• The maquis camps were given the names of the localities where they were located, Maquis de la Montagne Noire, Maquis des Glières, and others.

• Résistants had been hiding in forests and mountains since the start of the war, but did not constitute a military encampment until the formation of the Armée secrète(AS).

• Young men – *les réfractaires* – fled to the hills to avoid being drafted as forced labor in Germany. They sometimes knew of a résistance camp or if there were a number of them (some were former scouts) from the same area, they would establish an encampment, which later was integrated with a résistance maquis.

• A resistance member was a *maquisard*.

ii. Maquis and maquisard usage

• The terms *maquis* and *maquisard* were not widespread until the late summer 1943. At first, they were only used by résistants and rural folk. By the fall, the use of those words spread to towns.

• After the war, journalists and some historians used *maquis* as a shortcut to indicate any résistance fighter or group any time during the Occupation, despite the fact there were no maquis until 1943. Many résistance groups were not in maquis camps.

iii. National coffee

318

• There was no such concept in France of a *National Coffee*. The expression came into use under British influence only after the war by writers, journalists and filmmakers, partly due to a lack of research. During the war, people used the German term *ersatz* for coffee substitutes. The French equivalent is *succédané*. There is one mention of *café national* in a Pétain government document in the archives of the État Français alluding to the proportions of one third coffee, one third chicory and one third barley. Whether Pétain had intended this blend to become the model for a *Café national*, the term never caught on, not in Pétain's non-occupied zone or in the occupied zone. In the latter there was no coffee available at all – except on the black market – and people drank various concoctions of acorns, chickpeas, roots or grains, roasted and ground. They certainly had no notion of a *national* coffee.

iv. Nazi
• In wartime France it was not used to mean a *person*.
• The word refers to an entity, a regime, a political party. Various writers, historians, media find it politically correct to use *Nazi* instead of *German*. To be true to the era, it was not used in France to designate the occupying Wehrmacht soldiers, the SD-SS, the Sipo, the Schutzpolizei or the Gestapo. It was used as an *adjective* in its political sense, as in *the Nazi flag, Nazi party, Nazi policies, Nazi politics, Nazi regime, pro-Nazi*. Nazism – a shortened form for the National Socialist Workers' Party – was used when meaning the movement. The Germans in the Nazi party themselves avoided the term as in its origin it was a derogatory term for a foolish, awkward or backward person.
• Words you can use to avoid the term *German* might be *the Third Reich, the Reich, the MBF* or *the occupier(s)*or one of the nicknames. But there are instances when the use of *German* cannot be avoided. Nazi should only be used in its political sense, such as Nazi regime, or specific objects, Nazi flag, Nazi Swastika.

319

NOTE: Evolution of the language. After the war, and into the 1960s, hatred of everything German lingered among a large part of the adult French population and was picked up by children. Germans were still referred to by any of their pejorative names, *Boches* in preference. A change took place after the Traité de l'Élysée – Élysée Treaty – signed between President Charles de Gaulle and Chancellor Konrad Adenauer in January 1963 to establish reconciliation and friendship between the two nations. Writers, media and academics slowly began to use (incorrectly) the term *Nazi* in relation to the war to mark the distinction between the German people and the adherents of the National Socialist movement. This avoidance of the name German is reflected in many WWII novels and not faithful to the time period. I strongly encourage you to use an alternative.

v. Netherlands – Holland

• The most commonly used name for the country in the 1930s and 1940s was *Holland*. Though the name *the Netherlands* existed, do not use in your novel. The country officially adopted the name *the Netherlands* in January 2020.

vi. Résistance or résistance

• With a capital, it designates the abstract entity. General de Gaulle did not use a capital when he wrote of *the flame of résistance...* nor later in his memoirs. He meant the concrete resistance, people fighting back.

• All the other uses do not take a capital – *a résistance movement, a résistance cell, a résistance circuit, a résistance network.*

• The people were *resistants or résistants* – no capital.

• People joined a resistance group, a résistance cell or a résistance movement. They did not join the Résistance. You cannot join an abstract entity.

• The inclusion of the accent in English is discretionary.

vii. English terminology *not* in use at the time

- *abuse, abuser* – not used in the modern sense of maltreating someone but in the sense of deceit.
- *Alzheimer, dementia* –not diagnosed as such during this period. The condition was called *senility* or *dotage*.
- Not used – all the vocabulary related to climate change, environmental issues and carbon emissions, pollution, etc.
- *awareness* – not used in its modern sense of being culturally or politically sensitive, but in the sense of watchful, vigilant.
- *boss* – the term existed but was not in general use in Europe. More common in the U.S.A. perhaps to avoid the term *master*. Use any synonyms, leader, manager, director, commander, etc.
- *boyfriend, girlfriend* – used in the U.S.A. not used at the time in Europe.
- *collateral damage*– it came into use after 1968 in the accepted sense of the term.
- *color photography* – the process was not available to ordinary citizens in wartime France. Photos were touched up by hand.
- *concussion, concussed* – terms employed only by medical personnel.
- *disinformation* – the term came into common usage only circa 1955. In wartime, it was propaganda.
- *failure is not an option* – too modern an expression for a WWII novel. Use a sentence such as 'you cannot fail', etc.
- *food insecurity* – although the individual words are as old as the language itself, the expression is modern.
- *genocide* – the term was coined in 1944 by Raphael Lemkin, a Polish-American jurist. Certainly not in use in wartime France or Europe.
- *guy* – now universally adopted to mean any person, it was not in use in wartime France. Used by U.S. soldiers and came into widespread use only after the war.
- *hairstylist* – the term used at the time was *hairdresser*

321

• *hotty*, plural *hotties* – sorry, only available starting in 1995! If it is of any help, an earlier *hotty* meant a hot water bottle.

• *impact* – before 1955, it meant act of physically striking something. First used in psychotherapy in 1959.

• *impacted* – before 1955 it only meant something compressed into a space. Think wisdom teeth.

• *kid, kids* – the term was introduced in wartime Europe by U.S. forces and came into widespread use only after the war.

• *media* – Not in use. In the 1930s and 1940s, the terms used were *the press, newspapers, radios.*

• *need-to-know basis* – first came into use in 1952.

• *okay, OK* – this expression, in use in the United States since the nineteenth century, was introduced by U.S. troops to England only during the war. It was much later before it came into general use. From the lips of a character speaking French in a novel, the equivalent would be *d'accord.*

• *panic attack* – an expression that came into use only after WWII.

• *political correctness, PC* – the expression appeared in 1934 in an American English dictionary, but was not used until 1970. It was not in use in WWII Europe.

• *pollution* – not used until circa 1955.

• *PTSD* – Appeared in 1980. Before that, the syndrome was known as *shell shock* in WWI and *battle fatigue* in WWII.

• *recycle, recycling* – the term and concept do not fit a WWII novel. To *reuse* was the common term.

• *scam, scammer* – dates from the 1960s.

• *snafu* – meaning a mix-up, dates from 1942 U.S. military slang. Unlikely to be in use among civilians.

• *spa* – the term was in widespread use in the nineteenth century onward to denote a town or place offering curative mineral water to people of both sexes. Several locations were known as spa towns. Its modern use to denote a commercial establishment offering health and beauty treatments, mostly to women, dates from the early 1960s.

• *spam* – The only spam known to wartime Europe was the trade name *Spam*. The widely available canned ham, brought to England first, then the rest of Europe from August 1944 by U.S. forces. In the sense of *junk mail,* it dates only to the introduction of the internet (1983).

• *teenager* – although used in the U.S. the term was not used until after WWII in Europe. Consider using *adolescent, youngster, young man, young woman.*

• *tissue* – nose-wipes of the paper variety appeared on the market in the mid-1940s and were not mass produced until 1960. It did not exist in wartime Europe. Both men and women carried linen handkerchiefs which were washed with the laundry. Do not have fictional characters *reaching for a tissue.* Certainly not a Kleenex®!

• *virtual* – from the Merriam-Webster: being such in essence or effect though not formally recognized or admitted – a *virtual* dictator. Only use it in this sense.

• *war crime* – although the expression existed, it was not in the common vocabulary. Use massacre when writing about Oradour-sur-Glane, or the Vercors, or the maquis des Glières, etc.

• *water bottle* – today's ubiquitous water bottle that people carry everywhere was not around in WWII, France. For a picnic, people would take along water in an empty wine bottle. This would apply to someone in hiding.

• *woke* – not a concept in WWII.

vii. English terminology that changed meaning

• English words used at the time that have changed meaning but need to be used in the era's context. A notable example is the word *gay*, which until well into the second part of the twentieth century was a widely used term meaning *happy* or *joyous*. Today, of course, it is almost totally the preserve of the homosexual community. In a WWII era novel, the term *gay* in the sexual sense should be avoided, and such a character would be referred to either as *homosexual* or *lesbian*. There was no designation for other types of sexuality.

   • French law of the wartime era was much more enlightened on this subject than, say England, where homosexuality remained a punishable crime until as late as 1967. Despite this, homosexual activity, both male and female, in France carried a social stigma and was conducted clandestinely. People knew it existed but did not speak about it and treated homosexuals like any other persons.

Note:

   It is hoped that these few language notes will help prevent anachronisms creeping into your WWII novel.

34. Liberation
A. Allied Advance, June 6, 1944, Normandy landings
• In the week preceding the landings, June 1-5, 1944, the British Broadcasting Corporation(BBC) starting broadcasting radio messages to the French Résistance to standby, at 1230 hrs (12:30 pm) and every three hours until 2130 hrs (9:30 pm).

i. June 1, 1944
• The first message was *L'heure du combat viendra* – the hour of combat is approaching. This was followed by messages for each resistance cell to begin action, including a message in case of cancellation.

- Plan vert – Plan Green – the destruction of rail lines and rolling stock.

- Plan violet – Plan Violet – disruption of communication networks.

- Plan bleu –Plan Blue – sabotage of electricity infrastructure.

- Plan torue – Plan Tortoise – the blockage of roads and blowing up of bridges.

• The second and somewhat cryptic message was the most awaited – *"Les sanglots longs des violons de l'automne.."* which indicated that the landings would take place five days later.

ii. June 5, 1944
• *"Bercent mon coeur d'une langueur monotone."* – the message confirming the landings for the following day.

B. American maneuvers
• De Gaulle was aware that the American Administration had plans to set up a government of occupation to govern a liberated France. They had even printed obsidional money to replace the franc (See 21. Economy. Industries. Factories. Banks). General de Gaulle, being an ardent patriot, considered this to be totally unacceptable, as did his followers, especially the résistants.

C. De Gaulle's maneuvers
i. De Gaulle and the FFL
• De Gaulle and the FFL – Free French Forces – were not recognized by the United States as the legitimate government in exile, even after November 1942, when de Gaulle and his entourage set up the Provisional Government of France in Algiers, Algeria. Consequently, de Gaulle bypassed diplomatic and military channels. Many members of the civil service, ministers and military were unified behind him. He was the rallying figure of the French Résistance and he had the support of the population – ironically, the same population that had acclaimed Pétain two years previously.

ii. Thwarting the Americans
• To prevent the American administration from carrying out their occupation plan, the French Provisional Government was determined to be in Paris before the advancing Allies, and Paris had to be free of the MBF administration. De Gaulle ordered General Leclerc to press on to the capital, despite the Allied command's decision to bypass Paris. General de Gaulle and U.S. General Paton had a discussion.

• General Paton was convinced by de Gaulle's arguments and diverted some of his troops to help liberate Paris.

• The Paris uprising succeeded and von Choltitz surrendered to General Leclerc and André Parodi, representing the Provisional Government. The German forces had hastily retreated, except for a rear guard, by the time General Leclerc had entered Paris on August 25, 1944. He was soon followed by de Gaulle, who arrived by plane.

D. Importance of France for the liberation of Europe
• The French coast was of strategic importance to the Allied landings due to its proximity to England. There were miles of suitable beaches for landing craft.

• The Résistance was in place to delay the Wehrmacht from reinforcing its troops in Normandy. The French résistants had already proven their value in sabotaging targets that could not be bombed effectively.

E. Importance of the liberation of Paris

• Paris, the capital of France, had long held a special place in Europe. During the Occupation, it was the favored city of top German officials and military and the recreation hub for the troops. Hitler, himself, admired Paris and intended after the war to make it the "cultural capital" of the Third Reich. However, Albert Speer in his memoirs mentioned that Hitler wanted Berlin to be better and more grandiose than Paris and that afterwards Paris could be discarded, but would remain as a holiday resort for Nazi Herrenwolk.

• In the eyes of the French population in the non-occupied zone, Paris not Vichy remained the capital. Even the MBF viewed Paris as the capital of the whole of France, thus relegating Vichy to a minor role.

• It was widely held that Paris had to be liberated to affirm French sovereignty.

• August 11, 1944 –SNCF rail workers strike.

• August 15, 1944 – despite a general strike, the SS on their own still managed, in the middle of the night, to dispatch a deportation train bound for Auschwitz, carrying 2,400 prisoners and driven by German engineers.

• August 17, 1944 – political prisoners were released from the various prisons and joined the various résistance groups in the city.

• August 19, 1944 – spurred on by the FTP, the insurrection began and barricades went up.

• August 20, 1944 – Swedish diplomat Raoul Nordling negotiated a cease-fire to allow the wounded to be taken to hospitals.

• August 20 to 25, 1944 – The Wehrmacht and SS-units carried out executions in the suburbs. The Conseil National de la Résistance felt justified to break the truce. Fighting resumed. Entire units of the Wehrmacht withdrew.

• August 25, 1944 – at dawn, the French Second Armored Division, under General Leclerc entered Paris via the Porte d'Orléans, in the south of Paris, and took part in the final battles.

• At 1630 hours (4:30 pm), German General von Choltitz signed the surrender in the presence of General Leclerc.

• August 26, 1944 – celebrations took place, but at 2300 hours (11:00 pm), the Luftwaffe bombed Paris. Hôpital Bichat and the Halles-aux-Vins, wine market, were hit. One hundred dead. Many buildings damaged.

F. Major ports

• It was essential for the Allied troops to have access to ports, especially deep sea ports, for resupplying the advancing forces. The occupiers destroyed as much as they could of the port installations before fleeing or surrendering.

i. Bordeaux, 1944 – the occupiers planned the total destruction of the port and economic infrastructure. The résistance groups had been decimated, notably by the Grandclément's treason, in 1943, and the occupiers believed they were safe.

• June 2, 1944 – BBC Message was *Philémon réclame six bouteilles de Sauternes*, indicating the start of Opération Tortue involving the destruction of roads and all means of traveling to Normandy to counter the Allied landings. The occupiers were surprised. The fighting intensified.

• The occupiers' planned destruction of the port set for August 25, 1944, was pushed back to August 27, with the intention of laying explosives every fifty meters. But on August 22, a German soldier named Heinz Stahlschmidt deliberately blew up the warehouse containing the explosives.

TRIVIA: Heinz Stahlschmidt took the name Henri Salmide after the war and became a French citizen. Without his courageous act, the port and the town would have been obliterated and thousands of lives lost. The occupiers believed a résistant group was the perpetrator of the explosion.

• August 24 to 26, 1944 – the FFI maintained continued negotiating with the occupiers for them to leave without reprisals. Meanwhile, the occupiers sunk hundreds of boats in the Garonne River estuary to hinder its use by the Allies.

• August 27, 1944 – the occupiers left Bordeaux without further attempts to destroy the port and city.

• August 28, 1944 – official liberation of Bordeaux.

ii. Brest, 1944. Brest was a strategic port.

• August 14, the Germans accept to evacuate the population except for 2,000 persons deemed by them to be indispensable workers.

• As part of Operation Cobra, U.S. troops, guided by the FFI, fought house to house.

• September 19, 1944 – after forty-three days of continuous combat and siege, General Ramcke surrendered to General Middleton.

• The town had been razed to the ground. The port was heavily damaged. Six hundred inhabitants had been killed, 371 of them in the explosion of a bomb shelter, along with 500 Germans also sheltering there.

iii. Le Hâvre, 1944 – the port was considered the strongest along the Atlantic wall.

• September 4, 1944 – a surrender ultimatum was sent by the British commander, General John Crocker, to the German garrison, but Colonel Eberhard Wildermuth refused and requested the evacuation of the civilians.

• September 10, 1944 – General Crocker rejected the request to evacuate civilians and launched the attack. The town was heavily bombed, fires spread and many shelters collapsed. There were 2,053 civilian deaths – needless casualties had the town been evacuated as per the German request. The British later contested this figure, citing only a few hundred casualties. From a strategic point of view, the bombing of the town center – which was eighty-five percent destroyed – as ordered by British

Air Chief Marshal Sir Arthur Harris, was not necessary according to military leaders, including U.S. General Eisenhower.

* September 12, 1944 – the German garrison surrendered.
* The remaining population, who had been pro-British up to that day, did not welcome the liberating British troops. Windows in buildings that remained standing were shuttered. People did not even return greetings if they happened to meet them in the street afterwards. Some Hâvrais wished General Crocker could have been brought to justice for war crime.

iv. Lorient 1945 – as General Patton's forces entered Britany, German General Fahrmbacher ordered his forces to retreat to the fortified port of Lorient and its immediate hinterland to form a pocket with a 90 km (56 mi) front in which there were 26,000 German troops and 20,000 civilians.

* The Germans believed they were denying the Allies the use of the port.
* The Allies considered it of lesser strategic importance and did not launch a full assault on the fortress as they did on Brest, where it caused considerable casualties.
* The long siege was hard on the population during one of the coldest winters for the region with lack of food and fuel.
* Résistants were able to pass on intelligence to the FFI outside the pocket.
* General Farhrmbacher surrendered May 10, 1945.

v. Marseille 1944 – German General Schaëffer held the city of Marseille with 4,000 men, many of them older men and young Russians from conquered territories forced into the Wehrmacht. He had received orders to defend the city until the last man. The Allies entrusted the liberation of the city to the French General Joseph de Goislard de Monsabert.

* August 19, 1944 – the FFI led the insurrection, but they were sorely lacking arms.

• August 23, 1944 – General Monsabert and his troops reached Marseille. General Schaëffer refused to capitulate.
• August 28, 1944 – after five days of fighting, General Schaëffer laid down arms.
• August 29, – Marseille was officially liberated. Unfortunately for the Allies, the port installations had been sabotaged by the Germans and damaged by allied bombing.

vi. May 9, 1944, Saint-Nazaire – the German commander refused to surrender to the French FFI. The fighting continued.
• There were 130,000 civilians inside the Saint-Nazaire pocket, many of them evacuated during a truce by trains organized by the Red Cross. Others escaped and joined the FFI in the already liberated countryside. Many more were unable to leave and were forced to share the few remaining resources with the Germans during the coldest winter experienced in that region, without electricity.
• Since the Allies were not going to launch an assault on the fortress, FFI units were assigned to keep the Germans troops inside the redoubt to prevent them from breaking out and joining the forces on the Normandy front.
• A résistance group within the pocket passed on intelligence by crossing the front line to the FFI troops and on to the American troops.
• The Germans believed they were denying the Allies the use of the port. However, it was of lesser strategic importance to the Allies who wanted to avoid needless casualties.
• The prefect issued guidelines to the mayors of the communities within the pocket for evacuation. However, the occupiers were not willing to let civilians go for fear they would give the Allies valuable information on their deployment.
• **May 11, 1945** – the American General Herman Kraemer arrived and General Hans Junck surrendered.
• Saint-Nazaire was the last French town to be liberated. To this day, the inhabitants claim they had been forgotten.

G. Liberation of major towns
i. Amiens – liberated by the FFI, 1944
• August 30, 1944 – Allied armored divisions were directed to Amiens to protect the bridges essential to Allied troop movement to the north and Belgium.

• August 31, 1944 – the FFI engaged the Wehrmacht, who had already blown up three bridges, and succeeded in saving one essential bridge.

• Late evening, the FFI captured the town hall. Allied tanks entered the town and any German left surrendered.

ii. Lyon – liberated by the FFI, 1944
• There were not enough armed resistants in the city to sustain the insurrection, which started August 24 and ended August 27. Maquisards from the surrounding areas converged onto the city and fought alongside the U.S. Army that had arrived from the south.

• September 1-2, 1944 – the Wehrmacht fled.

• September 3, 1944 – Lyon officially liberated.

H. SS units and Wehrmacht reprisals (See 43. Retreating armies)
• Some towns and villages endured reprisals – later recognized as war crimes – from the occupiers, particularly in 1944 when German forces headed to Normandy. A brief list of towns and villages where crimes were perpetrated by the Waffen-SS, Totenkopf units,Wehrmacht and Kriegsmarine:

- Against civilians – Ascq, Buchères, Caen, Issendolus, Gouesnou (by the Kriegsmarine), Maillé, Mussidan, Oignies (one British officer burned alive), Oradour-sur-Glane, Saulx, Tulle, Vassieux-en-Vercors.

- Against Jews – Bron, Saint-Genis-Laval, Sainte-Marie-de-Chignac, Savigny-en-Septaine, Saint-Amand.

- Against POWs held on French territory being mostly colonial troops – Paradis-Lestrem, Chasselay (Senegalese battalion), Saint-Germain-Blanche-Herbe.

- Against résistants – Basse-sur-le-Rupt, Beyssenac, Janaillat, Meillan, Mont-Mouchet, Révin, Valréas, Glières, Vassieux-en-Vercors.

35. Media

• The word *media* in its modern sense denotes all forms of news distribution. It was not in use at the time. It was the *press* and *radio*.

• The French press was under the Propaganda Abteilung censorship and required permission to publish or broadcast.

A. Main newspapers at the start of the war

• *L'Illustration* – weekly, read by the bourgeoisie.

• *L'Action Française* – Catholic (monarchist tendency), extreme right wing.

• *Le Figaro* – moderate.

• *Gringoire* – right wing.

• *Le Populaire* – moderate, left wing.

• *Le Matin* – moderate.

• *Le Petit Parisien, Paris-Midi, Le Canard Enchaîné* – all left wing.

• *Je Suis Partout* – extreme right.

• *Ce Soir* – left wing, with communist leanings.

• *L'Humanité* – communist.

• *La Croix* – Catholic.

• *Paris-Soir* – popular for classified advertisements.

• *Le Merle Blanc* – satirical paper.

• *Paris Press* – moderate.

• *L'Intransigeant* – moderate, left wing.

ii. 1940, June – newspapers which chose to cease publication

• *Paris Press, Le Populaire, Le Figaro, Le Carnard Enchaîné, L'Intransigeant.*

iii. Non-occupied zone

• Newspapers from the non-occupied zone were banned in the occupied zone.

iv. 1944, August

• All collaborationist press was banned. Newspapers which had ceased publication reappeared. Some clandestine newspapers survived beyond the Liberation.

• New publications appeared: *L'Aurore, Le Monde.*

B. Role of the press

• Whether official or clandestine, the press filled the role of conveying information, false information and propaganda. Today, false information is referred to as *disinformation.* This term was not in use in the WWII era and its inclusion in novels of that time should be avoided.

• The press:
- Strengthened political power.
- Was subjected to censorship.
- Spread propaganda.
- Provided entertainment through articles, features and cartoons, as well as listing movies, shows and exhibitions.
- Women's magazines, besides giving advice on obtaining or growing food and recipes, also gave tips on beauty and fashion.
- *Signal* – a German-produced glossy color magazine, in several languages besides German. Both the French and German editions were available in France. It was a propaganda tool.

NOTE – The French edition was translated and some of the articles in the German edition were omitted in the French version or replaced by articles considered more appropriate for the French public. For example, articles on eugenics in the German edition were eliminated, as the editors knew they would not be well received by a French audience and would cause unfavorable reactions to Nazi ideology. The higher Nazi authorities were intent on collaboration and gave some consideration to the French in order to maintain it.
- The editors for the French were sensitive to French public opinion and stressed the collaboration between two *great nations* that would lead Europe together– no mention of the domination and occupation of France.

- Also, French translators were apt at using euphemisms.For the much-touted concept of territorial expansion known as *Lebensraum*, which would normally be translated in French as *espace vital* – essential living space, became *cadre de vie digne* – dignified lifestyle, which is perhaps not what the German propaganda officials intended.

- Although people were faithful to a newspaper, they read others so as not to miss any news.

- Women in particular scoured newspapers for announcements of the availability of foodstuffs.

- Newspapers could be bought from a street kiosk in Paris and in major towns or from a *librairie papeterie* – a bookstore that also sold stationery.

- The prewar *Le Journal Officiel de la République Française* was the official government gazette for the whole of France. From February 1941 until August 1944, it adopted the name – *Le Journal Officiel de l'État Français*.

- In London, the Free French Forces (FFL) published *Le Journal Officiel des Forces Françaises Libres*, which in 1942, after the installation of the provisional government in Algiers, changed to *Le Journal Officiel de la France Libre* and, finally as of August 1944, to *Le Journal Officiel de la République Française*, its original name.

i. Clandestine resistant press
• Resistance movements were established around the following newspapers:
- *Combat.*
- *Défense de la France* – centered on *Le Musée de l'Homme.*
- *Forces Unies de la Jeunesse.*
- *France Libre.*
- *La Voix du Nord.*
- *Le Franc-Tireur Parisien, Le Franc-Tireur.*
- *Le Père Duchesne.*

ii. Collaborationist press
• *Au Pilori*
• *Je Suis Partout* – banned in June 1940, allowed again in February 1941, and became the most widely read paper among collaborationists.
• *La Gerbe*

iii. Communist press
• *L'Humanité* – banned in September 1939, became clandestine, reappeared officially in August 1944, in Paris, later in all the regions.

iv. German publications
• *Pariser Zeitung* – German language paper for the Wehrmacht. Only in the occupied zone.
• *Signal* – both German and French editions. Only in the occupied zone.

v. Official publications
• *Journal Officiel* – published only legal, administrative and public service information, together with official decrees and laws citizens had to obey.

vi. Newspapers that voluntarily ceased publication until after August 1944
• *L'Intransigeant* – ceased publication in 1940, reappeared in August 1944.
• *Le Figaro* – ceased publication in 1940, reappeared in August 1944.
• *Le Canard Enchaîné* – ceased publication in 1940, reappeared in August 1944.
• *Le Petit Parisien* – originally enjoyed the largest circulation in the world. After
the arrival of German forces, the Propaganda-Abteilung Frankreich took it over for propaganda purposes. After the Liberation, it changed its name to *Le Parisien Libéré*.

• *Le Populaire* – ceased publication in 1940, reappeared in August 1944.

• *Paris-Press* – ceased publication in 1940, reappeared in August 1944.

vii. Non-occupied zone, newspapers censored by État Français

• *Gringoire.*
• *Le Merle.*
• *Le Nouvelliste.*
• *Le Petit Marseillais.*

viii. Newspapers published after the Liberation

• *Action* – a resistance paper.

• *L'Aurore*– a new publication, tendency Gaullist.

• *Le Canard enchaîné* – ceased publication in 1940, reappeared in August 1944.

• *Carrefour* – a resistance paper.

• *Combat* – a resistance paper.

• *Le Figaro* – ceased publication in 1940, reappeared in August 1944.

• *France-Soir* – a resistance newspaper founded in 1944 by Robert Salmonand and Philippe Viannay. The latter had founded *Défense de la France* at the *Musée de l'Homme.*

• *L'Intransigeant*– ceased publication in 1940, reappeared in August 1944.

• *Le Journal des Combattants* – a military veterans paper.

• *La Marseillaise* – a resistance paper.

• *Libération* – a resistance paper.

• *Le Monde* – founded after August 1944.

• *Le Parisien libéré.*

NOTE: *Le Petit Parisien* – had been taken over by the Propaganda Abteilung. After the Liberation, it changed its name to *Le Parisien Libéré.*

• *Le Populaire* – ceased publication in 1940, reappeared in August 1944.

• *Paris-Press* – ceased publication in 1940, reappeared in August 1944.

• *Voir* – an American propaganda newspaper, published 1944-1945 in France with the permission of the French Ministry of Information. Contained numerous photos depicting joyful populations liberated by U.S. troops.

ix. Periodicals, magazines

(a) Children's magazines were available in the occupied zone until 1942, when the MBF suppressed them due to paper shortages. The most popular for girls were *Lisette*, *Fillette*, *Les Grandes Aventures* and for boys *Pierrot*, *Fanfan la Tulipe*, *Gavroche*.

• Available in the non-occupied zone – *Robinson*.

• An anomaly appeared in 1942 in the occupied zone, in the form of a new glossy children's magazine, *Le Téméraire* – highly politicized, with anti-Semitic characters. It was founded in collaboration between the Propagandastaffel and Jacques Carlin, publisher of children's books. Despite the lavish use of paper, it was approved by the MBF authorities.

(b) Collaborationists magazines that disappeared after the Liberation:

• *La Semaine*.
• *Toute La Vie*.
• *Vedettes*.

(c) Women's weekly magazines

• *Candide, Eve, Fémina, Le Jour, Marianne, Pour Elles, Le Progrès*,
• *Le Petit Écho de la Mode, Modes et Travaux*
• *Marie-Claire*: moved to Lyon in the non-occupied zone.

x. Religious publications

• *La Croix*.

C. Role of the press at the liberation of the country

• Beside whipping up enthusiasm for the liberators, the press emphasized the search for justice by publishing the names of collaborators, particularly miliciens, with headlines such as *milicien-X, the murderer of innocent-Y, has been found.*

• Reporting the details of trials gave closure to people whose families had been harmed.

• The public was reeling from the violence of the Milice and was thirsty for justice. It was comforting to see that the justice system was working and was putting an end to the most despised and feared organization.

D. Role of the Radio

• The term *radio* at the time referred to the broadcasting station, not the actual receiver, which was a T.S.F. (*télégraphie sans fil*) set – equivalent to the English at the time of *the wireless*, meaning a radio set.

• Radio played a huge part during the Occupation. The competition among Radio Londres, Radio Vichy, Radio Paris – the latter controlled by the occupier, with programs with French announcers – and Radio Stuggart was fierce.

• They broadcasted a lot of music, information – and false information and rumors – as well as humorous sketches.

• 1940s-era radio sets were usually bulky items that had to be connected to a source of electricity. In a WWII-era novel, if referring to the apparatus in someone's home on which they listened to regular broadcast programs, it is advisable to use the term T.S.F. The term *radio* would be used if referring to two-way radio transmitters used for military-style communication and the transmitter-receiver used by the résistants and the SOE in London.

• Portable sets existed, but they too were cumbersome and operated on heavy, short-lived rechargeable wet batteries. Very few people would have one. Those were among the sets turned over to the MBF authorities when people had to surrender their T.S.F. sets, which had shortwave capacity.

i. Clandestine broadcasting stations listened to in France

• BBC Radio Londres, French broadcast – started every transmission with the opening bars of Beethoven's *Fifth Symphony*.

• Radio Sottens in Switzerland – a large audience, especially in the east of France.

ii. Official broadcasting stations in the non-occupied zone

• Radio Nationale de Vichy – Radio Vichy.

• Radio Montpellier – a local broadcasting commercial station, followed Radio Vichy.

• Radio Lyon – a local broadcasting commercial station, followed Radio Vichy.

iii. Official broadcasting stations in the occupied zone

• Radio Paris – began their broadcasts with a fragment of *La Cucaracha* – which soon had the humorists in London and in France singing *Radio Paris ment, Radio Paris ment, Radio Paris est allemand* (Radio Paris lies, Radio Paris lies, Radio Paris is German).

• Radio Stuttgart – German station broadcasting in French.

36. Nazi organizations in France
A. *Abwehr*
• The Abwehr occupied the Hôtel Lutétia in Paris. A counter-espionage organization. Pro-Allied elements of it had channels to the résistance groups.

• It specialized in the fight against resistants. Its plain-clothed agents were the secret Geheime Feldpolizei. They operated in Germany and occupied France – the Geheime Feldpolizei only until 1942, after which it was absorbed by the Sicherheitsdients(SD). Not to be confused with the Geheime Staatspolizei (Gestapo) who also operated in plain clothes. The Abwehr passed intelligence to the Gestapo who acted on it.

• Admiral Canaris headed the Abwehr and worked against the Nazi regime at the officer level, but this did not alter the hunt for résistants. The Abwehr's resistance work became known as *Die Schwartze Kapelle* – the Black Orchestra.

• There was strong antagonism between SS branches and Himmler, who wanted to control all the intelligence services.

• The Gestapo uncovered the anti-Nazi dealings of the Abwehr and Hitler abolished it in February 1944.

B. Gestapo – *Geheime Staatspolizei*
i. Nazi Gestapo
• The reach and the strength of the Gestapo were largely overestimated. Their harsh methods made them feared by all, hence why it was thought they had a kind of superpower.

• The Gestapo was a sub-office of the Sicherheitsdienst(SD) which also included the Sicherheitspolizei(Sipo).

• There were 2,500 Gestapo personnel for the whole of France after November 1942. They relied on the SD, Sipo's and their own informers among collaborators.

• Geheime Staatpolizei – plain-clothed secret police, some of whom were members of the SS but this was not a requirement. They pursued perceived political and racial enemies of the Reich namely, subversive elements, résistants, dissidents, communists and Jews from the SD intelligence.

• They also arrested and sent to concentration camps homosexuals discovered in the ranks of the Wehrmacht and all branches of the SS. In addition to punishment, they provided medical, psychiatric and educational therapies.

• The Gestapo occupied contiguous buildings on Avenue Foch in Paris – numbers 82 to 86. No. 84 was best known as the location for the torture of detainees. It was also there that the *Funkspiel* – the *radio game* in English – was located. Its role was to transmit false information to Britain by SOE radio operators who had been captured and forced to cooperate.

• One of the responsibilities of the Gestapo was the deportation of Jews to ghettos, concentration camps, execution sites and death centers.

ii. French Gestapo

• The French Gestapo, known as the *Carlingue* – from a slang word meaning *cockpit* in aviation – was not well-known by the general population.

• It was located on rue Lauriston with an annex on rue de la Pompe.

• The Reich did not have enough men to plunder the riches of the country. They could not rely on poorly organized collaborators, so they turned their attention to the criminal element of society, which they could pressure.

• Henri Chamberlin, who went under the name Henri Lafont, was its founder, along with a rogue police inspector named Pierre Bonny. The occupiers gave Monsieur Henri, as he was also called, a German police card, which gave him free rein to act.

• Initially, they set up French *bureaux d'achats* – buying offices – where at cut prices they bought anything people desperate for money were selling. The Carlingue then resold the goods to the German Bureaux d'Achats.

343

• The Carlingue also executed missions all over France for the Reich, including in the non-occupied zone, be it hunting specific people or dealing in trade.

• Dealing with the Carlingue, and for himself with the Reich, was Joseph Joinovici, a man of Romania origin and a non-practicing Jew. He never integrated with the Carlingue and kept his group independent. His business flourished during the Occupation. He also funded *L'Honneur de la Police* résistance group and saved countless Jewish lives. To this day, he remains a controversial figure.

• June 1944 – the Carlingue ceased operations, dispersed and tried to blend in with the general population.

• August 31, 1944 – Henri Lafont and Pierre Bonny were arrested.

C. SS – *Schutzstaffel*,

• The Schutzstaffel (SS) was the Nazi Party's dedicated paramilitary arm as well as its administrative branch. The Sicherheitsdienst (SD), the Geheime Staatpolizei (Gestapo) and the Schutzpolizei (equivalent to French police, made arrests, accompanied the deportation trains) were subordinate to the SS. The SS could be compared to an octopus with tentacles in every aspect of life, including Germany's own military units.

• It consisting of three units: The Leibstandarte which formed Hitler's personal guard, the Totenkopfverbände in the concentration camps and the Verfügungstruppen – the elite troops within the Wehrmacht.

• The SS ranks were more or less equivalent to those in the regular armed forces ranks but with different names.

D. *Sicherheitsdienst* (SD), *Sicherheitspolizei* (Sipo, SP)
i. The SD was the security and intelligence branch of the SS.

• They worked closely with the Gestapo. The SD gathered intelligence to ensure the security of the troops. Their units (Sipo) could arrest and imprison suspects. The SD also pursued criminals, such as black marketers, parallel to and in collaboration with French police. They used the same ranks as the SS. Usually plain clothes, when in uniform it was the gray SS uniform but without the runes. It displayed a black lozenge-shaped badge on the left sleeve with the embroidered letters *SD*.

• In addition, the Sipo, when in uniform, wore the gray SS uniform with SS runes on the left collar and a diamond patch on the sleeve. They also wore a gorget.

NOTE: a common confusion among writers is to call any German arresting squad *the SS*. You should use the SD or the SIPO.

• The SD wore the gray uniform with the distinctive SS runes on the right collar. The black uniform had been phased out by 1937 and was only occasionally used on ceremonial occasions and for official photos.

• June 1, 1942, the Sipo replaced the Wehrmacht security patrols.

• Due to tensions and rivalries among the various departments, lines of authority were sometimes blurred.

• German police units were not tasked with keeping public order. They only performed their special duties. French police and gendarmes kept order and dealt with crime, petty incidents, traffic, received denunciation letters and, when summoned, assisted with roundups.

NOTE: By the terms of the June 22, 1940 armistice, it was stipulated that the Reich had total power over the occupied zone. That included the French police. Biased historians have written that French gendarmes organized the roundup of Jews. Gendarmes are military. Like in all armies, soldiers obey orders. The prefect of police, as requested by the MBF, did give the orders that the gendarmes had to obey. The prefect of police's role has been controversial ever since. It must be remembered that except for the pro-Nazis, other administrators had no choice under the terms of the armistice but to obey in order to maintain the fabric of French administration and society. Individually, many of them found ways to beat the system.

345

ii. Police protection of deportation trains
• A detachment of the Ordnungspolizei – Order Police – and Schutspolizei accompanied the deportation trains, ensure order on stations' platforms. The Order Police wore a green-grayish uniform with a black collar, two bars but no runes, and a forage cap or casque. The Schutzpolizei wore a green uniform with the SS runes on the left collar.

iii. Schutzpolizei
• A branch of the Ordnungspolizei. Its members fulfilled police duties, accompanied the deportation trains, ensure order on stations' platforms and did guard duties. They wore a greenish uniform, which got them the nickname *vert-de-gris*, verdigris.

E. SS-Verfügungstruppe, Waffen-SS
• The SS-Verfügungstruppe was created in 1934 to be the combat arm of the SS.
• In March 1940, by Hitler's special decree, it officially became known as the Waffen-SS.
• They wore the same *feldgrau* – gray-green – uniform as the Wehrmacht.
• The Waffen-SS were elite panzer troops in the Wehrmacht. The 2nd SS Panzer Division received the name of Das Reich in the fall of 1940.
• At the beginning of 1940, Himmler recruited ethnic Germans from outside the Reich into the Waffen-SS. They wore an appropriate nationality patch on the collar.
• In 1942, the Waffen-SS accepted volunteers from Scandinavian countries and other countries. In 1944, in France, it became known as the Division SS-Charlemagne and was formed with the remnants of the Milice.

F. Lebensborn

- The Lebensborn program was created by the Nazi authorities to increase Germany's population. Women deemed racially pure were encouraged to give birth in special Lebensborn homes.
- A little known fact is that there was a Lebensborn in Lamorlaye in France's Oise department, which the Germans called The Westwald.
- It was organized in a small, isolated château the locals called *Château Ménier* belonging to the chocolatier Meunier but requisitioned by the occupiers.
- Lamorlaye itself was occupied by good-natured Wehrmacht mounted soldiers, who were strictly forbidden to approach the château, which was exclusively guarded by Schutzpolizei guards.
- The Lamorlaye Lebensborn began to function in 1943. French and Belgian women, deemed to meet the racial criteria established by the Nazis and made pregnant by SS officers, were admitted early in their pregnancy. After the birth, the mothers had the option of going to Germany with their child or having it sent to Germany for adoption.
- In August 1944, the center was evacuated to Steinhöring in Bavaria before the arrival of U.S. troops.
- The Lamorlaye Lebensborn was odd because the Nazi considered neither the French nor the Belgians superior races. But Hitler needed to increase the German population from which future soldiers could be drawn. Thus, official authorization came directly from Berlin.
- Its records were destroyed by the departing Germans. According to witnesses – gardeners, kitchen and cleaning staff – it is estimated that between twenty to thirty babies were born at the Westwald in Larmorlaye.

37. Occupation of France, June 1940
A. German occupation
i. Paris (See 2. Administration of France and 17. Daily life)
(a) June 14, 1940

• Upon arrival, the Reich authorities ordered the removal of protective sand bags from monuments. French POWs were assigned the work.

• Paris alone had 40,000 Germans in administrative and military positions, this plus large numbers of military personnel who came to Paris on short periods of recuperative leave.

• Other cities also had a large German presence in administrative and military positions, though not as large as Paris.

• Paris was the playground for the Reich Forces. Every soldier was entitled to a leave in Paris. The off-duty soldiers wore a forage cap or field cap, officers a peaked cap.

• There were regular patrols in the streets. They consisted of two men carrying rifles slung over the shoulder.

• August 28, 1940 – ban on public meetings, processions or demonstrations.

• September 16, 1940 – it was forbidden to take photos out of doors or to raise pigeons. French police were obliged to warn the occupier of any acts of sabotage.

• After 1941 and the increase of attacks – patrols were increased to three or more men, each carrying a rifle over the shoulder and a wearing a sidearm.

• Time change – when the Wehrmacht marched into France, it imposed German daylight savings time on a country normally one hour behind German time. As of June 14, 1940 clocks had to be advanced by one hour until October and in the following years of occupation from March to October. This put the country one hour ahead of its normal time both in summer and winter and caused additional disruption to daily life. France is normally one hour ahead of Greenwich Mean Time(GMT), the forerunner of today's UTC – Coordinated Universal Time.

• The requisition of buildings, food stocks, fuel supplies and other commodities was immediate.

(b) June 22, 1940 – the Germans viewed Paris as the cultural capital of the Greater Reich and of the whole of France. Despite Pétain's claim, even French citizens in the non-occupied zone did not recognize Vichy as being the capital.

• The Wehrmacht arrived with lists of addresses of buildings that had a front and back entrances – for security reasons – of hotels and places of entertainment.

• The lists were compiled with the help of the widely available tourist guidebooks and maps – *Les Guides Michelin* (See 2. Administration of France).

• The population's attitude to the new situation was either collaboration, resistance, or wait and see.

• With the Occupation came restrictions and rationing and the economy functioned at a slow pace (See 21. Economy. Industries, Factories, Banks).

ii. Public opinion. Résistance (see 33. Language)

• The restrictions imposed by the MBF and the rationing imposed by Pétain's government created deep resentment among the population.

• Those who collaborated did not suffer greatly from the rationing. The rest of the population did and resorted to various means to provide food and other items (See 17. Daily life).

• Until the summer of 1942, people were more concerned with their own wellbeing than that of others, such as Jews or Roma. When attacks began on officers, people disapproved because of the ensuing reprisals and execution of hostages.

• **June 1942** – the MBF imposed the wearing of the yellow star by all Jews six years of age and up. Public opinion was shocked. This is when people began to turn against the occupiers' policies. It culminated in July 1942 with the roundup and subsequent deportation of Jewish women and children. More people were ready to join a résistance group.

• **January 1943** – the creation of the Service de Travail Obligatoire (STO) was a tipping point. Youths took to the hills to avoid being sent to forced labor in Germany, and although a few did not integrate into a résistance group, the majority supported the résistance.

- The resistance camps thus formed became known as *maquis camps* by the locals or just *the camps*. By the summer, most of the population knew the term *maquis,* but it did not signify a specific place. People did not *join the maquis*, they joined *a maquis camp*. They took to the maquis.

NOTE: It is only after the war that journalists used the expression *'joined the maquis'*. The press, having a major influence on language, let it creep into people's memoirs and was even adopted by serious historians. (see 33. Language, C. Words not in use)

• January 1943 saw the creation of the Milice. Its nucleus was the Service d'Ordre Légionaire (SOL), which had been created by Marshal Pétain to keep order alongside the police in the non-occupied zone.

B. Rural areas in the occupied zone
i. France's special status

• Although France's resources were plundered and the imposed conditions of the occupation were harsh, the country did not suffer as badly as other occupied countries, like Poland or Holland. Hitler viewed the French as the *Alpine race* and acceptable enough to become a satellite of the Reich. He was convinced that the original Aryans had founded France. To prove this, he instructed German archeologists to conduct digs in places such as Carnac. He also ordered the construction of a fortified bunker headquarters at Margival in northern France, where traces of ancient people had been found.

• At the start of the war, no windows were left uncovered. The blackout was enforced. Dark blue cloth had been provided as the war became imminent.

• After the Germans occupied France, the blackout remained in effect but no longer strictly enforced and a blackout curtain might let through a crack of light. Enforcement depended on the local authorities.

• Urban areas suffered the most from the occupier's unfettered power.

• Cities were at an economic disadvantage as they were far from food sources.

• Many rural areas and villages only rarely saw German troops at the beginning and at the end of the war, when they were on the move.

ii. 1942 Secret constructions

• Construction of German secret structures began – the launch pads for V-1 and V-2 rockets in Eperlecques in the Pas-de-Calais region.

iii. November 11, 1942, Occupation of the former non-occupied zone.

• The Eastern Front was consuming too many men, which meant that fewer Wehrmacht soldiers were left to occupy the whole of France after November 1942 (See 3. Allied landings). This meant that some remote areas in the formerly non-occupied zone never saw a German soldier.

• There was only a small number of SD, SIPO, and Gestapo agents in France.

• Violent acts and war crimes were committed by the Waffen-SS, the Wehrmacht and the Kriegsmarine, especially in 1944, when the Reich's troops were attempting to move north to reinforce forces in Normandy.

iv. Postwar retrospective

• Due to the diversity of reactions and the varying degrees of occupation, France's occupation by the Third Reich was not viewed uniformly after the war. Attitudes toward the Résistance depended on a writer's political perspective, some being dismissive. Many writers and historians tended to calculate the number of résistants carrying out combat missions too narrowly and ignored the multitude of ancillaries involved as couriers, hosts of safe houses and radio operators or those who did not physically act but provided money, accommodation or food, as in the case of many farmers.

• From 1943 to February 1, 1944, the FFI counted 100,000 registered fighting members. That figure grew to 400,000 over the next four months. In August 1944, 252,000 FFI members were integrated into the regular French army and went on to continue the struggle.

C. Italian occupation

• November 1942 – Pétain's government was powerless to oppose the entry of the Wehrmacht and Italian troops into the non-occupied zone (See 30 and 31. Invasion).

• Mussolini claimed Corsica in 1940, but Hitler rebuffed him. In 1942, Italian troops were allowed to occupy Corsica – 85,000 troops for 215,000 inhabitants. General Humbert had orders not to resist and, in any case, did not have the means to oppose the Italian landings. Italian Admiral Tur assured him they were coming as friends.

• In Savoie and Haute-Savoie, the Italian troops – the *Alpini* and *Bersaglieri* – marched into villages and towns. No one was in the streets to welcome them and all the stores were closed and shuttered.

• The SNCF refused to drive trains for the Italians,which caused a setback in the Italians' agenda.

• Although Italy and Germany were Axis allies, the Italian government had little trust in Hitler, believing he had hegemony views over Italy. Likewise, Hitler's generals did not trust the Italians, who lacked the armored divisions necessary to hold off an Anglo-American attack.

• The German army marched on Toulon – even though the port was in the Italian zone – in order to capture the French fleet. They did not believe the fleet would scuttle itself.

• The État Français *Armée d'Armistice* was disbanded. In Corsica, the soldiers destroyed and sabotaged their equipment.

• Elsewhere in the Italian zone, *Alpini* and *Bersaglieri* troops pillaged *Armée d'Armistice* depots. The disarmed French soldiers sabotaged what they could.

i. The Principality of Monaco

• Despite its neutrality, which thus far had been respected, the Italians invaded Monaco on the pretext that they were protecting the principality from U.S. and British forces.

ii. Attitude of the French population in the Italian zone

• The population in both Corsica and mainland France felt humiliated at being occupied by the Italians, for whom they had only contempt.

• The Savoyards – inhabitants of the Savoie and Haute-Savoie regions – despised the Alpini and even more the Bersaglieri whom they considered pretentious and over-demanding. Savoyards had not forgotten that in 1940, their French Chasseurs Alpins had soundly beaten the Italian troops and won the battle of the Alps.

• In general, the Italian occupiers were mocked, especially in large towns and cities like Grenoble. The feathers on the broad-brimmed hats of Bersaglieri units were the butt of endless jokes. In other locations, Italian soldiers were met with an apparent total indifference.

• French citizens of Italian extraction had long cut ties with Italy and did not want to be reminded of their origins, while others went out of their way to welcome the occupiers.

• Derogatory nicknames were soon given to the Italian troops: *Macaroni* being the most common. In Corsica it was *Lucchese* – an inhabitant of Lucca, Tuscany. Other names included *Picf* – sparrow and *Pioulet* – small chicken. In Savoie, *Babi* – to cackle, and *Pianto* – young magpie in the southern Alps and the rest of the occupied Riviera.

iii. Attitude of the Italian occupiers
• The Italians recognized that the French had quickly guessed that on the whole, the Italians soldiers were tired of the war.

• The Italians understood that it was the German higher authorities not their own who commanded, and that their power was limited.

• The number of Italian deserters fleeing to Switzerland rose.

• If some troops had sufficient food, others were inadequately supplied. Italian soldiers tried to barter with the inhabitants but were not always successful.

• An army newspaper *IV Armata* tried to boost morale.

• Every week, the military postal service distributed postcards with slogans to help keep up the morale.

• Individual Alpini, dubbed with the reputation of being the *Latin lover,* engaged in relationships with local women.

• The brothel *Le Panier Fleuri* in Saint-Raphaël, was reserved for the exclusive use of Italian troops. Others were in Modane, Chambéry and Toulon, as well as Ajaccio and Bastia in Corsica.

iv. Résistance among the Italian troops
• Poor morale was common among the Italian occupiers. A clandestine newssheet, *La Parola del Soldato,* circulated messages to encourage the troops to desert and fight the Germans.

v. Differences between Italian and German occupation
• Co-existence took place between French citizens and Italian Alpini troops.

• The Italian occupier had orders to strengthen the coastal defenses. This meant the evacuation of several towns, which did not endear them to the population.

• They also enforced the blackout.

• As long as they were not the object of personal attacks, Italian forces did not take hostages or shoot people indiscriminately.

• To fulfill their needs, they adopted the MBF's methods of requisitioning.

• Despite the anti-Semitic laws adopted in Italy in 1938, the Italian occupiers refused to hand over Jews to the Reich. Jews who had previously escaped to the non-occupied-zone were now fleeing to the Italian-occupied zone. Although some incidents took place, the État Français police ended up transferring some Jews into the German zone and rounding up Jews in the Italian zone. After intervention at the government level, General de Castiglion ordered local prefects to free Jews, unless they were common criminals.

• Foreign Jews were assigned a residence and could not move but were otherwise free to shop and work. The État Français gendarmes were told in no uncertain terms that the foreign Jewish population fell under Italian jurisdiction. Fluctuations in food supplies affected everyone. Some locals resented having to share with the foreigners, and that included the Italians!

• Generally speaking, the French population showed a level of tolerance toward the Italians which they did not apply to the German occupiers.

vi. Franco-Swiss border question

• A fifty-kilometer zone had been demilitarized on the border with Switzerland. French border guards performed normal border duties.

• The Italians were to manage the border between Annemasse and Saint-Gingolf, but the Wehrmacht got there first on November 11, 1942 and only let the Italians take over six weeks later at the end of December.

• The État Français protested that the Italian border guards were disrupting communications with Switzerland. In a long tradition, Swiss farmers pastured livestock in French Savoie while French farmers cultivated land on the Swiss side.

• An agreement was reached for the French and Italian border guards to work side by side on goods and livestock crossing the border.

• Italian and French border guards patrolled together without animosity.

vii. Role of the résistance

• Initially, rather than attacking the troops, the résistants focused on the immigrant community that had shown an enthusiastic welcome to the Italians' arrival. Stores and informers were targeted as well as members of the OVRA – the Organization for Vigilance and Repression of Anti-fascism – Mussolini's secret police.

• The résistance groups' aim was to demoralize the Italian occupiers.

• Tracts were aimed at convincing Italian soldiers that Hitler's war was bad for everybody, that Mussolini had sold out to Hitler.

• In December 1942, a clandestine publication, *La Parola del Soldado,* circulated among the Italian troops, inciting them to desert and join the fight against the Germans.

• After the fall of Tripoli and Tunisia, the fascist arm of the Italian occupier executed a résistant in Corsica. Two thousand people attended the funeral. Résistant groups retaliated.

• On the continent, résistance groups kept the pressure on by targeting the Bersaglieri troops.

• The French population did not fully support the attacks on the Italians, who usually did not bother anyone.

viii. Service de Travail Obligatoire in the Italian zone
NOTE: There was a German presence in Toulon under General Scheer, though the area was under the command of Italian Admiral Tur.

• Admiral Tur did not share the Reich's point of view on forced labor. He refused to let French workers be sent to Germany, claiming successfully that he needed them for building the fortifications and working in other sections of the economy that called for intensive manpower. General Scheer gave in as Toulon was under Italian administration.

ix. Résistance in the Italian zone

• The Bersaglieri together with État Français gendarmes planned to destroy and disperse the maquis groups that had formed prior to the Italian occupation in order to recuperate arms.

• More often than not, they arrived to find the camps empty and took revenge on the local inhabitants. The Italian authorities condemned the violence. For their part, the résistants who did not take the Bersaglieri seriously enough were sometimes captured or wounded.

• When a résistance fighter was taken prisoner, often an Alpini or Bersaglieri soldier was reluctant to harm him because they might be related, as in the past the region had swung back and forth between French and Italian ownership. In fact, the Italian Admiral Victorio Tur's brother Paul Tur was French.

• The OVRA, with its black shirts, had no such qualms and aligned itself with Nazi policies of torture and reprisals.

• With the complicity of the OVRA, the Gestapo was able to make some raids into the Italian zone.

• Prisoners were taken to the sinister Villa Lynwood, avenue de Brancolar, in Nice.

• During the spring of 1943, talks took place between high ranking Italian officers and prominent leaders of the local résistance.

x. September 3, 1943 armistice

• Mussolini had been arrested and his government dissolved on July 10, 1943, when the Allies captured Sicily. Italy signed an armistice with the Allies on September 3, 1943, which took effect on September 8, 1943.

D. Special case of Alsace and Moselle
i. October 18, 1940

• October 18, 1940 – by an unpublished decree Hitler declared that Alsace (province made up of Haut-Rhin and Bas-Rhin departments) and the Moselle department (in the Lorraine province made up of four departments Meurthe-et-Moselle, Moselle, Meuse and Vosges) were a de facto part of Germany in direct violation of the armistice conditions signed June 22, 1940. The majority of French people refused to accept that Alsace and Moselle (mostly referred to as Lorraine) had been *annexed*. For them, it was *temporarily occupied*, like the rest of the country.

• Young Alsatian and Mosellan men were forcibly conscripted into the Wehrmacht and were known as *Les Malgré Nous* – Against our Will.

• Refugees with French names had been forbidden to return, except those few absolutely essential to the economy of the region.

• Any remaining Jews and any French sympathizers were expelled.

• Some people saw no alternative or did not have the means to escape, such as older people.

• Some Alsatians were enthusiastically pro-Nazi and welcoming.

• Storekeepers and businesses only saw the profits they could make, whether they shared the Nazi ideology or not.

• When the allowed categories of refugees did return, 100,000 non-Jews chose to remain in the south of France.

• In the non-occupied zone, the local inhabitants, having to share the burden of refugees, were not always welcoming, but the majority were.

• More violence erupted against the Germans in Lorraine, where there was a long history of war between German Prussia and the border departments.

• Of the 798 persons deported, 562 did not come back.

• At the Liberation, German POWs were accepted and better treated than the Allied prisoners had been in Germany.

ii. Résistance in Alsace and Moselle

• Massive yet passive resistance to germanization.

• From there came more active résistance, individual attacks and sabotage.

• The Alsatian and Mosellan résistance groups, although in contact with the German résistance movement, had little to do with it. They looked to the French résistance.

• Résistance began with 16-17- year-old students cutting telephone cables.

• People continued to speak French.

• They would not make the *Heil Hitler* salute. Instead, they said the derisive "*Ein Liter*" – one liter.

• Escape lines formed for POWs, résistants on the run and young men refusing conscription into the Wehrmacht and the Reichsarbeitsdienst – Reich Labor Service.

• Young men who did not want to be germanized and forcibly conscripted escaped to the free zone to travel on to England and join the FFL or they joined a résistant network.

• Escape routes with local *passeurs* were established over the Vosges mountains.

• Main résistant groups in Moselle – *Espoir Français, Réseau Mario, Réseau Derhan, Réseau Wodli* and *Réseau Mission Lorraine*.

• In Alsace – *Réseau d'Alsace* and the *Groupes Mobiles* formed several résistant combat units, namely *La Main Noire, Front de la Jeunesse Alsacienne, Feuille de Lierre, Équipe Pure-Sang, Tante Jeanne, Légion C40* and *Bateliers du Rhin* –Rhine Boatmen, the latter circulating on the river were able to provide much intelligence to the British.

• In 1942, Gauleiter Joseph Bürckel proposed to the Mosellans not belonging to the Deutsch Volksgemeinschaft, and to those who had been excluded, to register with the prefecture in order to leave the department.

    - They were tricked. In January and February 1943, ten thousand of them were rounded up and deported to Silesia. They were known as the *Patriotes résistant à l'Occupation*.

38. Police and gendarmes in both zones

• By the terms of the June 22, 1940 armistice, it was stipulated that the Reich had total power over the occupied zone. That included the police.

• In the occupied zone, although the day-to-day administration of the police and gendarmerie was overseen by the État Français, they were subject to the Reich's military authorities.

• Pétain decreed that there would only be one level of policing – by the *Police Nationale de l'État Français* – in every municipality except Paris, where the Police and Gendarmerie status was not changed.

• The prefects of police applied anti-Semitic laws sometimes zealously, sometimes with laxity.

• French police and gendarmes kept order, dealt with crime, petty incidents, traffic control, received letters of denunciation and when required assisted with the roundups. They answered to the prefects and, in Paris, to the Prefect of Police, which in Paris was a separate office to the administrative prefect – Paris had two prefects.

A. Municipal Police roles and activities

i. August 28, 1940 – ban of public meetings, procession or demonstrations.

ii. September 16, 1940 – it was forbidden to take photographs out of doors or raise homing or racing pigeons.
• Police must inform the occupier of sabotage acts.

iii. October 15, 1940 – the police must surrender any German citizen charged with a crime or offence.
• The police was a national organization and after the June armistice, an organization of the État Français. As a body, it had no autonomy.
• The prefect of police in all departments applied the directives from the Ministry of Justice.
• Individual police officers were required to obey orders.

361

iv. May 1942 to December 31, 1943

• During this period René Bousquet served as Secretary General of Police. Under the auspices of Pétain's government, he reorganized the existing security organization, known as the *Sûreté nationale*, a counterespionage and intelligence gathering body established in the previous century under the direction of the Interior Ministry, and brought it under police administration. To increase its efficiency, he created *Groupes Mobiles de Réserve* (GMR) – mobile reserve groups, effectively paramilitary units.

• June 18, 1942 – René Bousquet obtained from SS Karl Oberg, the chief of all German police units in occupied France, permission for his department to keep control of the French police forces, making the police autonomous of the occupying powers. Of course, this was in name only, as ultimately the German authorities called the shots.

• René Bousquet obtained permission to form the *Brigades Spéciales*(BS) – special brigades, tasked with tracking down and arresting anyone perceived to be an enemy of the state. They worked in close cooperation with German police units.

• Gendarmes – although engaged in civilian police work, the French *gendarmerie* was a branch of the French military, distinct from the police, which was a branch of the civil administration in French municipalities and in Paris.

v. July 2, 1942

• Bousquet and Laval decided to put the civil servants at the disposal of the MBF. The new arrangement suited SS Karl Oberg as he realized the French police would know exactly where to find Jews and other undesirables, such as communists and Spaniards who had fought in the French army. Besides, he would not need to ask for *labor*, as Pétain's government was eager to provide it.

• July 2, 1942. The Nazi regime demanded he hand over of 20,000 Jews. 27,391 registration cards of the persons to be arrested were taken out. Preparations were made for a massive raid in Paris (Vel d'Hiv) as well as in other cities. In Paris, René Bousquet was directly involved with SS Karl Oberg in the organization of the raid to take place on July 14, then changed to July 16 out of fear that a raid on France's national day would have caused riots.

• Despite the elaborate planning, only 13,152 persons were assembled at the Vel d'Hiv. For Bousquet and Laval it was a disappointing fiasco.

• August 26, 1942 – ten thousand Jews were requested by the Reich from the non-occupied zone. To supplement the raids planned for August 26, in the non-occupied zone, Bousquet ordered the arrest of women and children no matter how young. The children under five were taken from homes and orphanages and put on trains by themselves or with a few of their caregivers. There were non-Jewish caregivers who sacrificed themselves to accompany the young children.

vi. Public opinion
• Faced with a shift in public opinion, Bousquet tried to put the brakes on the apprehension of French Jews.

• December 31, 1943 – René Bousquet resigned and was replaced by Joseph Darnand of the Milice, who was an ardent proponent of Nazi ideology. An extensive hunt for Jews and other 'undesirables' was renewed.

vii. Résistance within the police forces
• Initially résistance came only from individual officers.

• Later this coalesced into four résistance movements – *Police et patrie*, *France combattante*, *Front national de la police* and *Honneur de la police*.

B. Gendarmerie nationale
i. Occupied zone

• Attached to the Ministry of Defense, the Gendarmerie was part of the army and therefore national. It remained so during the Occupation.

• The Gendarmerie had no autonomy in its work. Gendarmes of all ranks strictly obeyed orders.

• The job description of a gendarme, both rural and urban, was *guardian of the peace* and in cities, directing vehicular traffic – there were very few traffic lights, even in Paris.

• Gendarmes, as well as police officers, were employees just as factory workers were. All the factories worked for the Nazi regime, some enthusiastically – like Renault – others reluctantly – like Peugeot, and so did the police forces.

• It should be understood that when the occupiers requested the handover of a certain number of Jews, and later young workers for the STO, the actual number of arrests always fell short of the request. French National Archives show that only 52% of the planned arrests were successful. Witnesses testified that they received many warnings and tipoffs from gendarmes and police about pending raids. On the eve of Vel d'Hiv gendarmes and police officers toured the targeted districts, warning Jewish residents of the impending raid.

• This type of action was repeated outside Paris as well.

• Many a gendarme refused to separate mothers and children, even though they had participated in the arrests.

ii. Non-occupied zone

• On the failure of the gendarmes to round up the required number of Jews, the Pétain government accused the BBC of warning the Jews targeted, while the occupiers blamed the incompetence and corruption of the gendarmes.

• Pétain's government sent a memo to all prefects, encouraging them to break the resistance of the population and to indicate which civil servants were complicit in this lack of cooperation.

• In rural areas, the GMR – Groupes mobiles de repression – were not drawn from the areas involved and, consequently, had little hesitation arresting not only those targeted but many that were not.

iii. Police résistance
• 1942 – the raids on Jews marked the start of résistance among police ranks, only a minority at this stage, as most of the officers had been trained in the anti-Semitic institutions of the Third Republic.

• 1943 – the establishment of the Milice prompted more gendarmes to become résistants. In their view, the Milice was a disgrace to the police force.

• 1944 – by the end of 1943, police résistance had increased and culminated in Paris with the entire force on the brink of insurrection.

39. Propaganda (See 35. Media)

• The aim of propaganda was and is to influence public opinion.

A. British propaganda in France

• The British focused their propaganda efforts on radio transmissions. The BBC, broadcasting in French, with the popular program *Les Français parlent aux Français* – French people talking to French people – competed with the État Français' Radio Paris, which was under German control, and with Radio Vichy.

• In order to incite people to listen to Radio Paris in the occupied zone, the occupiers even used banned musicians' music.

• Besides passing information via personal messages, Radio Londres was geared to keep up the morale of the French people and energize the résistance groups.

B. État Français regime
i. État Français propaganda

• Anti-British propaganda, aimed at boosting morale, started immediately after the June 1940 armistice. It blamed Britain for the French defeat. Despite the occupier ramping up anti-British sentiment, it had little effect on the French population. After the first RAF bombing of collaborating factories in the Paris area, pro-British mood actually grew, confounding the occupiers who hoped it would have the opposite effect.

• In an effort to turn the French against the British, both Pétain's government and the MBF produced leaflets and posters showing one of France's patron saints, Joan of Arc, being burned at the stake, implying that the British were the enemy of France. Another anti-British slogan was *La perfide Albion*, – perfidious Albion, a dig at the British for being untrustworthy.

• In order to promote the idea of the Révolution Nationale, Pétain reorganized the Ministry of Information.

• The budget for the Ministry of Information was considerably increased.

• Propaganda centered around the *culte du maréchal* – the cult of Marshal Pétain – so that the people would look up to him as the savior of France and do his bidding.

• Propaganda used ceremonies to help spread the new order and enrolled the Catholic Church to support it.

• Besides the press and posters, cinema was the next powerful tool used by the Pétain government.

• In collaboration with the MBF, a widespread poster campaign boasted about the good life enjoyed by the French volunteer workers in Germany.

ii. Marshal Pétain's goals
• Build a new order, starting in the schools.

• To enhance masculinity.

• Fill school classrooms with Pétain's sayings to indoctrinate the young with the ideals of the Révolution Nationale.

• Have the population learn about Pétain's life and ideals.

• Make the marshal a model of masculinity (the childless man who, before he was 60, had numerous mistresses and visited brothels).

• To have school children participate in the Révolution Nationale by writing to Pétain and sending him patriotic drawings. The children's art would be displayed as propaganda and make parents proud that their children's work was being publicly shown.

• Promote his ideals with fairs and sporting events throughout the non-occupied zone. These events were forbidden to convey political or anti-Nazi messages. No such fairs were allowed in the occupied zone, except events – including Mothers' Day celebrations – permitted and controlled by the MBF. But sporting events were encouraged.

• To make the mother the feminine role model. Medals were distributed to mothers with five or more children. Mothers with ten children were lauded as the ideal.

• Such mothers would raise perfect children, keep the house spotless, cook her husband's meals and look attractive for his return from work.

iii. Symbolism

• In the occupied zone, prefects requested permission to fly the French tricolor flag on public buildings on ceremonial occasions, arguing that it would have a positive influence on the population, who would protest if the flag was not flown. The last thing the occupiers wanted was any kind of revolt – they were cognizant of the 1789 French Revolution. The flag was permitted, though the occupiers did not allow the last post to be played. Those in attendance were allowed to stand at attention.

• The État Français salute – arm extended in front, hardly different from the Heil Hitler salute – was required from the *Légion Française des Combattants*, the *Service d'Ordre Légionnaire* and the youth movements.

• Pétain's government was embarrassed by the July 14 Bastille Day celebration – the ultimate republican event – and converted it to a day of mourning for the military dead. Ardent collaborators were incensed, as they had wanted the day to be completely suppressed. The National Day remained a statutory holiday.

• November 11, Remembrance Day – a statutory holiday with processions at war memorials. It was abolished, but people and the Church continued to celebrate it with masses and wreaths on the monuments.

• November 11, 1940 – in Paris, students and citizens marched to the Arc de Triomphe in a gesture of defiance, an action repeated at the local level in other towns.

• May 1, Labor Day – Pétain's government put it at the center of its propaganda. Since it was also the day of the patron saint Philippe, it became focused on Marshal Philippe Pétain, with giant portraits of Pétain, awards of books, medals for deserving workers and parcels for POWs. It was all centered on the cult figure, Pétain.

NOTE: After the war, it became a statutory holiday, celebrating workers.

C. German Propaganda Abteilung
i. Goals
• The primary goal was to preserve the public.
• Prove the inferiority of the French and the superiority of the Germanic race.
• Show off the new Germany and the advantages of the Nazi regime.
• Showcase German accomplishments, especially in the social sphere.
• Underline German invincibility.

ii. Effect on the population
• People were not swayed. To the majority, the Germans were purely invaders.
• French citizens were very much attached to their native soil and resented the Occupation.
• While suffering under restrictions, with food disappearing from the shelves, coupled with a strong dose of innate chauvinism, many French people scoffed at the propaganda put out by the Reich.

D. Résistant propaganda
• Messages were discreet, often relayed orally or on bits of paper slipped into the pocket of an unsuspecting passerby, a woman's bag or inside a newspaper wrapping vegetables.
• Conveyed through posters, which the authorities hurried to remove. Symbols, such as the distinctive Cross of Lorraine, painted on walls. Scraps of paper, bus, metro or train tickets were left everywhere, cut or bent in the shape of a V for victory.

• French people did things that indicated disdain of the occupiers and the hope of an Allied victory, such as turning the head away when meeting soldiers in the street, pretending not to understand when asked for directions or sending the inquiring soldier in the wrong direction. People made cryptic jokes, such as a woman in a store stepping aside to allow soldiers to be served and saying the soldiers need to be served quickly as they are expected in England.

• Starting in Paris but spreading elsewhere were tongue-in-cheek *Conseils à l'occupé* – advice to the occupied by Jean Texcier – *Don't complain about the 10:00 pm curfew, it is so you can listen to Radio Londres* (the BBC).

• Publication of the patriot's prayer: *The rebel general –* General de Gaulle

Our de Gaulle who art on the front line
Hallowed be Thy name
Thy victory come
Thy will be done on earth as it is in the skies
Give them today their daily bombs
Carry on the offensive, without forgiveness
Against those you will demolish
And leave us not under their domination
But deliver us from the Boche.
Amen

40. Red Cross in France
A. Chronology

• Before the war – the Red Cross provided humanitarian aid in the internment camps, particularly in the south of France where most of the Spanish Civil War refugees were.

• Exodus, June 1940 – the Red Cross with its cars and ambulances traveled the roads helping the wounded, distributing the little food they could get and pulling aside the dead for burial.

• Winter 1939-1940 – during this extremely cold winter, the Red Cross organized warming centers for mothers and children in the occupied zone. Its social work in the non-occupied zone continued.

• Under pressure from the Reich, the État Français began interning foreign Jews.

• February 1942 – volunteers were no longer admitted in the camps for Jews. The Red Cross administration did not fight to maintain a presence in the camps.

• July 1942 – Vel d'Hiv. A dozen nurses volunteered to stay and remained for four days and nights.

• The Red Cross was suspected to have transmitted letters from camp and transit camp internees to families, which was absolutely forbidden and caused some Red Cross workers to be arrested, but released after a spell in prison.

• Despite applying or appearing to apply the anti-Semitic laws, the Red Cross unofficially hid Jewish children with other families and facilitated or financed their evacuation to Switzerland.

B. Status

• The Red Cross was not dependent on the État Français and was a neutral organization. Because it worked for French citizens, it was marginally funded and relied on donations.

• The Reich wanted to deal directly with the French Red Cross, not wanting it to come under Pétain's control and influence.

• Its red cross symbol evoked images of white-coated doctors and uniformed nurses. This was not always the reality. As well as the paid employees, there were also volunteers, the majority of them women, who wore drab brown skirts, a belted jacket and a brimmed felt hat also brown.

• Archives do not agree on the numbers of paid employees and volunteers, enough to say that there were many more volunteers than paid employees.

• Some volunteers were trained as social assistants, whereas nurses who had undergone rigorous training were remunerated.

• The *Secours National*, an organization founded at the start of the 1914-18 war to provide social assistance to needy civilians and send warm clothing and other aid to soldiers in the trenches, was re-activated in 1939 and in 1940. It came under Pétain's control. The Secours National gave the Red Cross the task of distributing milk and clothing to babies and children.

• In January 1942, when Jewish personnel had to be dismissed, the Red Cross decided the decree did not apply to them, at least in appearance. The charity applied all anti-Semitic laws – from this point on the archives become murky.

C. Work and responsibilities

• In peace time – the Red Cross helped with the health of disadvantaged families. In wartime, its task was to be on the front line, assisting the wounded.

• The Red Cross sent parcels to POWs and occasionally received permission to visit.

• It was criticized for ignoring the French prisons and not providing humanitarian aid to the prisoners.

• It failed to ensure that the few parcels they sent were actually delivered to the prisoners. Most times, they were not.

• The Red Cross members acted as social assistants in internment camps. They were volunteers. If they criticized the meager food supply and other conditions, they were posted elsewhere.

• Where a massacre took place, in particular after the Oradour-sur-Glane massacre, the Red Cross arrived and took charge of identifying bodies and preparing them for burial, aided by victims' families and friends.

41. Religion
A. Position of the Catholic Church during the Occupation
• The senior clergy – cardinals, archbishops and bishops – mostly supported Pétain and were legalistic in the sense they unquestionably respected the laws passed by the État Français.

• Many lay Catholics opposed the Church's position and engaged in résistance activities.

• At the parish priest level, the situation was more fluid, with some priests becoming or actively supporting résistants, while others claimed to be neutral, neither supporting nor denouncing the local résistance groups.

• This attitude changed after 1942, when a number of cardinals and bishops publicly denounced the inhumanity of the Nazi regime and the deportation of Jews, French or foreign.

B. Catholic liturgy or ritual
i. Note the particular characteristics of the Catholic liturgy of the period
• The Bible – Roman Catholic priests did not use a Bible. They carried a *Breviary* – as its name suggests, a breviary is an abridgement of the various services, prayers and psalms used in daily services.

• The congregation used a *Missal*, a prayer book containing the texts for the mass. Worshippers owned their own missal, which they brought from home and took back at the end of mass.

• There was no reading of *lessons* in the Roman Catholic mass, as in a Protestant service. During mass, to the left of the altar (right side seen from the congregation) an *Évangile* – the book of the four gospels of the New Testament – sat on a lectern open at the gospel that the priest would mention in that day's sermon. No one, clergy or lay, read from the *Évangile*.

• Catholic churches held a daily mass at 6:00 am and an Angelus prayer at 6:00 pm. On Sundays a mass was held at 6:00 am, 8:00 am and the *Grand-messe* – a high mass – at 11:00 am, the latter with organ music and a choir, and most of the time incense. In peacetime, the church bells were rung before and after services. On the decision of the clergy in the occupied zone, the bells were silenced during the Occupation. In the non-occupied zone, the bells rang as before.

• An altar boy – *enfant de chœur* in French – or more than one, assisted the priest during the service. In the period under discussion, these assistants were young males only. The altar boy was thought of as the point of contact between the priest and the people. The priest, incidentally, stood at the altar with his back to the congregation. The older form of the mass was conducted in Latin and the congregation intoned the responses, along with the *enfants de chœur*, in Latin to the priest. Other duties of the *enfants de chœur* included carrying the cross and censer in processions, bringing water and a cloth to the priest to wash and dry his hands before the communion – Eucharist – arranging items on the altar and handing the priest the communion wine.

• Communion – congregation members received the host, but no wine. A Catholic had to be free of sins to receive communion. The person had to have gone to confession in the days prior.

• On entering a church, people dipped their fingers into the holy water stoup and signed themselves and genuflected.

NOTE: Because of sweeping reforms worldwide to the Catholic church in the early 1960s, an author should be cautious about using the present-day church as a model of any church-related scenes set in WWII France. Also, churches that were damaged and subsequently renovated, have modern stained-glass windows – they are usually less ornate.

ii. Special celebrations (See 16. Culture, Traditions)
• **Christmas** – a traditional midnight mass was still celebrated during the Occupation, but was held at 10:00 pm. On that occasion, the start of the curfew was put forward to midnight. Many occupiers would attend the mass.

• **Easter** – Good Friday was a working day. Churches held processions following the Stations of the Cross in the late afternoon or evening. Saturday was a normal working day. Easter Sunday was a celebration with mass and all the pomp the church could muster. In peacetime, the church bells stopped ringing on Good Friday. In some locations they also rang to mark time, so the time 'stopped.' They rang again on Easter Sunday. In the occupied zone, the bells remained silent.

• **Ascension Day** – a statutory holiday. Pétain canceled Whit Sunday, but not Ascension Day.

iii. Physical arrangement of churches

• The furnishings depended on the status of the church, whether in a city, a town or a village and how ancient the church was. All had a stoup of holy water next to the entrance, one or more confessionals, votive candles in front of statues of saints and a box for alms. Churches had Stations of the Cross around the walls, marked by a picture, either elaborate or simple. Large churches might have statues depicting the Stations of the Cross. Churches had stained glass windows, sometimes extremely ornate.

• The majority of cathedrals and churches were furnished with rows of chairs. In better off churches, they may have had a prayer stool in front of each chair. Note wooden pews were *not* a feature of Catholic churches.

• Churches, especially those dating to the medieval period, might have wooden benches with or without a kneeling plank. There was no prayer book shelf, as worshippers brought their own missal (see above).

• Churches had a crucifix behind the altar and statues of saints located around the church. If there was only one statue in a small church, it would be of the Virgin Mary.

C. Church bells and the requisition of non-ferrous metals
(See. 21. Economy, Industries, Factories, Banks)
i. Pétain and the protection of the bells

• The reason behind Pétain's decision – he was not a practicing Catholic – to protect the bells was political, not pious. He wanted the support of the powerful Catholic Church.

• Carillons and bells had an important place in the Catholic liturgy.

• The Reich demanded the bells in occupied countries to melt down the bronze for armaments, but agreed not to take the carillons.

ii. Annexed and restricted territories

• Alsace, Moselle, the Nord and Pas-de-Calais lost their bells, though in places, the inhabitants hid their bells. In at least one village, the locals rearranged the bells, made a bogus connection to a keyboard and pretended they were a set of carillon. This may not have fooled the German inspector, but the village kept its bells.

• The Reich demanded all France's bells. The MBF strongly resisted the request, claiming that the bells formed an integral part of the very religious French society and that their seizure would increase resistance to the occupation and lead to civil disorder. This would result in added demands for manpower from the Reich.

• The État Français was also opposed to handing over their bells and offered instead bronze statues and art objects dating from the Third Republic and therefore unwanted by the new État Français.

• French people liked their statues and often the statues would disappear before the requisitioning commission workers arrived.

iii. Demands for metals

• In 1943, the Reich, desperate for war material, renewed their demands, and a few bells were lost to the Reich despite municipalities hurriedly reclassifying bells as dating before 1790, as bells made prior to this date were considered artefacts and protected, even by the Reich.

• A German commission began to inspect churches and their bells.

• In many municipalities, résistants found ingenious ways to hide bells, such as in bombed-out buildings and in water-filled bomb craters. Only the heaviest of bells, which could not be brought down, remained in the steeples and those were usually spared as the commission was instructed to leave one or two bells.

iv. Lost bells
• There were bells lost when a church and steeple were bombed by the Allies or destroyed by the Wehrmacht. Steeples were ideal places for resistant snipers and were also ideal places to install anti-aircraft batteries.

v. Silent bells in the occupied zone until the liberation
• After the June armistice, clergy in the occupied zone unanimously agreed that the bells would no longer sound until after the occupiers had been defeated and sent back to Germany.

• Whenever a town was liberated, all the bells were rung, sometime so frantically that some cracked.

D. Judaism (See 32. Jewish affairs)
i. Who were the Jews?
• Officially, in France, people did not refer to members of the Judaic faith as *Juifs* – Jews – but as *Israélites*.

• They were not considered a different people or race, but fellow French citizens.

• Most ordinary people used the term *Jew* without malice or prejudice.

• Anti-Semitic people called them Jews as an insult, as in *sale juif* – not with the derogatory sense of *sale* meaning *dirty* but rather the somewhat milder term *bad,* a term they applied equally to non-Jews, such as in *sale concierge* – when referring to a concierge they did not like, or *sale gosse* – a misbehaving bad boy.

ii. Position of the État Français
   • The État Français recognized Judaism as a valid religion. Synagogues remained open, as they did in the occupied zone, and services continued. The occupiers were conscious that public opinion would be offended and that would increase unrest in an already touchy occupation.

iii. Survival
   • The reason why three-quarters of the Jewish population of France survived was due to their dispersal throughout the country. There were no ghettos in France.
   • However, there were internment camps which made it easier for the Nazi powers to deport Jewish and other people considered undesirable.
   • In some areas, gendarmes and members of the local population provided help to the internees, including facilitating escapes.

iv. Persecution
   • Synagogues were systematically destroyed in the annexed regions of Alsace and Moselle and restricted zone from the Channel coast to the border with Moselle and Alsace.
   • In Paris, Nazi extremists destroyed some synagogues on October 3, 1940.
   • In July 1942, extremists from the Parti Populaire Français vandalized synagogues in the occupied zone.
   • The rabbinate organized spiritual help in the internment camps and held services in makeshift synagogues.

E. Protestant religion
   • Members of the Protestant churches in France were not numerous, with the majority being in areas south of the Massif Central.
   • Initially, Protestant pastors and congregations were supporters of Marshal Pétain and in favor of collaboration.

• A few pastors, spurred on by the influential letters of Karl Barth, the Swiss Reformed theologian, heavily censored but circulating underground, adopted a stance of résistance early on.

• As many others had, Protestants were first attracted by the ideals of the Révolution Nationale –healthy living, joy in work and respect of the mother figure. That changed when laws against the Jews were passed. As Protestants began questioning the anti-Semitism of the État Français, the 1942 roundups of Jews tipped them into sympathy with the résistance movement.

• There were no protestant resistant groups or maquis but they offered refuge to Jewish people, wherever possible, especially for children, such as those in Chambon-sur-Lignon under Pastor Trocmé.

42. Résistance

• The Résistance movement is often portrayed as a single entity working like a well-oiled machine. Far from it. Until the spring of 1943, it was a collection of disparate groups competing with each other and each group claiming to be the only true resistance unit. All of them played political games with London, BCRA, SOE and, later, the OSS. Each group sought control over the *Armée secrète* (AS) as well as over the other groups, and each claimed the right to govern France as soon as the Allies helped liberate the country. For the longest time, they refused to recognize General de Gaulle as head of the résistance.

• For his part, and for a long time, de Gaulle did not want an active résistance movement performing acts of sabotage by *amateurs*. He put his hopes in a reconstituted army composed of Frenchmen who had escaped occupied France and troops from the French colonies, whose elements were in England or fighting in Africa with the Allies. When he admitted the usefulness and validity of the résistance movements in the field, he realized that they had to be unified and organized as a combat force.

• At the end of May 1943, after Lyon, Paris became HQ of the résistance. Credit for unification is due to Jean Moulin, de Gaulle's representative. This was the time the résistance became *gaullist* and de Gaulle accepted what Churchill had understood from the beginning that the résistance movements and groups were invaluable.

NOTE: Considering the red tape, the bickering, the ambitions and aspirations to power of the players involved, it is amazing that the French résistance, the British and the United States forces coalesced into a whole that led to victory.

A. Definition of résistance movements and networks

• It is not easy to define the term *Résistance* when used with a capital. The concept suggests one vast organization run like a business. It was not, even after the various movements and networks were unified and regrouped under one command. It is the entity, the spirit, not the acts.

• In WWII France, resistance manifested itself in various physical forms. A person wishing to resist did not join the *Résistance*, rather, joined or connected with a résistance cell, a résistance network, a résistance movement.

• To be true to history and keep the French flavor in your novel set in WWII France, it is necessary to use *résistance* – no capital. The British Cambridge dictionary uses a capital, the American Merriam-Webster does not nor do French dictionaries, unless referring to the entity as a whole.

– Since you are writing in English, the accent is optional.

• To complicate matters, there was not just one form of resistance. For many people, the popular image of the résistance consists of the sabotage of factories, the blowing up rail lines and attacking the occupiers' road convoys. There was much more to the résistance movements than this. Armed résistance could not have occurred without the help of thousands of unnamed citizens who sheltered downed airmen, aided escaping Jews and résistance fighters on the run and other hunted persons. Résistance would have been ineffectual without the countless numbers of selfless women who secured food and clothing, carried messages, tracts, newssheets or grenades and weapons. Women spied on the occupiers as part of their daily work, whether in a store, an office or a brothel. In addition, there were several million people who did not belong to any group but performed individual acts of defiance, some quite small. They might tear down Nazi propaganda posters from walls or leave a few métro tickets in the shape of a V to remind others that victory was possible. Perhaps they merely gave wrong directions to soldiers. Those on farms hid requisitioned animals and crops. Sometimes, and often just as important, they observed and said nothing. For these and other acts of passive resistance, many paid with their life.

i. What is a résistance movement?

• Meriam-Webster defines a movement as *an organized effort to promote or attain an end.* By necessity, the French

Résistance movement had political overtones. Movements were formed by one or more individuals who wrote and distributed a clandestine newssheet to mobilize public opinion.

• Résistance movements bore names like *Combat* – Henri Frenay, *Confrérie Notre-Dame* – Colonel Rémy.

ii. What is a résistance *réseau* – network

• A *réseau* was the grouping together of like-minded persons sharing the same goals, namely the expulsion of the Nazi invader from French soil. The various groups – *réseaux* in the plural – were geared to action, no newssheets or tracts.

• There were different types of réseaux, each with a specialty. For instance, *Comet* handled escapes, *Alliance*, intelligence gathering, *Œuvre de secours aux enfants*(OSE) did charity work, *Réseau Garel* was involved with French intelligence and action. The *Marco Polo* network gathered intelligence specifically for General de Gaulle's *Force Français Libre* (FFL), while the *Agir* network focused on British intelligence.

iii. The beginnings of the résistance

• There were no precedents to draw on. WWI had seen the occupation of the northern part of France and the majority of the population there rejected the occupiers. They wanted to get rid of them as much as soldiers and politicians wanted to win the war. That résistance was non-violent. It took the form of gathering intelligence, organizing escape lines for escaping POWs, distributing underground newssheets and similar actions.

• In WWI, the majority of France did not suffer occupation and its citizens never had to learn the methods and strategies of those in the northern areas.

• In WWII, when the June 1940 armistice was declared, all those people who rejected both the armistice and subsequent occupation were untested amateurs. Some had heard stories from their families, but this war was nothing like the First. The résistants had to learn on the job.

• Being amateurs, the early résistants made mistakes, as did the British SOE, who at the start even lacked the concept of résistance by the people.

• To resist called for individual courage and self-denial, though the résistants themselves rejected the notion that what they did was heroic. For them, it was merely a normal reaction to a situation.

iv. Paramilitary actions

• From the end of 1942, résistance groups began systematic planned attacks and sabotage with the help of SOE and OSS agents.

B. Role of the French Résistance
i. Self-appointed

• Harass the occupiers to make them feel insecure.
• Make the occupiers leave the country.

ii. Under direction from London

• Sabotage the enemy's military materiel and equipment.
• Sabotage infrastructure and communications.
• Sabotage factories that served the Third Reich.

iii. Role in 1944. Mandate

• Delay German reinforcements en route to Normandy.
• Coordinate the disruption of enemy reinforcements.
• Provide intelligence to the Allied forces.
• Rescue strayed paratroopers.
• Sabotage infrastructure and lines of communication on a large scale.
• Support Allied troops through working as scouts.
• Support Allied troops in maintaining and defending captured positions.
• Support Allied troops by guarding German POWs.

iv. Secret Army. Formation

• The paramilitary branch of the resistance movements was mostly made up of and directed by French officers and soldiers who had rejected the armistice. After November 1942, the *Armée secrète* was joined by members of the *Armée d'Armistice* after it was disbanded by the MBF.

• Mid-1942 – the three largest résistance units – *Combat, Libération-Sud* and *Franc-Tireur* – joined the *Armée secrète*.

• Leadership was under General Delestraint.

• June 9, 1943 – General Delestraint was arrested by the Gestapo.

• In his absence, the staff of the Armée secrète directed the various regions until General Pierre Dejussieu – code named *Pontcarral* – was appointed head.

v. February 1, 1944
• The *Armée secrète* was integrated into the FFI.

C. Armed résistance
• Armed résistance involved harassing the occupier until help arrived to drive them out or eliminate them.

• Up to the spring of 1943, the résistant groups were not well equipped. Both the SOE and the OSS were frugal in delivering weapons out of fear that the résistants would attack the occupiers before being prepared and while the Wehrmacht was in a strong position. They encouraged guerrilla warfare and although they wanted to limit German retaliation on the civilian population, that could not be prevented.

• Initially, the work of the organized résistance was intelligence gathering and its transmission to London.

• The *Organisation Civile et Militaire* (OCM), created in Paris in 1940, permitted better liaison between the groups.

i. Forces Françaises de l'Intérieur (FFI)
• The term applied to metropolitan France only until the 1944 Liberation.

(a) Formation of the FFI.

• Résistance in France was divided into sixteen regions, each with its own command structure.

• By December 1943, there was a coalescing of the leadership of the Résistance, culminating in March 1944 when résistance groups came under a single command and being named *Forces Françaises de l'Intérieur* (FFI).

(b) Leadership of the FFI.

• General Delestraint – arrested by the Gestapo in May, 1944.

• General Dejussieu, code name *Pontcarral* – arrested by the Gestapo in Paris on May 2, 1944 and deported. In Dora-Mittelbau, he organized a resistance group to sabotage the V2 rockets.

• André Masseret, code name *Alfred* – killed in action on July 23, 1944 during an attack by *maquis Jimbert*.

• Alfred Malleret, code name *Joinville*.

(c) Delegates

• Each resistance movement had a delegate liaising with the FFI high command.

• Each resistance group had its own leaders liaising with the movement command.

ii. Francs-tireurs et Partisans(FTP) and communists

• The FTP regrouped résistants with a political leaning to the left. Their goal was action. Like other résistant groups, they were poorly equipped. The SOE was reluctant to supply arms to the FTP.

• Until June 1941, the French communists were pro-German. There were party members who were more patriotic than communist and joined FTP groups.

• After June 22, 1941 – the Communist party made a reversal, overnight becoming anti-Nazi.

• In 1942, its members were absorbed into the FTP.

D. Maquis
i. The word *maquis*

- The term *maquis* was not in use until the 1943 spring-summer. It does not take a capital. The word comes from the French island of Corsica and refers to hilly and rugged terrain covered with prickly bush and sparse vegetation, where anyone escaping the law went to hide from the police. The expression *prendre le maquis* – take to the maquis in English – would be the equivalent of *going on the run*.
- In the context of the war in France, maquis referred to a hideout in the mountains or forests and, only after the war's end did it denote the actual military group of résistants.
- Former military personnel, especially after the Armée d'Armistice was disbanded by the MBF – *Militärbefehlshaber in Frankreich* – in November 1942, gathered in remote locations and trained in well-organized camps in preparation for the day they could fight the occupiers ahead of and alongside the Allies.
- Urban and rural résistant groups operated as required, mostly at night, and went home once the task was over.
- The edict for the *Service du Travail Obligatoire* (STO) prompted many young men to flee into the forests and mountains as early as December 1942, though the law only came into effect in February 1943. There had been much pressure put on the young to work voluntarily in Germany –*la Relève* – which did not bring the desired results, and it was generally known that the young would soon be *forced* into working in Germany.
- They were called *réfractaires*, the closest English equivalent would be *the reluctant ones*
- They were untrained and not equipped for living outdoors.
- The résistant groups realized that these young people posed a danger to their security and set up various camps along the lines of scout camps with the aim of training the young men militarily. They also integrated them into the existing hidden military camps where they were looked after and also trained for combat.

• Not all the *réfractaires* had what it took to become fighters and some went home to hide or find other ways to avoid the STO.

ii. A *maquis* is not a person (See 33. Language, i. Maquis)
• In your novel, do not call a person a *maquis*, as the correct term is *maquisard*, plural *maquisards*.

• Also avoid having a fictional character say, *I'll go to the Maquis,* although you may find such an expression used by less rigorous writers. The character ought to say, *I'll take to the maquis* in the sense of absconding to the bush country. Alternately, the character could say, *I'll find a maquis in* – and insert the name of the region. It would also be acceptable to say, *I'll make my way to the maquis of* – and insert the name of the unit.

iii. Spanish maquis groups
• There were some twenty-five maquis groups that were composed either completely of Spanish citizens or having a majority of Spaniards. These men were predominantly former soldiers who fled Spain after the defeat of the republican forces at the end of the Spanish Civil War (1936-1939). The résistance units so-formed carried names like *maquis de Perighut, maquis de La Montagne noire, maquis de l'Aveyron, maquis de la Loche, maquis de Belves* and *maquis de Privas.*

• Spanish maquis fighters were also present in the *maquis du Mont-Mouchet* and the *maquis du Vercors*, where they fought to the death.

• The Spanish units did not receive the same recognition as the French maquis, yet they took part in some of the fiercest battles and paid a heavy price during the struggle to liberate France, their adopted country.

E. Résistance in Alsace-Lorraine – annexed territories
• Alsace was made up of two departments, Bas-Rhin and Haut-Rhin

• Both departments, were commonly referred to as Alsace – the name of the province – together with the Moselle department – in the Lorraine province – were annexed by German forces in 1940.

• The résistance in the annexed territories was unlike that in the occupied and non-occupied parts of France. Nor was it like the German resistance within Germany.

• There was a massive, if somewhat passive, résistance to the Nazi-enforced program of Germanization of the area.

• Although forbidden to they continued to speak French.

• Just like elsewhere, there were pro-Nazi sympathizers.

• The first résistance group, *Espoir Français*, was created by young people. Their first action was the sabotage of telephone lines.

• Some of the major résistant groups in Moselle included *Espoir Français*, *Réseau Mario*, *Réseau Derhan*, *Réseau Wodli* and *Réseau Mission-Lorraine*. In Alsace there were the *Réseau d'Alsace* and *les Groupes Mobiles* – which comprised several combat units – *La Main Noire*, *Front de la Jeunesse Alsacienne*, *Feuille de Lierre*, *Équipe Pure-Sang*, *Tante Jeanne* and *Légion C40*. One group named *Bateliers du Rhin* – literally, *Rhine Boatmen* – on the River Rhine, were able to provide valuable intelligence to the British.

• August 15, 1940, Assumption Day – in Metz, the population deposited bunches of flowers blue, white and red, at the foot of the Virgin Mary statue. They sang a hymn, *Queen of France, pray God for us*... The Germans did not interfere.

• Fall 1940 – former militaries led by Commandant Scharff formed the résistance group *Mission Lorraine*. They did not engage in open combat but specialized in sabotage.

• People favoring résistance in Alsace and Moselle adopted the habit of not making the Nazi salute and saying *Heil Hitler*. Instead, they mocked by saying, *Ein Liter* – one liter.

• The réseaux created and maintained escape lines for POWs, résistants on the run and young men refusing the enrolment into the Wehrmacht and the *Reichsarbeitsdienst* – Reich Labor Service.

• The young men who did not want to be germanized and be forcibly enrolled in the Wehrmacht escaped to the free zone to join a résistance network or to join the FFL in England.

• Escape routes aided by local *passeurs* were established over the rugged Vosges mountains.

• In 1942, Gauleiter Joseph Bürckel proposed to those Mosellans who did not belong to the Deutsch Volksgemeinschaft – people's community– and those who had been excluded, to register with the prefecture in order to leave the department.

• It was a trick: in January and February 1943, ten thousands of them were rounded up and deported to Silesia. They were known as the *Patriotes résistant à l'Occupation*.

F. Jewish résistance (See 44. Social organizations)
• At first Jewish résistance organizations concentrated on providing material help to their co-religionists with the creation of the *Comité de la rue d'Amelot* in Paris, the *Comité de Bienfaisance Israélite de Paris*(CBIP), *Solidarité* and the *MOI-Yiddish* – Jewish immigrant labor organization.

• After July 1942, the Comité de la rue d'Amelot and Solidarité, which had been extensively involved in the fabrication of false identity papers, moved on to armed résistance.

• In August 1942 – a FTP-MOI battalion was formed with Jewish volunteers, who all spoke Yiddish.

G. Foreigners in the résistance
i. *Main d'Oeuvre Immigrée* (MOI) – Immigrant labor organization
• The immigrant workers were loyal socialists and communists. Many were Jews.

• Workers of different nationalities had been employed in France for many years and considered France their home. Most had been granted French citizenship.

• They shared the common goal of wishing to crush fascism and were prompt to form or join résistance networks.

ii. Polish refugees

• Poles had come to France as refugees from Nazism. Some had come earlier because of a cultural connection. Poles enjoyed a long-standing association with France. They enrolled in the French army, the air force in particular, and were determined to beat the Nazi regime and either went to England to join the FFL or joined resistant groups.

iii. Spanish refugees – *La Retirada* (retreat or exodus)

• After the fall of Barcelona, Jamuary 26, 1939, a wave of refugees, close to half a million, led by former republican soldiers fled across the Pyrenean, in terrible conditions. It became known as the *Retirada*.

• They were former soldiers who had fought against General Franco's fascist Nationalist Forces. Following Franco's victory, the defeated republican soldiers, many of them communists, began to be systematically executed by the Franco regime.

• They did not receive a particularly warm welcome but were tolerated and lived freely in refugee camps until the war was declared. Most immediately joined the French Army.

• After the June 1940 armistice, the État Français treated them as enemies. The refugee camps now became prisons.

• Most men avoided or escaped from the camps and soon joined resistance groups and brought valuable experience of three years of guerrilla style warfare.

• There were some maquis in the Ariège and Dordogne regions totally made up of Spaniards.

• For the Spaniards, fighting fascism was a conviction and a question of survival. They even had contacts in Spain with ready-to-fight maquis units – they had been beaten but not conquered – should Franco decide to reciprocate the military aid the Nazi government had sent him.

• This never happened. With Spain still crippled from the savage Civil War, Franco maintained Spanish neutrality.

iv. The Irish connection

• Although the Republic of Ireland remained neutral during WWII, there was a strong connection with the French military dating as far back as the seventeenth century. In 1690, following the defeat of Irish Catholics by British Protestant forces, hundreds of Irish soldiers sought refuge in France, where they eventually settled and became citizens. Successive generations of their descendants formed contingents in the armies of French kings, participated in the French Revolution and continued the tradition under the French Republic, right up to and including WWII.

• At the outbreak of war in 1939, there were several hundred Irish Republic nationals residing in France. Many of them became résistants, performing valuable roles, among them intelligence gathering and helping stranded Allied servicemen make their way to England.

H. Branches of résistance
i. Communications: PTT (See 14. Communications)

• The *Poste, Téléphone et Télégraphes* (PTT) – the state controlled postal and telephone service – was a public service centrally administered from Paris. Its mission was to ensure communications were not interrupted.

• At the outbreak of hostilities, many of its male employees were conscripted into the army and the functioning of the service throughout the war fell on the women employees.

NOTE: The role of the postal women does not get the recognition it deserves.

• Retired postal workers were called back into service
• Individually and collectively, postal workers took part in the résistance by intercepting mail, sabotaging transmissions and

listening in and reporting vital information to the résistance groups. The workers faced enormous risks as there were collaborators working alongside them. In addition, they were under the constant surveillance of MBF inspectors.

• Postal workers soon organized a résistance network which took the name of *Résistance PTT* and in 1943 *État-major PTT*.

• They were skillful at finding letters of denunciation. In small towns, they would warn the person targeted who would be able to move away. Only once the person was sheltered would the letter be delivered to the police. In a city, a similar scenario took place. Some denunciation letters simply disappeared. The résistance workers took care not to shred the letters systematically, as it would have endangered the network.

• They installed secret telephone lines, unknown to the occupiers and the inspectors, solely for the use of résistance groups.

• They organized attacks on their own post offices to seize money and ration booklets, which were then passed to the local résistance groups.

• The mobile postal workers had a traveling Ausweis and were able to penetrate the forbidden areas and gather intelligence, for instance, along the Atlantic coast.

• The *État-major PTT* played a crucial role prior to and during the Normandy landings, with *Plan Violet*. Messages were sent out to give advance warning of the landings, among them *Allô, allô, James. Quelles nouvelles?* – Hello, James, what's the news? and *Je n'entends plus ta voix.* – I no longer hear your voice.

• 2,000 communication cables were cut, totally isolating Normandy and the Wehrmacht, leaving the Allies with the secret lines and their field telephones.

• Many postal workers were arrested, tortured and sent to concentration camps or shot.

• The État-major PTT even issued a stamp where the face of Pétain was replaced by that of de Gaulle. It took a keen eye to detect the false stamp, which was called *Faux de Nice*.

• They turned a blind eye to the false postage stamps produced by résistant forgers.

• They hid whole sheets of stamps and passed them onto the local résistance groups to post newssheets or tracts. Buying too many stamps would have looked suspicious to the Reich inspector.

ii. Highways department, civil engineering – the *Ponts et Chaussées*

• After the declaration of war, and some time prior, the *Ponts et Chaussées* – literally, the Department of bridges and highways – prioritized the highway work of military interest.

• The Highways Department was in close contact with the Allies while ensuring passive defense during the Phoney war, and remained so during the Occupation, with résistant workers passing on information about roads, bridges and the occupiers' movements.

• Lighthouses were under the Maritime Service of the Highway department (See 6. Armed Forces) *Service des phares* (Lighthouses service).

iii. Noyautage des administrations publiques(NAP) réseau – the infiltration of the civilian administrations network

• Its mission was to infiltrate the civil administration in order to ensure a smooth transition of power after the Libération when civil servants of the Vichy État Français quit or were made to quit.

• Another mission was to provide original official stamps and blank identity papers.

• Résistance réseaux had to ensure the security of their agents with foolproof false identity papers and other documentation, such as Ausweis, demobilization certificates, ration tickets and baptismal or marriage certificates. All documentation needed to be officially rubber stamped. The artisanal production of documents could not keep up with the demand and it became imperative for the résistance groups to infiltrate the administration and recruit members who were willing to risk handing over copies or originals of the stamps and blank forms and papers to the résistants.

iv. Paris transport

• The *Société des Transports en Commun de la Région Parisienne* (STCPP) – Parisian regional transit company controlled the bus network until January 1, 1942, when it was absorbed by the *Compagnie du Chemin de Fer Métropolitain*(CCFM) – Paris métro.

NOTE: It was renamed the *Régie Autonome des Transports Parisiens* (RATP) in September 1944.

• There was no résistance network within the STCRP. Individual workers belonged to one of the many Parisian groups.

(a) Métro.

• The Paris Métro is often thought of as an *underground* rail network. Much of it is, but large sections of the lines, together with the stations, are above ground.

• The full name was *Compagnie des Chemins de fer Métropolitains* (CCFM), renamed *Compagnie des Chemins de Fer Métropolitains* or Métro for short. Many of its workers formed a résistance group. The Métro, with its long corridors, presented an ideal location for the distribution of tracts and other résistance work. Saboteurs could quickly disappear into the labyrinth of tunnels, where maintenance chambers and other hidden places were ideal for stashing arms. The Métro played a vital role during the liberation of Paris. By then, not even the SD and Gestapo personnel dared venture into the bowels of the Métro.

• To travel the Métro, a passenger had to buy a ticket or a book of tickets. Once used, those were found on the ground or on shelves, often folded in the form of a defiant V for victory.

• The long corridors and the walls of the stations were plastered with posters. The État Français posters and those of the German propaganda machine were regularly torn down or defaced.

• The myth of the Wehrmacht's discipline exploded when it came to the Métro. There were multiple incidents between the occupiers and the Métro personnel due to the drunkenness of soldiers and the destruction of property. The incidents took place in and around the stations in areas with a high concentration of soldiers, namely the 5th Arrondissement, district of La Bourse – the Paris Stock Exchange – Champs-Élysées, Opéra, 16th and 7th Arrondissements.

• The occupiers conducted searches and raids for Jews in the Métro, which could easily become a trap or an escape route.

• Attacks on officers began in the Métro. Barbès-Rochechouart Métro station was the scene of the first such attack, August 21, 1941.

• The résistants launched eighteen attacks on the occupiers in the Métro.

• Bombing of factories, including the Renault auto plant, caused damage to the nearby Métro stations and lines, some of which were above ground.

(b) *Société Nationale des Chemins de fer Français* **(See** 19. Deportation)

• The SNCF formed the national rail system.

• The occupiers requisitioned SNCF locomotives and cars.

• The MBF authorities warned the train engineers and other staff that they would incur the death penalty if they refused to obey orders.

• There were 410,000 employees, 40,000 of whom became active resistants. An unknown number were not actively engaged but facilitated the résistants' actions, while others turned a blind eye.

• Engineers of trains carrying deported Jews drove the train only as far as the French border with the Reich. There, the French locomotive was detached and replaced by a German one, driven by a German engineer.

• A comfortable passenger car or sometimes two, for Ordnungspolizei detachment was attached to each train of deportees, with a machine gun mounted on the roof.

• As in every other area of French society, there were collaborators among SNCF staff, as well as many who sat on the fence and those who did not want to take part in the résistance but did nothing to stop it. And there were the resistants.

• Thanks to resistance activity, railroad rolling stock had a habit of disappearing. After 1942, cars and locomotives were systematically damaged. The Reich was obliged to fill the gaps with its own cars.

• When the résistants wanted a train to go through, the *cheminots* – the rail workers – quickly repaired a switch or a bridge to allow the train to pass. Some of the controlled damage looked impressive but was easy to fix and unfix. They then re-sabotaged the line to prevent the passage of the occupiers.

• German railroad cars had separate compartments, each with a door opening directly onto the platform. In contrast, French cars, though made up of compartments, each seating four passengers in First Class and six in the other two classes, the compartments opened onto a corridor running the length of the car and exiting by a door at each end. The passenger cars were equipped with lavatories at each end of the car.

• Some regional trains had cars without compartments. They had wooden slatted seats back to back. Such trains were feeder lines for larger urban centers.

TRIVIA: The *Wagon de l'Armistice* – was actually a former dining car belonging to the International Wagon-Lits Company. It was parked on a spur line in a clearing in the Compiègne forest just north of Paris and was famous as the location for the German surrender and signing of the Armistice of November 11, 1918, that ended WWI. In 1940, Hitler deliberately chose the site for Fance's surrender and the signing of the June 22, 1940 Armistice. During WWII, the Compiègne rail car was transported to Berlin and put on display. Later, it was moved for safety. In 1945, it was destroyed in a fire deemed accidental, but deliberately set by SS troops. Today, a replica currently sits in the Compiègne clearing.

(c) The hidden face of railroad résistance (See 45.Transports)

• Violent reproaches have been made by biased journalists and some historians against the railroad workers for having driven the deportation trains without exploring the history of the SNCF and the tens of thousands of its workers who, often through small of sabotage, disrupted the functioning of the railroad and saved lives. This attitude ignores the 1,500 railroad men that were shot or died in deportation for acts of resistance. It also ignores those who made escapes possible and carried messages to families of deported.

• It must be remembered that the occupiers had no hesitation in shooting an engineer who refused to drive his locomotive or blackmailing him by holding his children hostage. They could also, and did, bring in armed German engineers who shadowed the French engineers.

• In addition to the constraints, there was surveillance by MBF inspectors, as there was in every other industry.

• Just as in the rest of society, there were collaborators among rail workers, especially at the management level where there was little if any of the résistance found in other industries.

• When approaching a suitable station, pre-arranged with the local résistance on the ground, the engineer would slow the train and blow the whistle. This was the signal for résistance prisoners to jump out, the doors having been previously unlocked by rail staff. Some Jews also jumped, but the majority were too scared. Those who had family on the train stayed on.

• The railroad resistants passed on information about train movements, timetables, troop deployments and what goods or passengers were being transported.

• A résistance cell had to choose between derailing – the least damage – or blowing up a train.

• Despite the Allied landings in Normandy on June 6, 1944 and increased pressure from résistance groups, the Nazi authorities in Berlin still issued deportation orders and the État Français complied, while railway men did what they could to prevent the trains from reaching their destination.

• Germany was desperate for workers to continue its war and did not want the captive labor in the internment camps to be liberated and take up arms against them.

• In preparation for D-Day, both resistant cells and rail workers sabotaged lines.

v. FTP and Communist résistance groups

• Until June 21, 1941, the French police actively hunted communists. Because of Germany's non-aggression pact with the USSR, the German occupiers did not. In contrast, Pétain's government in the non-occupied zone banned the Communist Party and its newspaper, *L'Humanité*.

• After June, 1941, this changed and communists became the enemy of the Third Reich and were hunted by both the occupiers and the État Français.

• Despite anti-communism and the distrust of the Allies toward the FTP and communist maquis, their strict military organization was recognized and they were supplied with weapons and explosives.

I. Civilian résistance

• Civilian resistance – also called passive résistance – was driven by the will to survive, to save what could be saved. The goal was not to defeat the occupiers, as it lacked the means, but to co-exist with them while performing small acts of defiance behind the enemy's back.

i. Individual résistance
• People who did not agree with the State were classed as *dissidents*. For the most part, they did not take up arms or act violently. Their acts of résistance may have gone no further than hiding hunted persons.

ii. Spontaneous résistance
• Civilian resistance showed moral strength. The next level was disobeying orders. The résistance groups recruited among the latter.

• Civilian resistance involved spontaneous disobedience – miners' strikes, street protests by housewives, offering hiding places to hunted persons be they Allied servicemen, *refractaires*, young men refusing forced conscription into the Wehrmacht in Alsace-Lorraine and in Italy.

• Various strata of society – doctors, dentists, lawyers, grand couturier dress designers, storekeepers, civil servants, factory workers – all performed small gestures of résistance, from tearing down propaganda posters to writing and distributing anti-Nazi tracts and underground papers.

• Civilian résistance could adhere to a political party line, as with Communists, or be purely patriotic. Both had the aim of booting the Germans out of France.

iii. Escape networks
(a) Specializing in saving Jewish children.
• *Réseau Garel*, based in Lyon, specialized in taking Jewish children to Switzerland. It was helped by Catholic and Protestant church organizations and individuals.

• *Réseau Marcel*, in the Nice area, received help from the Bishop of Nice, Monseigneur Rémond.

• OSE (See 32. Jewish organizations)
(b) Escape lines on French territory.
• The numerous networks that ran escape lines for compromised people are well-known and well-documented. Some réseaux were exclusively dedicated to the journey of

compromised people to safety out of the country. Others were résistance réseaux that also occasionally helped lead people to safety.

• Then there were the hundreds of *passeurs*, acting altruistically or for profit, who did not belong to any particular group.

• Some of the well-known escape routes were Pat O'Leary, Comet, Shelburne, Bourgogne, Grimaud, Marie Odile, Brandy and Bordeaux-Loupiac.

J. Exterior résistance
i. London
(a) Why London?

• London was not occupied and was close to France. It was the gathering point of all those who succeeded in leaving France to join the Forces Françaises Libres(FFL) or to be trained to return to France for special missions (SOE). There was also a need for people for administrative tasks.

• New arrivals in London were able to report with accuracy on the situation in France.
Broadcasts in French were deemed essential.

• To hear familiar voices was a boost to the morale of French citizens under the yoke of the Third Reich.

(b) SOE Section F – goals (See SOE section below)

• Trained agents to go into France to gather specific intelligence.

• To train groups of resistants and in 1943 train whole groups of maquisards.

• Although a great deal of good work was done, criticism was leveled at the Home Station for not respecting schedules, being condescending to radio operators and ignoring pre-arranged signals that indicated a radio operator had fallen into the hands of the Gestapo. Most of the time, this was due to the lack of understanding of the situation in occupied and non-occupied France.

• There was also criticism for not sending all the arms requested.

ii. General Charles de Gaulle
• Head of the Résistance, de Gaulle's idea of résistance was *armed* résistance, the creation of a government in exile and the establishment of its military – the Forces Françaises Libres (FFL).

• He believed in the strength of the French empire and hoped the colonies would join him in the fight against Hitler. After the fiasco at Dakar, he made no further attempts to rally the colonies by show of force. Many joined the FFL voluntarily.

• The intelligence section of the Free French was initially the *Service de Renseignement* –Intelligence Service – becoming the *Bureau Central de Renseignments et d'Actions* (BCRA) in January 1942. The BCRA, under the leadership of Captain, later Colonel, Dewavrin using the code name Passy, was in charge of coordination among the résistance groups in France, the Free French and the Allied forces.

• General de Gaulle delegated the minutia of the organization. This enabled men with a clear vision to fashion Gaullism and unify résistance movements.

• Jean Moulin's work unified individual movements into a *Conseil National de la Résistance*. De Gaulle became the head of all résistance movements and networks.

• After Jean Moulin's arrest and death in June-July 1943, Émile Bollaert was appointed his successor.

iii. Special Operations Executive (SOE) – British
(a) Methodology.
• Trained agents to go into France to gather specific intelligence.

• Trained groups of resistants and in 1943 undertook the wholesale training of maquis units in order to build up an additional military force behind enemy lines for when the Allies landed.

(b) Communications.
• Today's easy and efficient phone and internet communication makes it hard to appreciate fully how limited and difficult communication was during the war years. In fiction, radio communication with London tends to be idealized, where in reality it was disorganized, difficult and dangerous.
• The Home Station frequently did not respect schedules, was condescending toward radio operators and ignored alert signals.
• Everyone learned on the job. New arrivals from France could only report on the situation in the limited area they had last been in, making it difficult for the British to comprehend the situation and the mood in the whole of France.

(c) Details.
• Since it was imperative that agents hid in plain sight, they had to blend in with the local population and surroundings where they were assigned.
• In Europe, and particularly in France, clothing styles were distinctive and people, women in particular, were prompt to adopt the lasted fashion.
• Secondhand clothing and accessories, often bought from new arrivals, were soon insufficient and the SOE had to begin manufacturing authentic 'used' clothing.
• Refugees with sewing and tailoring skills were in demand. Original garments were carefully unpicked to learn the manufacturing methods and copy them with accuracy, all the while taking into account regional differences.
• Current French hairstyles were also carefully followed.
• Whereas female agents sent to urban areas were to look stylish, agents in rural areas, where simplicity was the norm, usually had to forgo makeup and elaborate hairstyles and clothing.
• Diversity in clothing became more difficult as the war progressed and the number of agents sent out increased. Shoes were the biggest problem, as they were difficult to replicate accurately.

(d) The L-pill.

• Agents were provided with a lethal pill of cyanide should they be caught and chose to end their life rather than speak under torture.

• It was the symbol of the agents' sacrifice. They knew their survival chances were extremely poor.

iv. Role of the American Office of Stragegic Services(OSS) in the French résisance

• It was created June 13, 1942 in the United States.

• The OSS goals were to gather intelligence, execute clandestine actions that were not ordered by other organizations and support the résistance in France in preparation for the Allied landings.

• Whereas the SOE had long been working behind enemy lines and had acquired much experience, the OSS had to devise their own approach.

• After Operation Torch, it garnered major successes in North Africa with the French résistance in areas where the SOE had not made inroads.

• With an office in London, the OSS endeavored to coordinate with the SOE.

• The Special Forces Headquarters(SFHQ) wrote to Washington – *Appreciating the Potentiality of French Résistance* and requested massive arms drops to various maquis groups.

• Clandestine *Jedburgh* teams – first formed in May 1943 – were dropped before, on and after D-Day to conduct offensive actions behind enemy lines and carry out specific tasks as dictated by the military situation.

• A Jedburgh team was made up of three members – two military officers and one radio operator. One of the officers would be native to the occupied country they were dropped into, the other either British or American. The radio operator could be of any nationality as long as he could code and transmit in English. Bilingual operators were an asset.

- Unlike SOE agents operating individually, Jedbugh team members were armed and wore uniforms.
- On being parachuted behind enemy lines, they made contact and operated with the nearest résistance group.
- They were dropped with arms, explosives and stores.
- The aim of Jedburgh teams was to carry out sabotage and guerilla activity. They equipped and trained maquis groups in the use of arms and explosives, communicated by radio with London and led and assisted in operations against the enemy.
- Many résistance groups were already trained and self-sufficient and directed the Jedburgh teams to more needy résistance groups.
- The Jedburgh teams were also dropped where there were no résistance groups in order to protect or demolish vital installations.
- They were also positioned to help prepare for the arrival of airborne troops
- The SFHQ made extensive drops of arms and explosives.

43. Retreating armies

• Although massacres perpetrated by the Nazi forces were more numerous during the closing stages of the war, atrocities had also occurred early in the Occupation when troops and other units committed needless killing of civilians (See 29. German invasion 1940).

• In 1944, as widely dispersed military contingents began to withdraw from their positions in a bid to reinforce the Normandy front, the troops engaged in massacres, which continued as they were retreating ahead by the Allied troops. Old men, women, children were easy targets. In 1944 alone, from April 1 to September 27, excluding the shooting of hostages and captured résistants, there were no less than 293 massacres – a massacre defined as the killing of five or more people. Of these 293 massacres, 38 were of 50 civilians or more, including at Saint-Amand where 73 Jews had lived in security for five years. Tulle 99. Oradour-sur-Glane 642.

• Those massacres were perpetrated by diverse units – Waffen-SS, Wehrmacht, Gestapo, SD-Polizei, Schutzpolizei, Feldgendarmerie, Kriegsmarine and Milice.

44. Social organizations

A. *Le Secours national* – organization for national security

• Created in 1914 to help people in need, particularly women with children left alone while their men were on the front lines, the Secours national was revived in 1939. When Marshal Pétain came to power, he subsumed the Secours national into his propaganda machine. Posters commissioned by Pétain, showed benevolent miliciens working in a soup kitchen for bombed-out people, with the marshal's portrait conveniently positioned on the wall.

• Being largely independent under Marshal Pétain's auspices, the Secours national made its own rules.

• It received part of the funds from the National Lottery.

• Pétain added the name *Entraide d'hiver du Maréchal* – Winter Help from the Marshal.

• The Secours national was indispensable to prevent millions of people from dying of starvation.

• The Secours national was allowed to raise funds by any suitable means.

• Due to an upsurge in the outbreak of turberculosis, it became imperative to ensure more people, children in particular, received adequate nutrition. That was the theory. The practice was quite different.

• Some of the Secours national's work was in schools, providing meals. It also opened soup kitchens in deprived districts and provided additional food to hospitals. Despite being government sponsored, the food supplies were inadequate.

• The Secours national fell short of the demands made on it. In big cities, such as Lyon and Marseille, mayors asked the Secours national to take over some restaurants and their food stores to provide meals for disadvantaged people. Again, meals were barely enough to sustain life.

• An innovation of the Secours national was the distribution of a pill containing vitamins C and B_1 as well as vitamin-fortified biscuits to schoolchildren.

• In rural areas, where food was more accessible, there was still a need to supplement the diet, as the occupier's requisition of crops, cattle and produce left insufficient to feed those who were unable to work for various reasons, many having lost their jobs, the elderly and the indigent, as well as the refugees and those in hiding.

• Despite these efforts, the majority of French children were undernourished. Workers also suffered.

• Deaths from starvation ran into the thousands, directly or indirectly from diseases brought on by poor nutrition. Psychiatric hospitals were particularly hard hit.

B. Jewish organizations

• There were three main organizations in France devoted to saving Jewish children and three others of a more general nature.

  i. *Éclaireurs Israélites de France* – Jewish Scout Movement.

ii. *Mouvement des Jeunesses Sionistes* – Zionist Youth Movement.

iii. *Œuvre de Secours aux Enfants* (OSE) – Children's Aid Work. It had its origins in 1923 Saint-Petersburg, Russia. It transferred to France, with headquarters in Paris, but maintained its international character. With the Occupation, the UGIF dissolved it but the OSE continued to operate unofficially.

• OSE workers created a vast network of shelters for Jews and others at risk. They organized the emigration of vulnerable children. Thousands of children were smuggled out of internment camps and saved from deportation.

iv. *Comité d'Assistance aux Réfugié*s (Car) – Committee for Assistance to Refugees.

v. *Fédération des Sociétés Juives de France* (FSJF) – Federation of Jewish Societies in France.

vi. *Service Social des Jeunes* (SSJ) – Social Service for Youth, under the direction of the *Éclaireurs Israélites*.

45. Transport
• People never traveled as much as they did during WWII. Paris outdid all other French cities in the ratio of occupiers to citizens.

• In Paris, *Société des Transports en Commun de la Région Parisienne* (STCRP) – the transit system of the Parisian Region – was privately owned. The Métro was an independent entity, also privately owned, known as the *Compagnie du Métropolitain de Paris*(CMP).

• The Pétain government, having suppressed all unions, merged the two under its own authority and appointed the CMP to the management, January 1, 1942. In actual fact, the STCRP and the CMP had each their own management, but only the CMP was imposed a Reich *counselor*.

A. Buses – in French, *Autobus*
• The last Parisian streetcar went out of service in 1938.

• At the outbreak of WWII, all transit buses were requisitioned to take French troops to the frontline. Many were destroyed.

• With the Wehrmacht advancing rapidly, the remaining buses were used for the evacuation of the population. Brought back to Paris, the buses transported personnel and refugees to Toulouse and Clermont-Ferrand where the STCRP moved its administration.

• It was not until the end of August 1940 that the MBF began authorizing the return of the buses that were still operational to the capital.

• Despite adapting the buses to different fuels, service was limited. During the Occupation, the STCRP did not have enough buses in running condition and canceled more than half the bus routes in Paris. Most of the available vehicles were used to servicing the suburbs, which in that era did not have Métro lines. This enabled workers to reach their factories.

• The lack of parts and rubber tires meant that more and more vehicles were disabled. The company ran into financial difficulties. Under pressure from the occupiers, the STCRP placed its autobusses at the occupiers' disposal, one benefit being that it enabled the vehicles to be repaired.

• In January 1943, electric-powered trolleybuses were brought into service. They were withdrawn after August 1944.

B. How the bus functioned

• Parisian transit buses were painted in a distinctive subdued yellow and green livery. Passengers boarded the bus at the rear via an open platform. A *poinçonneur* – ticket-puncher – wearing a punch machine on a belt watched the people climb aboard. He then fastened a security chain across the platform entrance and pulled the bell equipped with a light chain and wooden handle to signal the bus driver to continue on the route.

• The same bell pull while moving indicated that someone wanted to get off at the next stop.

• A repeated pull of the bell chain alerted the driver that an accident had taken place.

• From the open platform, the people moved forward down an aisle, with pairs of wooden seats on each side. The ticket-puncher then took the passenger's ticket, slipped it into a slot on his punch and turned the handle. The ticket was now printed with the date and the number of the route. He then gave the ticket back to the passenger.

• The bus route was divided into sections. To travel within one section, one ticket was required. Multiple tickets were required for journeys over more than one section.

• Tickets were sold individually or in booklets at Métro stations or could be obtained on the bus from the *poinçonneur*. The top part of the ticket had a pre-printed running serial number.

• The Nazi authorities requisitioned buses in order to conduct the raids on Jews in Paris on July 16-17,1942.

• Buses were also used to bring help to bombed areas. The Red Cross used them for the evacuation of the injured.

• The Allies requisitioned buses for troop transport and the Red Cross commandeered any available buses to evacuate the wounded.

• In 1945, buses were pressed into service to ferry returning prisoners, deportees and refugees.

NOTE: There are pictures of buses with an enclosed rear platform which are labeled as being used during the Occupation. The enclosed platform was introduced in 1949.

C. The Métro – *Compagnie des chemins de fer métropolitains* (CCMP) had been renamed *Compagnie du Chemin de fer Métropolitain*(CMP).

• The Métro was an essential part of Parisian life. There were stations and sections of lines that were not underground – *Métro aérien*. The second class Métro cars were the same green as the buses and had a large Roman numeral II in the middle of the car. The seats were made of wooden slats with a slight curve to make them comfortable. The first-class cars were red and had a large Roman numeral I in the middle. The seats were padded leather.

• The Métro ran on electricity and was not affected by fuel restrictions until the supply of electricity became erratic. Some lines closed. Others were maintained by generating sets.

• The wheels were steel and therefore were not affected like the autobusses by the shortage of rubber.

• At the start of the war, the above-ground sections of the Métro were closed for fear of bombing. Some of the lines affected were Étoile to Nation, Châtelet to Lilas, Invalides to Porte de Vanves.

• A German technician was appointed to oversee the management of the Paris Métro. The well-being of the occupiers had priority.

• The Métro had to cope with two different types of clientele – French citizens and the occupiers, the latter further divided into military and civilian.

• Since Parisians had to share *their* Métro, they often expressed their disdain for the occupiers through subtle insults, nothing dramatic, as the occupiers had the upper hand. Examples were completely ignoring the presence of Germans on the train by turning their backs and avoiding eye contact. A pretty woman, particularly when a German smiled at her, would purposely not smile and would glance away. A man might deliberately step off the train at a station when a German entered the car. The Germans, ever-fearful of contracting diseases, would be unsettled when the French people around him deliberately started coughing.

• The rail company was instructed to keep order in the Métro and was obliged to report every incident to the management, who then forwarded it to the Préfecture de police.

• All the Métro workers were instructed in this new way of working.

D. How the métro functioned

• The métro had two classes.

• First Class was reserved for officers and certain selected Parisians, such as collaborators. An attractive Frenchwoman might be invited into First Class by a German officer. Soldiers were also permitted to travel First Class but usually did not, perhaps not wishing to crowd their officers.

• Second Class was for everyone else. After June 5, 1942, Jews were required to travel in the very last car of the train.

• Passengers purchased a ticket or a book of tickets at a booth at the entrance to the Métro and proceeded to the gate of the platform where a *poinçonneur*, or sometimes a *poinçonneuse*, punched a hole in the ticket. The ticket agent opened and closed the gate. Some stations had a ticket-puncher and automatic closing barriers.

• A First Class ticket was green, Second Class was a nondescript beige.

• A Métro train ran on steel wheels on steel rails and created a lot of noise. One ticket took a passenger anywhere in Paris. There were a number of stations where several lines converged to enable passengers to change direction.

• Métro trains were habitually over-crowded. People who before the war owned automobiles or took taxicabs now, like everyone else, traveled by Métro. A few better off Parisians traveled by vélo-taxi. People carrying sensitive documents preferred the vélo-taxis as the occupiers occasionally made raids in the Métro.

• The occupier traveled for free in the Métro. Soldiers were easily identifiable and the gatekeeper promptly opened the barrier, but when it came to German civilians or collaborating civilians, equally recognizable because of being better fed and dressed and having an air of arrogance, the ticket agents derived pleasure from meticulously demanding to see the passenger's Ausweis. This often led to confrontations which were rarely settled in the ticket agent's favor, though this did not deter him or her from doing it again.

E. The bicycle
i. La Petite Reine

• Since there were so few bus routes in service, with fewer buses, travel frequently involved long waits. Parisians soon adopted the most common mode of transport, that of the bicycle, especially in good weather.

• People affectionately dubbed the bicycle *la petite reine* – the little queen.

• There was not a great deal of traffic on the streets as Parisians were not allowed to own a car. Even if they had, the lack of gasoline would have made car ownership pointless. Only German officers traveled in cars. French medical doctors were allowed a car but suffered from the same lack of gasoline as all civilians. To get around the gasoline shortage, vehicles were converted to *gazogène*. In wartime, Paris traffic jams were not a problem and bicycles ruled the streets.

• The few commercial vehicles deemed essential ran on *gazogène*.

• Taxis had disappeared. French ingenuity created the vélo-taxi. Invented by one Monsieur Fidèle Outterick, the vélo-taxi consisted of a bicycle with a trailer capable of carrying one or two sitting passengers or a quantity of luggage. Some trailers were enclosed and much in demand in rainy weather.

ii. Traffic lights

• There were few traffic lights at the time. In Paris and in major towns, white-baton waving gendarmes, standing on a low platforms, directed traffic. To emphasize his signals to motorists, the gendarme gave sharp blasts on a whistle.

• Exterior lights, both on buildings and lamp standards, were made of brass. To prevent the brass from being requisitioned by the occupiers for munitions, the Paris electricity company painted the metal lamp housings with dull brown paint.

• On a historical note, the first traffic light in Paris was installed in 1923 at the junction of Boulevard Saint-Denis and Boulevard Sébastopol, consisting of a red light and a bell. Lights with green, amber and red came into use in 1933 when eleven major junctions were equipped with them.

• The lights' function was coordinated by an electric timer.

• There was no pedestrian push button or a pedestrian crossing signal. Pedestrians crossed between two rows of large-headed nails in the street. Hence the term for pedestrian crossing – a *passage clouté*.

• The development and expansion of traffic lights was halted by the Occupation.

• The occupiers extinguished the existing traffic lights as a security measure. They were deemed superfluous, since civilian vehicle traffic was greatly reduced. Traffic light standards were painted with white stripes to make them more visible to indicate a pedestrian crosswalk.

F. Outside Paris

• Bus, trolleybus and streetcar services were not particularly affected except where fuel was concerned.

• The bicycle was already a habitual mode of transport in villages and rural areas.

G. Existing road network

• There were no four-lane highways. The largest and busiest road, the *Route nationale*, was only a slightly wider two-lane highway, with shoulders in many places but not everywhere. On flat land, the roads were lined on each side by a row of tall poplars. The concept of multi-lane freeways, circular roads, beltways and bypasses did not see the light of day until after the end of the war, and only then slowly as the country recovered.

• Secondary roads, *routes départementales*, were narrow and bordered by local trees and poplars.

• Local roads, *routes municipales*, were even narrower and also bordered by trees or hedges. In small towns and villages, houses toed the edge of the roads, as they were built long before the invention of the automobile.

• Very few people among the middle-class and working-class owned a car. Even among affluent families, car ownership was rare, because the French rail system was excellent and cheap. It was supplemented in those rural areas without a rail line by coaches and later buses serving villages and hamlets on a regular schedule when there was no secondary local line.

• On roads there were no rest areas, pull outs, or highway service stations. In prewar days, gas was obtained in towns or larger villages and so it was during the Occupation – if there was any fuel available.

H. SNCF (See 19. Deportations, 43. Résistance)
i. Trains

• During the Occupation, people of any level in society took the train into the country, no longer to have a picnic on the bank of a river but to seek out a farmer willing to sell them food, if they did not have rural relatives.

• In this era, trains on all major lines were hauled by steam locomotives. Secondary lines were often electrified. There were three classes of travel:
(a) Cheapest tickets

• Third Class cars had compartments, each fitted with two facing, straight-backed wooden benches. Each bench was separated by an armrest in the middle, with four places on each side, eight places in total. The narrow space between the benches did not permit much leg room. Overhead were two luggage nets, the lower one narrower for small parcels, the larger upper net for suitcases. Nazi police exercised more control over Third Class in the belief that résistants and Communists would be scruffier and more inclined to mingle with ordinary workers. Third-Class cars were identified by a painted Roman numeral number III on the doors.

(b) Reasonable priced tickets

• Second-Class compartments were more or less the same as Third Class but with some padding on the seats. The backs of the benches were slightly inclined and provided more comfort. Also, there was marginally more leg room. A Roman numeral number II on the doors marked this class.

• Second Class was favored by those resistants more likely to fit in with the middle class passengers, who for the most part, dressed well.

(c) Highest priced tickets

• First Class compartments had upholstered bench seating with three places on each bench, each separated by a padded armrest. Two nets for luggage, as in the other classes. More room to stretch legs between the benches.

• Only German Officers, collaborators and female spies traveled First Class. First-Class compartment doors were marked with a Roman numeral number I.

(d) Pullman wagons-lits.

• The Pullman wagons-lits were luxurious long-distance sleeping-car trains operated by the private *Compagnie Internationale des Wagons-Lits*, usually having two berths per compartment, with a sink, hot and cold running water and a toilet. In WWII France, they were used by German personnel and spies. The dining car was the spies' favorite place.

• Wagons-Lits trains were pulled by locomotives of the country they traveled through, as the company did not operate their own locomotives and were fitted with a dining car. Regular French trains rarely had dining cars.

(e) Layout of train cars.

• Main lines – train cars were made up of compartments, each with a sliding door opening onto a windowed corridor running the length of the car. There was no direct access or egress to or from the compartments to the platform.

• A lavatory was situated at each end of the car.

• Two doors for boarding and exiting the car were located on either side of the car at the front and rear

• A door at each end enabled the conductor and anyone needing to pass from one car to another, crossing precariously in the open over two steel plates which slid over each other and were constantly moving with the train motion. Sometimes the open space was protected by a folding *soufflet*, a bellows-like rubber contraption.

• In each compartment, under the window, there was a folding tablet, the length of the width of one seat and thus only usable by the two window passengers.

• At night a blue light that could be extinguished illuminated the compartment. A heavy blind blacked out the window when needed.

• A conductor – a *contrôleur* – visited each compartment to check tickets.

• Secondary lines – trains were either hauled by steam or sometimes electric locomotives which drew power from overhead gantry lines. They consisted of two classes only, First and Second.

• Similar design as the major lines.

• Some short secondary lines had cars with wooden benches in Second Class.

• There was a class of train popularly called *Micheline* – after the inventor Marcel Michelin, son of André Michelin of the tire company. They were diesel-powered rail cars that ran on

417

wheels equipped with special tires. The official name was *auto-rail*.

• Only one class and open design as in a bus.

• As the occupation continued, the shortage of fuel and rubber obliged the SNCF to take the Michelines out of service and put them into storage.

(f) Telegraph.

• Telegraph wires ran alongside the railway. Every station had a telegraph office.

ii. Locomotive engineers (See 42. Résistance, H. Branches of résistance)

• The MBF authorities had warned the employees of the Société Nationale des Chemins de fer Français (SNCF) they would incur the death penalty if they refused to obey.

• After the war, the train engineers were reproached for having driven the deportation trains, an unjust criticism that ignores the thousands of rail workers who often by small acts of sabotage disrupted the functioning of the railroad and saved lives. It must be remembered that the occupiers had no hesitation in shooting an engineer who refused to drive, or blackmailing him by holding his children hostage. Two Order Policemen traveled in the locomotive to watch the French engineers.

• As in the rest of society, there were collaborators, especially at the management level.

iii. *Les trains de la honte* – the trains of shame.

CAUTION in using this expression as it came into use only *after* the war. The expression denoted those trains that early in the Occupation carried French writers, artists, intellectuals and other prominent French citizens who had accepted invitations from the Third Reich to visit Berlin and other German cities. After the war, some journalists used the expression to include deportation trains carrying Jews and others to Nazi death camps. It was not in general use.

• August 15, 1944 – *Le convoi de Pantin* or The Last Transport, when SS police emptied the prisons and camps in and around Paris and sent 2,600 men and 400 women to Nazi concentration camps. Rail workers, Red Cross officials and even members of Pétain's government, whilst fleeing to Germany, tried unsuccessfully to stop the trains and free the prisoners. The SS commander refused to listen.

• August 17, 1944 – *Transport N. 79* departed from Royallieu station near Compiègne with 482 prisoners on board. Despite all efforts, diplomatic and resistant, the train arrived at Buchenwald.   - August 22, 1944 – a number of prominent Résistance figures were on board. 130 of them did not return.

• During the Occupation, people turned a blind eye to what was happening around them. Those who did not live close to a station or a rail line were not necessarily aware of the trains. Many people, even among supporters of the résistance, knew of such trains only through the rumor that the Jews were being resettled in the east. By the summer of 1943, news of concentration camps and mass killings reached some resistants, but it was so horrendous that many assumed it must be grossly exaggerated and did not believe it.

I. Towns and transport
i. Lyon
• An underground funicular railway, built in 1860, went from rue Terme up to the plateau of Croix Rousse. It was transformed into a road tunnel in 1960.

• Streetcars were replaced in 1941 by trolleybuses.

ii. Marseille
• A large network of streetcars was in service until 1942.
• A trolleybus network was in service from 1942 to 1944.

iii. Bordeaux
• A trolleybus network was in service from 1940 to 1954.

iv. Nice
• A trolleybus network was in service from 1942 to 1970.

v. Poitiers
• A trolleybus network was in service from 1943 to 1965.

vi. Rouen
• A trolleybus service was brought into service in 1933 and was operational throughout the war, only withdrawn in 1970.

J. Waterways
i. Canals and rivers
• France had 18,500 km of waterways. At the start of the war 12,054 km were navigable. There was a well-developed network of canals and navigable rivers in the Nord, Pas-de-Calais and environs, in the Seine basin, the Moselle basin, the Saône and Rhône basins, in Brittany and Charente. In the south, canals linked the Atlantic Ocean to the Mediterranean Sea.

• Barges were either towed or pushed by a tugboat. Just before the war, barges were still powered by steam engines but also some diesel engines.

• Travel by water was slow, a little faster when floating downriver. Cargo tended to be restricted to that which was not time sensitive.

• There were many locks to permit vessels to navigate gradients.

• In some places during the Occupation, barge operators returned to using horses walking along the towpath at the edge of the canal to haul their barges.

• Barges were divided into six classes according to their tonnage capacity. Class One being the smallest.

ii. 1940, River traffic
• When the Wehrmacht invaded France, many barges were gathered on the canals in the northern regions, having brought

supplies and reinforcements to the French troops. The Kriegsmarine requisitioned the majority of the barges that had not been damaged by bombing and shelling. The idea was that once France was defeated and occupied, Hitler would invade Britain. Since the Kriegsmarine lacked the necessary transport vessels, the requisitioned barges would transport troops and materiel across the English Channel, this according to German archives. They had obviously not factored in the danger and unsuitability of using river craft to navigate the treacherous, stormy waters between France and Britain.

• In the Bordeaux area, the occupiers destroyed all seven locks on the Canal des Landes and replaced them with wooden dams that could be easily removed to flood the area in the event of a British invasion. There is a twenty-meter (some sixty feet) difference in elevation between Lake Cazaux and Arcachon. It would have been a major catastrophe.

iii. The Rhine's special status

• The River Rhine had been made into an international waterway in 1815 and was controlled by the *Commission Centrale pour la Navigation du Rhin* with headquarters in Strasbourg. Although flowing through annexed regions, freedom of navigation as per its charter was left unchanged by the occupiers, and French river crews, in particular the Alsatians, continued to use the Rhine.

• They had permission to cross the Swiss border to unload their cargo near Basel.

• The résistants among them passed on valuable information to the Allies on targets and the effectiveness of bombing raids.

• They may have carried fugitives to Switzerland, but there is no official confirmation of this.

iv. Inland navigation

• In 1942, the État Français created a register of all river barge operators in an effort to keep track of them. Previously, rivermen had a tradition of independence, answering only to themselves.

   • After that, river boatmen had to carry a booklet in which all movement was recorded at the river and canal checkpoints. It included details of merchandise carried and the names of mariners and any passengers on board.

46. War and men
A. Patriarchal French society
• Prior to and during WWII in a French household, the man's status was one of perceived superiority. His word was law.

• A man worked and earned the money and gave the wife an allowance to run the house.

• He expected to come home to a clean house, clean children and a meal on the table.

• He expected to be informed of his children's misbehavior and to mete out the appropriate punishment.

• Among the lower classes, children, both male and female, were commonly physically punished with a strap.

• In other classes, the *martinet* – a small whip with many thin leather strands – was used in the worst cases of misbehavior.

• The man did not help with the housework or with the children.

• Fathers were barred from birthing rooms, whether at a hospital or at home.

B. Opinions
• The man was expected to have and express an opinion on everything, whether it be the Americans, the British, the army, collaboration, the Occupation or the résistants.

• Men who had fought in WWI had a strong allegiance to Marshal Pétain, but were ambivalent about the policy of collaboration. Some rejected it outright while still admiring the marshal. Others believed or pretended that Pétain had a plan to rid France of the Germans.

• The majority of WWI veterans rebelled against criticism of the French army and took pains to explain away the rapid defeat of 1940.

• The majority of demobilized soldiers expressed the same opinion and deflected the blame onto politicians and the military brass who had not been in the field and had not adapted their strategy to the new ways of war, that is, a fast moving war.

C. Collaborators

• Except for the ardent collaborators, men of all classes tended to be favorable to the résistance movements, especially after July 1942, even if they personally did not get involved.

47. War and Women
A. Social classes
• Prior to the outbreak of war, there were marked distinctions between the classes.

• Women in the lower classes worked in factories or in retail trades until they married and had a child, after which, they ceased paid work and accepted the man's superiority. A working class woman was not expected to hold an opinion other than about domestic matters or child rearing.

• Upper-class women did not work outside the home. They took part in discussions on any subject and could express an opinion, though in the end, the man's point of view prevailed (!) They did could be found raising money for charities.

• Bourgeois or middle-class women might discuss the economy or politics as long as they were circumspect about it and acknowledged that the man's point of view prevailed. They did not work outside the home, but did volunteer work.

• Women working with their husbands, such as in stores and small businesses, were more likely to share responsibilities, but demurred to the man in decision making.

• Single working women often ran a seamstress business from home. They were also employed in hairdressing salons.

• Educated unmarried women were increasingly sought after as secretaries. Nursing was an acceptable profession. Few women succeeded in becoming doctors unless they had an influential sponsor, such as her father, or an uncle, being a doctor. School teaching was another profession open to women until they married, when social pressure pushed them out. Some women chose to remain single, while others remained single after the loss of a fiancé on the battlefield.

B. Working women
• The Occupation dramatically changed women's lives soon after the June 1940 armistice. With 1.8 million men made prisoners of war, and some eighty to a hundred thousand killed

on the battlefield, many households found themselves without a man.

• Many women, especially in the middle- and upper-classes, were already engaged in health services and in community work.

• During the Occupation, it was accepted as normal that women went to work outside the home. Some viewed it as their patriotic duty. For others, it was a necessity.

C. Survival

• Common to all women was a fear of the future, fear of hunger when rations proved to be inadequate and fear for their children.

• In their fight for survival and their need to find paid work, they developed a deep hatred for the occupiers. It led many of them to help résistance groups in various ways, sometimes small, like leaving a loaf of bread in a certain location, or a more active participation working as couriers and occasionally belonging to a maquis group.

• Working-class women were also involved in résistance work. Traditionally in France, the working class was socialist or communist. During the war, young women were assigned roles by their political parties.

• Although disapproving and blaming the black market for the inflation, many women bartered goods for food and bought food on the said black market, especially when they had children.

D. Women, fighters without weapons

• Women had little hesitation in confronting the occupiers and the French police when it came to food. Several street demonstrations – reminiscent of the 1789 French Revolution, which also began over bread – erupted, with women demanding bread and other foodstuffs.

• It is impossible to estimate the number of women who were active résistants. The majority went home after the liberation and never spoke of the war and their role again.

• They all scorned the occupiers in ways big and small. As an act of defiance, a woman would dress in her finest clothes to line up at a food store, pretended not to see soldiers in the street and crossed to the other side or promptly left a store, café or Métro car if a soldier entered.

• Young women, in particular, took risks to resist the enemy. They participated actively in résistance groups. The SOE recruited agents from among them.

E. *Collaboration horizontale* – the meaning is obvious

• There were women who found themselves alone at the start of the Occupation and accepted the fact the enemy had won and they should make the best of it. The occupiers were young soldiers eager for female company. The occupiers offered perks. Genuine attachments did take place.

• For other women, the attraction of food and better clothing provided by a soldier or officer was irresistible. Among them were mothers who saw a liaison with an occupier as a way of providing adequate food for their children. No romantic feelings were involved.

• Among aristocratic and upper-class women, some embraced the ideals of Nazism and were openly pro-Nazis. They saw refugees, Jews and others as riff-raff that needed to be swept away. A liaison with an officer, himself often of aristocratic or upper class, was not frowned upon and even encouraged in their milieu.

• Whereas the poorer and less affluent horizontal collaborators after the liberation were caught and head-shaved as retribution, an upper class woman had the means to vanish abroad discreetly until tempers settled down.

F. Emancipation of women

• In France, WWII marked the beginning of women's emancipation. They received the right to vote in 1946, which meant they were finally recognized as full citizens.

• More women chose full-time employment after the war. Among the middle and upper-classes, paid employment was no longer considered something beneath them. Change did not happen overnight. It took many years and much struggle before French women narrowed the equality gap between themselves and French men.

48. Weather – by years and months

• Mainland France enjoys a temperate climate, with regional variations according to elevation and latitude. During WWII, the country, as did Europe in general, saw many unseasonable weather events, such as prolonged spells of freezing temperature. The weather mentioned below applies to the majority of the regions. Mountainous regions, such as the Vosges, the Alps, Pyrénées and Massif-Central were no strangers to snow and frigid temperatures, but during the war, they experienced abnormally normal cold and above normal snowfalls.

• The weather below was taken from the *Archives Météorologiques de France* – France's Meteorological Archives.

• January 1940. Extreme cold. Snow. Minus 13°C (8°F) in Paris and colder in other regions. Freezing rain and flooding at the end of the month in many places.

• February 1940. Extreme cold. Rivers froze. Snow in Paris.

• March 1940. Rain and snow. -21°C (0°F).

• April 1940. Rain and snow, with a wave of powerful storms with hail and extreme winds on April 18.

• May 1940. Dry and sunny.

• June 1940. 30°C (86°F) short heatwave, followed by thunderstorms and rain, then a second heatwave and more thunderstorms.

• July 1940. A mix of fine weather and colder days.

• August 1940. Very dry and hot.

• September 1940. Extreme rainfall with a short heatwave 33°C (90°F) in Paris.

• October 1940. Starts off very cold. Record rainfall, flooding in the eastern Pyrenees.

• November 1940. Unending storms. Tidal wave on the Côte d'Azur.

• December 1940. Extreme cold, water pipes froze in apartments and houses, fog, snow in some regions. Most rivers froze over.

• January 1941. Snow and extreme cold continue, rivers froze over.

• February 1941. Extreme snowfall, with power outages in many areas. Successive cold fronts caused freezing in Corsica. Extreme storm with hurricane-strength winds from the Atlantic Ocean.

429

- March 1941. Sunny and mild. Mid-month, a hurricane-strength storm from the Atlantic Ocean struck the northern part of France.
- April 1941. Cold.
- May 1941. Unseasonably cold and rainy.
- June 1941. Cool until mid-month, then a heatwave with temperatures of 36°C (near 100°F), thunderstorms and flooding in places.
- July 1941. Short heatwaves with temperatures up to 39°C (103°F).
- August 1941. Rainy, warm, stormy.
- September 1941. Mixed, near-normal weather.
- October 1941. Heatwave early in the month, extreme rain mid-month. Landslides and flooding in south-east France. Then snow.
- November 1941. Mixed, near-normal weather up to mid-month, then extreme storms. Tidal wave on Mediterranean coast.
- December 1941. Cold front with unseasonable freezing temperatures.
- January 1942. Extreme cold front with temperatures -35°C (-31°F) in places. Major avalanches in the Alps.
- February 1942. Dry conditions with freezing temperatures. Freezing rain in the northern regions at the end of the month. In Paris 5cm (2in) of ice on the roads.
- March 1942. Dry, mild.
- April 1942. Dry, mild.
- May 1942. Dry, mild.
- June 1942. Dry, warm, with occasional high temperatures.
- July 1942. Dry, warm.
- August 1942. Normal warm weather up to August 19 then storms with hail in latter part of month.
- September 1942. Warm, stormy.
- October 1942. Dry, sunny, mild.
- November 1942. Dry, cold, down to -40°C (-40°F). Extreme cold in every region. Rivers froze over. Corsica and the Mediterranean coast experienced unseasonable freezing temperatures.
- December 1942. Extreme snow in every region.
- January 1943. Mild.•
- February 1943. Dry, mild.
- March 1943. Dry, warm, sunny.
- April 1943. Dry, warm, sunny.

- May 1943. Warm, with scattered showers and a heatwave in mid-month.
- June 1943. Sunny, warm with thunderstorms.
- July 1943. Warm with thunderstorms, heatwave at month end – up to 37°C (99°F).
- August 1943. Intermittent heatwaves, cooling at the end of the month.
- September 1943. Warm, rainy.
- October 1943. Dry, warm, sunny.
- November 1943. Dry, cold.
- December 1943. Dry, cold.
- January 1944. Dry, mild.
- February 1944. Dry, with snow in eastern regions, cold.
- March 1944. Cold. very dry.
- April 1944. Dry, drought conditions, warm, sunny.
- May 1944. Dry, drought conditions, warm, sunny.
- June 1944. Stormy conditions at start of the month, particularly north of the Brittany coast, with massive waves. D-Day landings delayed by one day. Conditions improved for Normandy D-Day landings, June 6.
- July 1944. Dry, drought conditions.
- August 1944. Successive heatwaves.
- September 1944. Rainy, cool.
- October 1944. Rainy, cold.
- November 1944. Extreme rain, with widespread flooding.
- December 1944. Rain, with cold front close to Christmas.
- January 1945. Extreme cold front with temperatures -35°C (-31°F) in places, persistent snow up to 40 cm (16 in) in the east, 20cm (8in) in Paris.
- February 1945. The mildest February since 1937.
- March 1945. Dry, warm.
- April 1945. Very dry, warm, with a heatwave mid-month.
- May 1945. May 1 saw a spectacular drop in temperature. Snow in Paris and most everywhere else. Freezing temperatures destroyed crops and vineyards. May 6 – rapid return to normal temperatures. Long-lasting heatwave mid-month.
- June 1945. Extreme heat.

• July 1945. Storms with hail in first half of month. Second part heatwaves.
• August 1945. Cool and damp, often below average temperatures.

49. Annex I
French first names

The following is a concise collection of male and female first names that would have been common in France during the period covered by this book to help you name your fictional characters appropriately. In French society traditional names that had long been in use were popular. Naming tended not to follow fads as they did in other cultures, and in modern times. Another feature was that names were never abbreviated, no matter the social class. A boy called Frédéric was always referred as Frédéric, never Fred. Many girl's names were hyphenated with Marie, as in Marie-Claude, Marie-Thérèse. In a similar fashion, boy's names were compounds of Jean – Jean-Guy, Jean-Pierre. Note that the boy's name Jean is the French equivalent of John not the English girl's name Jean. The girl's equivalent of the English Jean is Jeanne. Just to make your life a little more difficult, the name *Marie* can be both female and male, but in the latter case only if it is compounded with another name. When the girl's name Marie is compounded, it always is the first of the pair. French Catholic families often gave the name to boys, as in François-Marie, Paul-Marie, with the Marie in second place. The compound name was more often than not used as a middle name. A number of names were the feminine version of a male name.

Feminine names
Agnès – Adrienne
Berthe – Brigitte
Cécile – Charlotte – Christiane – Claire – Claudine – Colette
Éloïse
Françoise
Geneviève – Ginette – Gisèle
Hélène
Irène
Jacqueline – Jeanine – Jeanne – Jeannette – Julie
Louise
Madeleine – Marguerite – Marie – Marie-Ange – Marie-Claude
Marie-Louise – Marthe – Michelle – Monique
Nicole
Odette – Odile
Paulette – Pierrette

Rose
Simone – Solange – Suzanne
Thérèse
Violette
Yolande – Yvette – Yvonne

Masculine names

Adrien – Antoine – Armand (F=Adrienne, Antoinette, Armande)
Baptiste – Blaise – Bruno
Charles-Marie – Christian – Claude – Cyprien (F=Christiane,
    Claudette, Claudine)
Damien
Eugène
Fernand – François (F= Fernande, old-fashioned. Françoise)
Gaston – Germain – Gustave – Guy (F=Germaine)
Hector – Hugo (F=Huguette)Jacques – Jean – Jean-Baptiste
Jean-Guy – Jean-Jacques (F=Jacqueline, Jeanne)
Jean-Louis – Jean-Marie – Jean-Pierre
Jules (F=Julie)
Louis (F=Louise)
Marius – Matthieu – Maurice – Michel (F=Mauricette, Michelle)
Nestor – Noël (F=Noëlle)
Paul – Pierre (F=Paulette, Pierrette)
Rémi – René – Roland – Romain (F=Renée, Rolande)
Sébastien – Simon (F=Simone)
Victor – Vincent (F=Victorine)
Yves (F=Yvette)

50. Abbreviated Bibliography

Alary, Eric; Vergez-Chaignon, Bénédicte; Gauvin, Gilles. Les Français au quotidien 1939-1949, Paris, Perrin, 2006.

Amédée-Mannheim. Gérard. *Le marché de la viande en zone non-occupée depuis la guerre 1939-40*, thèse de doctorat en Droit, université de Toulouse, 1942, p. 46.

Amouroux, Henri. 1 *Le peuple du désastre: 1939-1940*, Paris, Laffont, 1976.

Amouroux, Henri. 2 *Quarante millions de Pétainistes: Juin 1940-1941*, Paris, Laffont, 1977.

Amouroux, Henri. 3 *Les beaux jours des collabos: Juin 1941-juin 1942*, Paris, Laffont, 1978.

Amouroux, Henri. 4 *Le peuple réveillé: Juin 1940-avril 1942*, Paris, Laffont, 1979.

Amouroux, Henri. 5 Les persécutions et les haines

Amouroux, Henri. 7 *Un printemps de mort et d'espoir: Novembre 1943-6 juin 1944*, Paris, Laffont, 1985.

Amouroux, Henri. *La vie des Français sous l'occupation*, Metvox Publications, 2018.

Archives du Groupe Société Générale. *Histoire des banques françaises pendant la Seconde Guerre Mondiale.*

Astier d', Emmanuel. *De la chute à la libération de Paris: 25 août 1944*, Paris, Gallimard, 1965.

Azéma, Jean-Pierre. *De Munich à la Libération* (1938-1944), Paris: Éditions du Seuil, 1979

Azéma, Jean-Pierre. *1940: L'année noire*, Paris, Fayard, 2010.

Azéma, Jean-Pierre; Bédarida, François. *La France des années noires: De l'occupation à la Libération*, Paris, Seuil, 2000.

Bauer, Alain; Dupuis-Danon, Marie-Christine. *Les Protecteurs : La gendarmerie nationale racontée de l'intérieur*, Jacob, Odile, 2019, présentation en ligne

Bérard, Armand. *Au temps du danger allemand: Un ambassadeur se souvient*, Paris, Plon, 1976.

Berlière, Jean-Marc. *Policiers français sous l'Occupation*, Paris, 2001.

Bernard, H.; Chevallaz, G. A.; Gheysens, R.; Launay de, J. *Les dossiers de la seconde guerre mondiale*, Verviers, 1964.

Bertin, Celia. *Femmes sous l'Occupation, Mémoires*, Paris, Stock, 1993.

Bonet, Gérard. *Les Pyrénées-Orientales dans la guerre: les années de plomb 1939-1944*, Lyon, Horvath, 1992.

Bourdrel, Philippe. *Histoire des juifs de France*, vol. 2, Paris, Albin Michel, 2004.

Bourne-Patterson, Robert. *SOE in France 1941-1945*, 1st ed. London, 1946. 2nd ed. U.K. Barnsley, 2016.

Broch, Ludivine. *Contemporary European History, French Railway Workers and the Jewish Deportations, 1942-44*. Vol. 23, No 3, pp. 359-380. Cambridge University Press, August 2014.

Browder, George C. *Hitler's Enforcers: The Gestapo and the SS Security Service in the Nazi Revolution*, Oxford and New York, Oxford University Press, 1996.

Butler, Rupert. *The Gestapo: A History of Hitler's Secret Police 1933-45*, London, Amber, 2004.

Catala, Michel. *Les relations franco-espagnoles pendant la Deuxième Guerre mondiale: rapprochement nécessaire, réconciliation impossible, 1939-1944*, Paris. L'Harmattan, 1997

CIA *Government Archives: SO, OSS, War Planning, ETO, WWII*. Freedom of Information. Electronic Reading Room.

Cobb, Matthew. *The Resistance: The French fight against the Nazis*. London: Simon & Schuster, 2009.

Collins, Larry; Lapierre, Dominique. *Is Paris Burning?*, U.S.A. Simon & Schuster, 1965.

Collins Weitz, Margaret. *Sisters in the Resistance: How Women Fought to Free France, 1940-1945*, Wiley & Sons, 1995.

Cüppers, Martin. *Les Éclaireurs de la Shoah*, Paris, Calmann-Lévy, 2018.

Curatolo, Bruno. *Écrire sous l'Occupation : Du non-consentement à la Résistance, France-Belgique-Pologne, 1940-1945*, Presses universitaires de Rennes, 2019.

Degliame-Fouché, Marcel; Noguères, Henri; Vigier, Jean-Louis. *Histoire de la Résistance en France: L'armée de l'ombre: juillet 1941-octobre 1942*, vol. 2, Paris, Robert Laffont, 1981.

Drake, David. *Paris at War 1939-1944*, Cambridge, Harvard University Press, 2015.

Eismann, Gaël. *Le Militärbefehlshaber in Frankreich*, pp.109-180. September-October 2009.

Flonneau, Jean-Marie . *Législation et organisation économiques au temps des restrictions (1938-1949)*, dans D.Veillon et J-M Flonneau (dir.), *Le temps des restrictions en France (1939-1949)*, Cahiers de l'Institut d'Histoire du temps présent (IHTP), 1996, p. 46.

Foville de, Jean-Marc. *L'entrée des allemands à Paris (14 juin 1940)*, Paris, Calmann-Lévy, 1955.

Francos, Ania. *Il était des femmes dans la Résistance*, Paris, Stock, 1978.

Garçon, Maurice. *Journal (1939-1945)*, Paris, Les Belles Lettres/Fayard, 2nd ed. 2015.

Gauvin, Gilles; Vergez-Chaignon, Bénédicte; Alary, Eric. *Les Français au quotidien · 1939-1949*, Paris, Perrin, 2013

Gildea, Robert. *Fighters in the Shadows: A New History of the French Resistance*, Belknap Press: Harvard University Press; 1st edition 2015.

Gildea, Robert. *Marianne in Chains: Daily Life in the Heart of France during the German Occupation*, Macmillan, 2002.

Glass, Charles. *Americans in Paris: Life & Death Under Nazi Occupation*, New York, Penguin, 2009.

Glass, Charles. *American Hospital of Paris: Brave Volunteers and Heroes of the Resistance.*

Grynberg, Anne. *Les camps de la honte : Les internés juifs des camps français (1939-1944)*, La Découverte, 2013 (ISBN 9782707176189, présentation en ligne <https://books.google.com/books?id=ofQSZ3FJp7AC&pg=PAPP6>

Guéhenno, Jean. *Journal des années noires 1940-1944*, Paris, Gallimard, 1947 & 2002.

Hogan, David W., Jr. U.S. Army Special Operations in World War II

Humbert, Agnès. *Résistance: Mémoires.*

Kastell, Serge. *Dictionnaire du Français sous l'Occupation*, Paris, Grancher, 2013

Lacroix-Riz, Annie. *Les élites françaises entre 1940 et 1944 : De la collaboration avec l'Allemagne à l'alliance   américaine*, Armand Colin, 2016, présentation en ligne

Lang, Peter. *Documents Diplomatiques Francais, 1940 : 1er-janvier - 10 Juillet*, vol. 1, 2004, présentation en ligne

Leroux, Bruno; Levisse-Touzé, Christine; Marcot, François (ed.). *Dictionnaire historique de la Résistance*, Paris, Robert Laffont, 2006.

Levisse-Touzé, Christine. *L'Afrique du Nord dans la guerre: 1939-1945*, Paris, Albin Michel, 2016.

Lieb, Peter. *La répression en France, 1940-1945*. Caen, Centre de recherche en histoire quantitative, 2007.

Marcot, François; Leroux, Bruno; Lévisse-Touzé, Christine. *Résistance: Dictionnaire historique, Résistance intérieure et France libre*, Paris, Laffont, 2006.

Marrus, Michael R.; Paxton, Robert O. *Vichy et les Juifs*, Calman-Lévy, 1981.

Mcdonough, Frank. *The Gestapo: The myths and reality of Hitler's secret police*. U.K. Coronet, 2015.

Meinen, Isa. *La réglementation de la prostitution et des relations sexuelles par l'occupant*. Travail, Genre et Société, 2003/2. No 10, pp 49-54, 69-82.

Michel, Henri. *Paris allemand*. Paris, Albin Michel, 1981.

Michel, Henri. *La Défaite de la France: Septembre 1939-juin 1940 Que sais-je?*, Presses universitaires de France

Ollier, Nicole. *L'exode: sur les routes de l'an 40*, Paris, Robert Laffont, 1970.

Paxton, O. Robert. Porte Rémy. Entre dissidence et résistances. Les officiers face à la défaite de juin 1940. *Inflexions*, 2015/2 No 29, (pages 15-34)

Rosbottom, Ronald, C. *When Paris Went Dark: The City of Light under German Occupation 1940-1944*, Little, Brown & Company, London, 2014.

Sauvy, Alfred . *La vie économique des Français de 1939 à 1945*, Flammarion, 1978, p. 45.

Sebba, Anne. *Les Parisiennes: How the Women of Paris Lived, Loved and Died Under Nazi Occupation*, New York, St. Martin's Press, reprint ed., 2017

Schoenbrun, David. *Soldiers of the Night: The Story of the French Resistance*, Meridian, 1981.

Semelin, Jacques. *Sans armes face à Hitler*.

Semelin, Jacques. *Persécutions et entraide en France occupée*.

Semelin, Jacques. *La survie des Juifs en France, 1940-1944*. CNRS, Paris, 2018

Stafford, David. *Britain and European Resistance 1940-1945: A survey of the Special Operations Executive*, London, MacMillan Press, 1980

Sweets, John, F. *Choices in Vichy France: The French under Nazi Occupation*, Oxford, Oxford University Press, 1994.

Veillon, Dominique. *Le Franc-Tireur: Un journal clandestin, un mouvement de Résistance 1940-1944*, Paris, Flammarion, 1977.

Veillon, Dominique. *Vivre et survivre en France (1939-1947)*, Payot, Paris, 1995

Vomécourt de, Philippe. *An Army of Amateurs* (1961), U.K. Pickle Partners Publishing, 2016.

Wahl, Alfred. *Les résistances des Alsaciens-Mosellans durant la Seconde Guerre Mondiale 1939-1945 : actes du colloque organisé par la Fondation Entente Franco-Allemande à Strasbourg (19 et20 novembre 2004)*, FEFA, 2006

Walton-Kerr, Philip, ST. C. *Gestapo: The History of the German Secret Service*, 1st Ed. London, Hale. 1939, 2nd Ed. London, Bracken,1996.

Wieviorka, Annette. *Ils étaient juifs, résistants, communistes*, Paris, Perrin, 2018

Solitude Publishing
solitudepublising@gmail.com

About the Author

Genevieve has spent many years researching, gathering original documents and unpublished diaries about WWII in France. Memories she spent years burying floated up to the surface . To help fellow writers she attempted to put together as much information as possible in WWII France, A Writer's Guide.

Among her body of work in romance, children's books and poetry, she published a trilogy All the Silences.

www.ingramcontent.com/pod-product-compliance
Lightning Source LLC
Chambersburg PA
CBHW062145080426
42734CB00010B/1568